THE EMERGENCE OF THE PAST

THE EMERGENCE OF THE PAST

A Theory of Historical Explanation

Dale H. Porter

The University of Chicago Press
Chicago and London

DALE H. PORTER is associate professor and
chairman of the Department of Humanities
at Western Michigan University.

The University of Chicago Press
Chicago 60637
The University of Chicago Press, Ltd.
London

Library of Congress
Cataloging in Publication Data

Porter, Dale H
   The emergence of the past.

   Includes bibliographical references and index.
   1. History—Philosophy.   2. Chronology.   I. Title.
D16.9.P75   901   80-27165
ISBN 0-226-67550-5

To the Memory of
Robert M. Limpus

Contents

Preface

The genesis of this book was a symposium on "Time" that met in 1970 under the aegis of the Society for Values in Higher Education. Biologists, physicists, psychologists, and philosophers offered definitions and applications of the concept of time from their various perspectives. Finally, the group turned to the historian in their midst. "Since time is obviously a central concern of historians," said the chairman, "they must have thought about it a great deal. What is their view?" A bit confused and embarrassed, I had to admit that, so far as I knew, historians don't think much about time at all. The notion of a "temporal event," which should be basic to historical explanation, seemed utterly mysterious.

Convinced that I was simply ignorant of a systematic body of thought known to more senior historians, I set off in pursuit of an answer. I wanted to show that history has a respectable theoretical framework; that the framework was compatible with those used by the other disciplines represented by my symposium colleagues; and that, after all the theoretical questions are settled, traditional historical narratives are the most effective way to express our understanding of temporal events.

There wasn't a systematic body of thought that would do those things.

Any historian can describe, in detail, a multitude of temporal events. Yet very few can explain why they talk about events the way they do. Terms such as "cause" and "effect," enshrined by nineteenth-century positivists, are ragged with misuse, and the theoretical context that once made them intelligible has been thoroughly eroded by modern discoveries in the sciences and arts. In short, historians are working without a viable theory of explanation. Their individual investigations cannot be related to each other in any systematic way, and they are largely irrelevant to studies in other disciplines.

Paradoxically, however, historians may be closer to a modern, scientific understanding of events than many of their philosophical and social-scientific critics. The structural and dynamic features of their narrative explanations are strikingly similar to features of explanatory models proposed by physicists, biologists, psychologists, and art critics to deal with complex temporal developments in their fields. These researchers, in turn, lend support to the "process" philosophy developed by Alfred North Whitehead earlier in this century in response to the breakdown of scientific positivism.

Process philosophy provides one conceptual framework for this book, but this is not a book of philosophy. The focus is always on narrative explanations of the past: how they work, how they can be talked about, compared, and improved in a systematic, critical, and intelligible way. It will be obvious that the author is a historian, not a philosopher. Each major part of the argument represents an accommodation of philosophical doctrine to the craft of historical reconstruction. I have provided many examples of historical writing to illustrate problems and alternatives, and from these examples the reader may gradually realize that the proposed approach entails substantial changes in historians' assumptions and practices.

It is inevitable that my review of scientific research into temporal processes, presented in Chapter 4, is not up-to-date. The work in this field is mushrooming, especially in the biological sciences, and a mere historian cannot keep up. But though a few examples are subject to revision, the general argument is, I believe, valid. The exact definitions of terms like "process," "emergence," "development," and "perception" have yet to be determined, but the terms do represent an emerging paradigm of twentieth-century thought of great significance to historians.

I have also not tried to review all the arguments between analytical philosophers of history and their critics, even though I have indicated some of the main areas of controversy. Some readers will no doubt see this as a serious weakness in the book; but I believe that the controversy is misguided, and that historians would be better served by a conceptual approach that has practical application to their research and writing.

This book was made possible by a year-long fellowship for independent study from the National Endowment for the Humanities, and by the support of research grants from Western Michigan University. I wish to thank Louis O. Mink and Lewis Ford, who gave advice and encouragement during the early stages of inquiry, and Arnold Gerstein, William Fowler, William Gallagher, and Jay Mandt, who read parts of the manuscript and generously offered their advice. Finally, a note of appreciation to my long-suffering typist, Colleen McLeod.

1. The Dual Character of Historical Narratives

To live in any period of the past is to be so overwhelmed with the sense of difference as to confess oneself unable to conceive how the present has become what it is.
V. H. Galbraith, *An Introduction to the Study of History*

The narrative account is the form of understanding and expression used by most historians, and accepted by the public as the typical mode of historical explanation. Monographs and statistical studies in the discipline serve chiefly to lay the foundation for more intelligible and complete narratives, and the narrative mode is employed within such studies to give them a typical pattern. Prior to the twentieth century, when problems of historical explanation were not treated so analytically, considerations of cause and effect, determinism and novelty were woven into the basic story to provide transitional stages for reflection and anticipation. But in the twentieth century such considerations have been increasingly subject to separate and intensive study. As one result, traditional narrative has come under fire as an imperfect, immature, and even irrational mode of explanation.

The main difficulty with narrative accounts is that they involve two kinds of understanding of events. There is, first, the kind of understanding one gets by following a sequence of incidents in a given duration. For example, if one asks how English monasteries came to be disbanded and looted in the 1530s, one can follow the story of Henry VIII's confrontation with Rome and the subsequent actions taken against remnants of independent church authority throughout England by the king and by people related to him. One could also choose a longer duration, say from 1066 to 1530, through which to follow the conflicts between monarch and monastery. The kind of understanding gained from following such a sequence is difficult to categorize. On the one hand, there is an increased awareness of some pattern of development, a continuity of action and reason spanning the whole duration. On the other hand, the perceived pattern stands in contrast to other patterns which might also have developed from the same initial situation. The contrast between patterns, moreover, is not fully apparent until the story is done, that is, until one reaches the stage of development previously chosen as the focus of inquiry. Any pattern abstracted from the narrative is therefore meaningful only by reference to what actually happened.

1

There is, however, a natural tendency to use the pattern abstracted from the story as a heuristic device that prompts questions about the similarity or difference between one sequence of events and another. This second kind of understanding is analytical. It assumes that people possess a relatively modest repertoire of behaviors normally conditioned by their cultural environment and heritage, which includes institutional, religious, economic, and other forces of a general nature. By analyzing these forces, one can show that there is a logic to the sequence of development, a logic that applies to other sequences as well. One can understand a particular event as an illustration of a general lawlike hypothesis about human history. However interesting the particular human actions may be, they are meaningful only by reference to some such hypothesis. From an analytical viewpoint, Henry VIII's attack upon English monasteries in the 1530s need not be approached by way of an extended reconstruction of concrete antecedent events; a better understanding of its significance is achieved by showing that it expressed a centralizing tendency required as the foundation for the modern state, or that it paralleled incidents in other countries with similar antecedent conditions.

These two modes of understanding, by following and by analyzing, appear to be antithetical. The fact that both are involved in traditional historical narrative accounts has led to a great deal of anxiety among historians and their critics in recent years. In other disciplines, especially in the social sciences, advocates of concrete narrative exposition have gone their own way, and advocates of lawlike hypotheses have followed suit. History is perhaps unique in still possessing a traditional form of exposition that tries to combine the two modes. That they appear antithetical, however, is only due to the assumptions made about the priority of one kind of understanding over another. If one assumes that complete understanding requires *reciprocity* between hypothesis and empirical evidence, between pattern formation and following, between historical forces and human behavior, then the traditional form of narrative appears most appropriate.

Reciprocity is the underlying theme of this book. In the earlier chapters, the different ways of understanding will be reviewed in order to clarify their contributions and limitations, and in order to arrive at a definition of historical events that permits abstract analysis to function in the service of improving sequential narrative. In the later chapters, the definitions will be expanded into a general scheme of analysis and criticism, with suggested applications to particular events and problems.

I have attempted to provide illustrative examples for almost every part of the scheme. This is done partly because the scheme is unfamiliar to many readers; but also because any theory of explanation should have real implications for people working in the field. If one accepts the assumption that following and abstraction are reciprocal modes of understanding, then any change or clarification of the scheme of abstraction must change the way historians reconstruct events and write their narratives; and no analytical framework can be accepted which denies the validity of a large portion of the historian's craft. At present, this kind of mutual support is virtually nonexistent in the discipline: historians generally ignore the blandishments of analytical critics or fail to see the implications of their own forays into theoretical matters, and the critics, mostly analytical philosophers, often begin by dismissing the craft of narrative as an impediment to understanding.

This chapter will focus on the first of these two problems, the awareness by historians of the theoretical implications of their work and of the "craft" implications of their theory. As one considers events in history, one may reflect that what appears in perspective as an *arrangement of experience,* with a definite form, must at one time have been an *experience of arrangement,* with an indefinite form. That seems to be the way events emerge for us in the present. For example, one attends a concert. While listening to the music, one is aware of oneself perceiving the sounds, sitting in a seat, looking at the conductor, feeling sleepy. Because one has been at concerts before, one knows that the experience will gradually assume an overall form similar to the forms of previous concerts. One hopes that this concert, and the individual works on the program, will prove different in certain respects, but not so different as to be unrecognizable. One is therefore looking backward and forward simultaneously. The *form* of one's experience at the concert is conditioned by one's own past, and by the past of a lot of other people (who one hopes will cooperate in presenting a reasonable facsimile of a concert). But the form is not definite, excluding other possibilities, until the concert is over.

The fact that our experience of events has to arrange, formulate, or organize itself within an extended duration is a commonplace of perceptual psychology, and is also (without the human element) part of the foundation of modern physics and biology.[1] What is not so commonplace is the notion that events in the past must display some evidence of that organizing process. That is, their relatively definite form is not just a spatial one, like that of an object, but must also be a temporal form, like that of an event. If one looks back upon a concert from some future duration, one "sees" not just a cross section of the experience, perhaps one second, in which everything is arranged in a certain way, but rather a sequence of images, each of which involves some feeling of development or perception. In other words, past events have definite forms, which we can relate in terms of labels and dates (e.g., the murder of Thomas Becket). But they also have temporal structures that reflect the process through which they emerged into definite form. The formal relationships between historical events may be analyzed on various levels of abstraction. The temporal relationships have to be described concretely, in a narrative, because abstraction is inherently spatial in its orientation.

The historian knows that an event such as "the murder of Thomas Becket" is a shorthand label for a whole sequence of incidents which, as Carl Becker remarked a half-century ago, we do not care for the moment to consider.[2] The label refers to the overall form of the event, which has characteristics the historian can isolate and compare with those of other events. Thomas Becket was archbishop of Canterbury; he had been chancellor to the king of England; he had fought for the independence of the church; the papacy was involved; and so on. Using the formal approach, the historian can show that the murder is perfectly understandable in terms of its context, and that its context is understandable by comparison with others involving prelates, kings, and conflicts between them.

But no matter how many characteristics are sorted out and compared, the historian never forgets the whole sequence of incidents which makes up the temporal structure of the event. The two approaches to historical understanding proceed simultaneously in most cases, or become so interwoven that distinctions are impossible. Most people can sympathize with the habit of isolating and comparing characteristics—it's done all the time. And many people can grasp the notion of temporal sequence if they simply try recalling their own past adventures. But few would agree that the historians can have it both ways.

Another example of everyday experience will draw out more clearly this dual mode of understanding. Recently I went to a local salvage yard to buy used lumber for a cabin, to be built in some woods near town. It was to be a makeshift affair, useful in the summer for a few seasons, but, for all that, I wanted it sturdy and square. In my head, and on paper, there was a design for the cabin that included the lengths and thicknesses of the necessary boards, the probable sequence of construction, and an image of the finished building. All of these were projected patterns which I used for prediction and control. At the same time, being an amateur at cabin-building but not naive, I knew that the job would be more complex and difficult than I could imagine.

Now when I looked back on my previous experience with building projects, two things were clear. First, I needed some plan or design, however general, in order to proceed with any effectiveness; and that design would be based on a comparison between what I wanted and what others had done. Second, I needed to be aware of the complexity and indeterminateness of the job so that I wouldn't give up or go crazy the first time a nail bent or a board refused to fit. That awareness, too, was based on past experience.

When a historian looks at the past, he wants to derive from the study some kind of design or pattern with which to face the future. He makes certain assumptions about the way people behave, which are really hypotheses about the way people will behave. And he uses the assumptions to study the past with the traditional caveat that the past may be different. While doing that, however, the historian also develops a sense of the indeterminate, accidental, complex nature of the historical process. And this sense is extremely important, because it enables people to face the future and cope with it on a personal level. Again, a critic would say that one can derive patterns, or learn to cope with indeterminacy, but not both. Yet the historian demands both. He wants, in effect, to follow through a process of emergence from general pattern to particular event, so as to understand and appreciate the relationship between the two.

This dualistic approach to events is reflected in the peculiar style of writing affected by historians in modern time. It is ostensibly a nontechnical style using ordinary language to evoke in the reader's mind an experience of the past as vivid, complex, and ambiguous as the historian's. But any discipline requires some refinement of language. Rather than invent jargon, historians have developed certain conventions of style that attempt to combine evocation with explanation. For example:

> In view of its century-old diplomatic tradition, the papal see could not fail to recognize that conditions in the great Roman Empire were moving toward a crisis.[3]

Using "ordinary" language, this historian has attributed to an institution, or group of people, a judgment regarding the probable course of events. He implies that this judgment was to be expected in view of the past experience and behavior of these people, and alludes to a probable future situation which, one can believe, he is about to describe more fully.

Most people, of course, do not use "ordinary" language in quite this fashion. Historical discourse seems to have more than its share of allusions, attributions, and euphemisms, which somehow obscure as well as embody the explanatory principles of the discipline. In consequence, one would expect critics of historical explanation to focus on this rather peculiar style. But with few exceptions, the historians and philosophers who argue about the validity of narrative accounts rarely provide examples to back up their assertions.[4] One can read through months of professional history journals and dozens of manuals on the craft of historical research without finding a single close examination of actual paragraphs from published historical writing. Apparently, although the logic of historical explanation is open to attack from all sides, the style of narrative presentation is taken for granted. Perhaps it is just dismissed as the sloppy, second-rate style expected of academics. Unfortunately, the gap between arguments and examples has produced theorists who, after struggling painfully with the difficulties of their favorite doctrine, arrive at discoveries that research historians learned in graduate school. And, as will be seen later in this chapter, there are plenty of historians who dismiss philosophy as a nuisance, only to deliver themselves of generalizations that would embarrass a first-year student of logic.

If one is to appreciate the subtlety with which traditional narrative deals with the dual aspects of history, one must look at some respectable published accounts. As an illustration, I have selected two studies of the coronation of Charlemagne, which occurred on Christmas Day, A.D. 800. This event was chosen because it has been the subject of decades of excellent research and writing, and because I know little about it. What I say about the two studies, therefore, implies no criticism whatever of the authors' erudition and insight.

The first example, "The Coronation as the Expression of the Ideals of the Frankish Court," is a translation of a work by Louis Halphen.[5] His argument runs like this: (1) by the end of the eighth century A.D., Charlemagne had emerged as master of the West; (2) under these conditions it was expected that a more general title should be added to the Frankish king's collection, to reflect his full power, whenever conditions were appropriate (this "expectation" implies a general hypothesis, that people will tend to bring social forms into line with changing facts whenever they sense a significant discrepancy; (3) local conditions in Rome demanded the intervention of an emperor in December 800; and (4) Byzantine imperial power was, at the time, temporarily disrupted and incapable of intervening in Rome. Therefore, concludes Halphen, Charlemagne was acclaimed emperor by the pope, by his own Franks, and by the Roman people because the prevailing conditions made it both obvious and advantageous for this to be done. It was simply a matter of legitimizing what was already accomplished in fact.

Halphen's approach to this argument is not so straightforward as the above summary suggests. After listing Charlemagne's previous conquests as evidence of his power, he introduces the main theme with a rhetorical question: "Under these conditions, was it not to be expected that" the king should add the more general title commensurate with his authority? Then Halphen proceeds to a second level of generalization, not so sweeping as his initial statement, but broad enough to be summarized in a paragraph:

> One fact of capital importance dominated the whole question: in the course of the events which had unfolded in Italy since the intervention of Charlemagne in the affairs of the Lombards, the West had, around him and through him, come to be conscious of its unity as opposed to the "Roman Empire" which, following its eight-century old career in the Eastern Mediterranean, continued to embody the tradition of ancient Rome. Forced back on the Bosporus in "New Rome," that Empire had conserved only a few isolated pieces of its ancient territories to the west of

the Adriatic and Ionian seas, and the future held little in store for these fragments. The papacy itself had ceased to look to the descendants of Constantine and Theodosius and was turning instead resolutely to the Carolingians with whom it felt from this time on a close solidarity. And along with the papacy the West, or at least all the continental West, had finally realized that by ranking itself around the Conqueror of the Saxons it would gain in strength and in its prospects for the future.[6]

Even when one allows for the awkwardness of the translation, this passage is remarkable for its obfuscation of the theme. The barebones argument is that "the West" and the papacy realized their autonomy and estrangement from the weakening Byzantine rulers, and turned to Charlemagne as the stronger alternative. This is not a restatement of the initial assertion about the legitimization of Charlemagne's power. It contains many of the same elements, but it is presented from a different perspective. The terms of the argument have been shifted.

But the rhetorical devices in this paragraph far overshadow its logic. In fact, they tend to take the place of logic, and it is worth looking closely at how this is done. First, institutions and abstractions are personalized by the use of expressions of feeling and thinking. An entity called "the West" is said to have "come to be conscious of its unity." It "finally realized" that it could profit by "ranking itself around" Charlemagne. In contrast, "the Empire" is "forced back" into small areas. The papacy, meanwhile, "ceased to look to" Byzantium, and "turning resolutely" toward Charlemagne, "felt a close solidarity" with him. Using one or two images like this in a long passage might be considered apt. But this is a systematic conjunction of vaguely defined institutions with specific, personalized behavior.

One could call such a style "subjective shorthand" because of its close attention to subjective feelings and its use of shorthand labels to denote the people who had the feelings. If one accepts the historians' belief that immersion in documentary evidence is the best path to knowledge, one can realize that the shorthand (papacy, West, Empire) refers to masses of detail that this historian is well aware of, but prefers not to mention. Either Halphen is taking the reader's knowledge of the period for granted or he considers the objective details irrelevant at this point. The real intent of the paragraph seems to be the clarification of subjective feelings involved in the situation.

A syllogism regarding cause and effect can be abstracted from Halphen's prose, but it is evident that the empirical warrant for its premises must lie elsewhere. One can see why some critics have denigrated narrative explanation. But is such a passage really the place for logical rigor? Halphen is trying merely to establish one basic condition for the coronation, namely, a complex, dynamic relationship among the three or four equally significant powers. One needs to grasp that relationship as a whole before one can understand the behavior of any one participant. That is why subjective feelings are emphasized over objective details. The passage is in fact preceded by a factual account of Charlemagne's rise to power, and it is followed directly by a detailed explanation of the papacy's "resolute turn" toward the West.

Second, there is a suggestive use of capitalization and quotation marks, as well as of epithets, to contrast the power of Charlemagne with the weakness of Byzantium. The West is allowed to stand on its own, without quotation marks, but the "Roman Empire" at "New Rome" is apparently less real, more pretension than power—just what Halphen is trying to argue. Also the mention of the Byzantine emperors as "the descendants of Constantine and Theodosius," evokes only bygone glory, while Charlemagne is the more recent, more virile "conqueror of the Saxons." Clearly this overall contrast is to be felt, not reasoned. It cannot even be disproved by contradicting the facts.

Third, the description of conditions is buttressed by the historian's hindsight, masquerading as the anticipation of clever contemporaries: "the future held little in store for these fragments. . . ." and "it would gain in strength and in its prospects for the future." There is no special reason to adopt this device. Halphen could have separated his own hindsight from the views of his subjects. But the narrative form constantly tempts authors to confuse the two, and to shift the point of view from present historian to past participant. In a fictional narrative (which is not really so differnt in this respect) we would be disappointed if the author failed to do this, because it helps us identify more closely with the subject. In nonfiction, where such an identification is felt to be unscientifically subjective, the technique is less admired.

Fourth, a relativistic use of time augments the subjectivity of the passage. Past, present, and future are interwoven so as to produce the impression of movement within a formal time period. For example, the papacy *"had* ceased to look. . .," "then *was* turning. . .," and finally "felt *from this time on*. . .," all in the same sentence! This may be just poor construction. But it has interesting parallels with that sense of emergence that one experiences in the developing events. Rather than dismiss such constructions as nonsense, one should consider how to justify them in theoretical terms.

Now let us return to the general structure of Halphen's argument. Having restated his basic thesis, Halphen summarizes the complex conditions existing before the coronation. Next follows a more specific narrative of growing contrast between Charlemagne's assumption of authority over the church and over Pope Leo III's political troubles in Rome. The two developments occur simultaneously, and so are not causally connected. Yet the sequential character of narrative makes them seem vaguely related in that way. *"Post hoc, ergo propter hoc"* is built into the structure of many languages, and especially into English, where position within a sentence often replaces word endings as an indicator of relationships. It might have been more accurate to express Charlemagne's growing power, and the pope's growing troubles, in the manner of contrasting musical themes that are played at the same time.

Halphen next describes the change in thinking which resulted from the pope's appeal to Charlemagne for help. The cause-effect bond seems quite evident here: pope seeks Charlemagne's help, which causes change in thinking. But look how Halphen qualifies the argument! The key sentence says, "From the moment when the pope decided" to meet Charlemagne, the writings of Alcuin and others "sounded a note that was in part new." Moreover, though Halphen cannot draw a direct line between those writings and any change in public opinion, he asserts that Alcuin's use of new terms "acted little by little in the manner of an influential and persuasive idea, and, consciously or not, prepared contemporaries for the events for which Rome would soon be the theater." This is not a historical statement at all. It is a revelation of the author's own intent to gain credibility by suggestion.

Following this almost unwarrantable cause-effect assertion, Halphen restates his argument in a brief transition to yet more documentary evidence: "In the meantime, everything had worked together since the since the summer of 799" to produce "a powerful impression." At the conclusion of this detailed description, the author attributes to his Frankish sources his own first premise: "Charlemagne, placed at the summit of the earthly hierarchy, had become the direct agent of God over all the Christians of the West, the sovereign pontiff included." The clarification—that *this is what Halphen read in the sources,* or that *this is what he imagines certain people might have said if asked at the time to summarize their view of the situation*—is missing.

This section of the argument provokes two observations. First, the illustrative data for the argument are at the same time the only evidence to support its own interpretation. The historian says, in effect, "here is what I meant by my argument," and "here is the evidence for it," all in one. There is no other coronation from which we may draw additional supporting data for the degree of particularity sought in this one. This problem is common to most historical narratives, for reasons discussed above, and is the chief reason why critics regard such narratives as logically defective. Yet Halphen and other historians are not ignorant of the rules of logic. What are they trying to do?

The second observation may provide an answer to that question. Halphen's persuasive arrangement of evidence and assertion, with all its allusions, attributions, and selective punctuation, forms an analogy to the temporal development of the events he wishes to explain. Rather than use the nebulous concept of causality in a deductive manner, he has provided a means for the reexperiencing of the event by the reader, in such a way that the reader feels for himself the emerging impetus toward Charlemagne's coronation. One can deny the validity of such an analogy only if one rejects the notion that events are initially and primarily formulations of subjective experience. If one asks, What are the chances of such an arrangement occurring again? then the answer might be couched in terms of some analytical scheme with lawlike hypotheses. But if one wants to know how *this* arrangement came to be what it was, instead of something else, then the subjective analogue is preferable. It may be that the two forms of presentation are incompatible within the structure of the narrative and must be separated for proper treatment. But that possibility does not deny the validity or effectiveness of either one.

Having established Charlemagne's credentials, Halphen picks up the detailed narrative of events in December 800, when Charlemagne came to Rome, subjected Leo III to trial and purification by a church council, and entered the Basilica of St. Peter to be crowned. At this point, Halphen's intuition works overtime. The coronation is said to be the work of "secret deliberations which had been in process for almost a month," led by Charlemagne himself. Secret deliberations, of course, leave no evidence. What we do have is the word of Frankish annalists that "all the Christian people," including the pope and his priests, desired the change. Halphen's comment on the annals forms a general hypothesis of the kind apparently desired by analytical philosophers, although not worded in their style: "It was not the first time in history nor would it be the last that an emperor brought about his own election by the people." In other words, one could predict that any emperor in a similar situation would do the same thing. Halphen does not support this hypothesis with data from other historical periods. Instead, he reminds the reader again of that pre-Christmas council, led by Charlemagne, whose deliberations were so mysterious. And he wraps up this selection with yet another summary of the main theme, regarding

> the incontestable interest which there was in the year 800 to bring legality and reality into accord by conferring on Charlemagne the imperial title, circumstances at the moment permitting one to dispose of the matter without risk of serious opposition.[7]

This conclusion explains away several minor but awkward discrepancies in the evidence that had just been presented. Halphen's purpose, however, is not to demonstrate the necessity of the case but to provide an intelligible "fit" between hypothesis and data. That is, the explanation is not intended to demonstrate an invariant relationship between typical causes and typical effects, but to show that *this* particular set of events appears most intelligible if one looks at it *this* way. Most hypotheses in the natural sciences begin with the same kind of "fitting" process, and most scientists are content to leave the business of working hypotheses into coherent theory to philosophically minded colleagues.

In terms of coherence, Halphen's argument has some drawbacks. For one, the recorded consequences of Charlemagne's coronation do not, by Halphen's own admission, fit the hypothesis as well as the alleged causes. The crowning of a new emperor was intended to clarify the situation. Instead, two new ambiguities appeared. Externally, the Byzantine emperors reacted with hostility, as was expected, and Halphen finds the ultimate resolution of this problem (by designation of Charlemagne as "brother" instead of "son" of the Byzantine rulers) very unsatisfactory. Internally, the exact nature of Charlemagne's new authority was never adequately defined, although in Halphen's view a consensus about it developed prior to the coronation. Halphen seems disappointed that "the Empire" turned out to be "no more than a sort of personal apotheosis of Charlemagne." Despite his previous argument that the coronoation simply legitimized an existing authority, he appears to regret that "of the new perspectives opened by the coronation of the year 800, not much was left, as one can see, less than six years after the event." Those new perspectives, adumbrated by Halphen's knowledge of future developments, are not described. And yet, by mentioning them, the author reminds readers that all historical events involve a realm of possibilities, derived from the conditions of the antecedent world, that cannot all be realized at the same time. This realm of possibility, of potential form, is relevant to what actually happens, because it provides the contrast one needs to assess the historical significance of actual events. How else than by reference to such a realm could one explain the continuing fascination of historians for the coronation of Charlemagne?

Nevertheless, there is disagreement among historians about the importance of examining unrealized possibilities. Generally, the science-oriented writers disregard anything that did not actually materialize, whereas the more subjective types stress contrasts with what might have been. E. H. Carr, for instance, whose purpose in research is to gain rational control over the environment, believes that "History is, by and large, a record of what people did, not of what they failed to do." For Carr, the "essence" of the historian's job is to give "an appearance of inevitableness" to an existing order.[8] Carr's attitude is directly opposed to that of Marc Bloch: "the unsuccessful act is one of the essential data of human evolution."[9] One is reminded of certain scientific experiments whose "failure" opened the way for a more comprehensive understanding of phenomena. Perhaps if one paid more attention to "unsuccessful" events, one could state more clearly how and why they differ from more "successful" ones, and thus satisfy both sides in the dispute. In many cases, the successful actor in history is the person who is most aware of the many possibilities of a situation; and the dramatic quality of historical events does seem to depend on there being alternative outcomes to consider.

Louis Halphen's work has been quoted extensively in order to uncover some of the dynamics of explanatory narrative. Though some difficulties in his argument have been indicated, they are not meant to denigrate his work, which is highly regarded. It is a good example of what most historians try to do. Yet one can see the consequences of trying to apply two incomplete and apparently incompatible theories of explanation. On the one hand, there is evidence of a lawlike hypothesis regarding the causes and effects of the coronation. It is an incomplete hypothesis, a mere "sketch" (as some critics put it) lacking corroborative data for establishing a principle of regularity. Also the terms used by Halphen would be difficult to generalize and apply to other events of the same type. On the other hand, there is a literary approach, using detailed description, narrative summary, and documented scenes, which produces a subjective analogy to the temporal development of the events surrounding the coronation. Instead of leading the reader to expect the coronation to occur as it did and no other way, the literary approach evokes a number of plausible possibilities which then stand in significant contrast to what actually happened.

The two forms of explanation, by analysis and by emergence, can be equally effective and valid ways of understanding a historical event. But in Halphen's account, they tend to weaken each other. The analysis is weakened partly by the use of literary devices which suggest indeterminacy, and partly by the fact that the consequences of the coronation are not wholly consistent with its alleged causes. And the gradual emergence of the coronation as a complex event with extended duration is obscured by attempts to establish definite, limiting causes. The solution to this problem is either to remove analysis altogether from narrative, as has been done in other social sciences, with a probable loss of credibility for narrative; or to create a mode of analysis more appropriate for the process of emergence.

Lest the argument seem to rest on a single example, let us briefly examine another view of the same historical event. Werner Ohnsorge, a German medievalist, approached the coronation of Charlemagne from the perspective of the Byzantine court, thus offering several correctives to the "Western" orientation of previous studies. His argument is instructive because, instead of concentrating on the immediate causes of the coronation itself, he surveys the whole pattern of Charlemagne's behavior from about 754 to 814, the year of Charlemagne's death. He is thus in a better position to show the contrast between what was expected by contemporaries before the coronation, and what happened afterward.

In the relevant chapter of a work on Frankish politics, Ohnsorge sets out the conditions which, taken together, made the imperial coronation a strong possibility.[10] Prior to the year 800, (a) Charlemagne sought recognition of the equality of his Frankish domain with that of (Roman) Byzantium; (b) the Byzantine emperors, while recognizing the growing power in the West, refused to accord Charlemagne equal status, writing to him as "son" instead of "brother"; (c) the papacy sought independence from Byzantine authority by alliance with the Franks, in the context of a Roman imperium; and (d) for all three powers, relative political status was believed to be obtained and expressed through sacred rituals, traditional symbols, and forms of address including titles. One may note that the first three conditions are "dynamic" lines of development, whose conjunction at any place or time might be sufficient to account for a coronation. When one adds the further condition, that the only form of imperial power then known was that of the Roman Empire, the conclusion follows, that it was to be expected that Charlemagne would be crowned Roman Emperor in a traditional ceremony, initiated by the papacy, whenever Byzantine influence weakened and when local or immediate conditions presented an opportunity consistent with tradition. Such conditions prevailed, the argument continues, at Christmas 800. Pope Leo III required Charlemagne's judicial authority at Rome, and the Byzantine throne was temporarily occupied by a female usurper. Therefore, the coronation of Charlemagne as Roman emperor on or near Christmas 800 could have been predicted. And though the conclusion to a strictly deductive argument needs no empirical warrant for its validity, so long as the premises are warranted, there is documentary evidence that several important contemporaries did anticipate, if not predict, such an event.

Thus a fairly good causal hypothesis may be abstracted from the narrative Ohnsorge presents. Its premises are empirically warranted by documentary evidence that he displays in narrative form. But Ohnsorge is not content to demonstrate necessary or sufficient conditions. He also wishes to describe the significance of the event; to do that, he must analyze its subjective form. It is his contention that the coronation ceremony was planned and perpetrated by the pope and his advisors, against the will of Charlemagne, for the purpose of reconstituting the Roman Empire on a Western, Roman foundation. He further maintains that Charlemagne's displeasure, recorded by his confidant Einhard, arose from his desire to create a separate but equal Frankish imperium, unentangled with the effete snobbery and ulterior motives of papal and Byzantine officials. This is the subjective side of the event, the side concerned with the feelings and perceptions of the participants, which the causal hypothesis ignores almost completely.

Yet the two forms of explanation are interdependent. The terms used in the causal hypothesis have been abstracted from a vast array of particular data, while the subjective description of those data is necessary to justify the formulation of Ohnsorge's initial premises. For example, to support his premise that Charlemagne, prior to 800, sought recognition for a separate but equal Frankish empire (a generalization abstracted from dozens of empirical observations), Ohnsorge describes the king's reaction to his coronation, after the event. That reaction was, according to Einhard, negative. The historian goes on to narrate Charlemagne's subsequent efforts to disengage his authority from the taint of Rome and, at the same time, to assert its validity against the continuing arrogance of Byzantine agents. Thus, instead of treating the coronation as the conclusion of a deductive argument, Ohnsorge uses it as a focal point for composition. Its "causes" and "consequences" are ranged on either side as elements of a single complex event having an extended duration. The content of the narrative, illustrating the emergence of that event, is also the empirical warrant for his causal hypothesis.

In such a dualistic mode of explanation, the initial conditions are not "given" prior to one's interpretation of subsequent developments. The whole form is understood before its parts. Once a reader follows through the complete narrative, grasping its overall meaning, he can arrange its parts according to their appropriate functions, as he would the elements of a story. Such an arrangement represents a temporal pattern of emergence whose internal relationships are interdependent. In other words, Charlemagne's intentions prior to the coronation, and his actions afterward, are not to be understood as cause and effect but as different versions of the same pattern of behavior. Each version gives meaning to the other, and the contrast between them gives meaning to the coronation.

It was pointed out above that in analytical explanations the meaning of an event is invested in the lawlike hypothesis which it illustrates. In a narrative explanation, the meaning is invested in an event's relationship with other events. As a pattern of events emerges, the meaning of any element in the pattern may change from what was expected at an earlier stage, and cannot be determined fully until the whole pattern has developed. Understanding events in this way requires a shift from *prediction* to *retrodiction*, or reasoning from present to past. Sir Isaiah Berlin has discussed retrodictive reasoning in some detail, contrasting it with other modes of inquiry as a valid tool for history.[11] Given a set of events A, B, and C, and a hypothesis stating that such a set is usually found to originate from another set of conditions R, S, and T, one can retrodict the actual existence of the second set in some period antecedent to the first. And one can go look for the second set in the surviving documentary records. This is what Werner Ohnsorge did when trying to figure out why Charlemagne and the pope behaved the way they did after the coronation. And this is what most historians do when they go about their most characteristic and, to some people, most inane task, the search for origins.

Paradoxically however, retrodictive reasoning is often obscured as well as prompted by the temporal flow of narrative. Ohnsorge does not appear to be looking backward in his account of the coronation. He begins with a review of Frankish conquests as far back as the beginning of the eighth century, then describes the first confrontations with Byzantium over territory and religious doctrine, the Frankish claims to prominence, the usurpation of the Imperial throne by Irene, and the visit to Rome by Charlemagne in December 800. After the coronation scene, quoted almost verbatim from the annals, the narrative continues with the negotiations between Charlemagne and the successor of the Empress Irene. This pattern forms a temporal analogue to the sequence Ohnsorge discerned in the documentary evidence. The techniques by which he discerned it, including the use of retrodiction, are not explicitly mentioned in the account. But they are definitely implied, and the structure of the narrative itself provokes in the reader a constant reflection backwards in order to qualify previous images of the significance of events. Ohnsorge, like any other historian, has selected and arranged his narrative material so that the reader's retrodictive reasoning will imitate his own. But the reasoning flows in an opposite direction to that of the reading: it is as if one started with the conclusion of a syllogism, and then discovered the premises. Only at the end of the reading does a definite pattern of relationships become distinguishable from the general field of possibilities.

Let us look, for example, at one or two of the possibilities that Louis Halphen saw in the coronation, which were left unrealized when Charlemagne died. At one extreme there was the possibility that the Frankish king would repudiate the coronation and the title. That he did not might be explained by the fact that the ceremony was sacred and traditional, hence irrevocable. But Charlemagne's subsequent actions are ambiguous enough to suggest, to some writers, that he found the title distasteful and inconvenient. Other historians believe that he salvaged as much authority as he could in the face of Byzantine hostility. Either way, when one interprets the later events one is bound to infer a pattern of significance for the precoronation events as well.

Another possibility discoverable in the coronation is the domination of the whole Christian world by Charlemagne. In this scenario, the Frankish ruler persuades the Empress Irene to marry him, return to the iconoclastic doctrine, and move her court to Rome. Werner Ohnsorge says such a project was discussed in the year 802 with enough enthusiasm to cause a palace revolt against Irene.[12] Yet if Charlemagne had succeeded in reunifying the Christian world around Rome, how different would be our interpretations of the previous half-century! One would scarcely credit Ohnsorge's contention that Charlemagne tried all along to gain recognition for his Frankish empire.

Does the historian weaken his case by mentioning potential lines of development that fail of realization? The answer is no: rather the opposite is true. It is possible to construe the initial conditions of Charlemagne's era in a number of plausible ways, depending on which general hypothesis about human behavior one wishes to invoke. As Carl Hempel pointed out, the notion of a complete explanation of some concrete event is self-defeating, "for any particular event may be regarded as having infinitely many different aspects of characteristics, which cannot be accounted for by a finite set, however large, of explanatory statements."[13] If, despite Hempel, one should demand a single hypothesis so subtle, so complex that it does justice to all conditions, one will end up with a description of the whole antecedent world, a "law" with but a single instance. The more successful hypothesis is one derived from the temporal pattern surrounding the focal event, before and after. It is that whole temporal duration that reveals which of the several plausible possibilities emerged into actuality.

Few of the experts on Charlemagne claim he was so single-minded (or simpleminded) as not to have entertained alternatives, both before and after his coronation. The pope and the Byzantine rulers must also have changed their minds along the way. If one presents a picture of causal determinism by means of a lawlike argument, one denies the obvious intelligence of the participants and the meaning of the event itself. That meaning is revealed by the contrast between what did happen and what might have happened. Charlemagne's coronation is worth investigating primarily because of the vividness of its contrasts. Leo III's initiative in the ceremony appears contrary to Charlemagne's assumption of church leadership; Charlemagne's negotiations with Byzantium involved religious doctrines unacceptable to his supposed ally, the pope; the omission of the imperial title in the division of Frankish domains in 806 contrasts ironically with Charlemagne's diplomatic offensive against Byzantium, and with the resumption of the title when, at his death, there was only one legitimate heir. A form of explanation that cannot deal with contrasts like these has lost touch with historical reality.

The above observation brings us back to the dispute between those who champion the narrative mode of explanation, seeing the process of emergence from possibility to actuality as a subjective experience to be followed and reconstituted by the reader, without interference from abstract analysis, and those who champion abstract analysis as the more effective mode of explanation, capable of deriving from particular events those patterns of regularity which alone make sense out of the world of experience. It is evident from the examples discussed above that both modes are used by most historians, in different ways and to different degrees. It may also be evident that no satisfactory approach has been found to allow the two modes to complement each other. Rather, an ad hoc use of regularity hypotheses interrupts the flow of narrative without really clarifying the meaning of events.

The problem of complementarity is not limited to these examples. It is evident throughout historical writing, and is especially noticeable in the reflections on history and in the manuals produced by the much-published elders of the discipline. Offering distillations of long experience, these manuals serve chiefly to impress young scholars with the necessity of mastering documentary evidence. All of them stress the importance of immersing oneself in factual details until a narrative thread begins to emerge; and then they emphasize the desirability of correct writing. Most, however, are weak on analysis and its theoretical framework. As J. H. Hexter says (justifying his own effort): "Instead of the tightly constructed, precise delusional systems characteristic of some of the philosophies of history produced by logicians, the meditations of historians on the fundamentals of their craft have been with rare exception turbid and rather messy."[14] (Perhaps if such meditations were written at the outset of a historian's career, instead of at the end, they would be more venturesome regarding problems of explanation, and less inclined to rationalize a lifetime of prejudice.) The theoretical shortcomings of craft manuals are most evident in discussions of causal analysis, and in recommendations for incorporating such analysis into the narrative. In general, such authors reject any strict interpretation of causality, defend the use of intuition to understand processes of development, emphasize the subjectivity of ordinary language, and (most importantly) see little relationship between their opinions on theory and their strictures on writing.

G. R. Elton is a good example of the immersion-and-intuition school. In the preface to his *The Practice of History* he dismisses philosophy of history as the work of men ignorant of archival treasures and of the possibility for their transformation into historical prose. His book "embodies an assumption that the study and writing of history are justified in themselves, and reflects a suspicion that a philosophic concern with such problems as the reality of historical knowledge and of the nature of historical thought only hinders the practice of history."[15] Elton's own pronouncements on theory reveal a naiveté that would indeed undermine practice, if ever applied. Historical truth, he says, is a product of "understanding what the evidence really says," which requires "the analytical eye of the investigator," and of "understanding how it fits together," based on the "comprehensive eye of the story-teller." Controlling this interaction so as to ensure the truth is a matter of asking the right questions and of applying "informed standards of probability."[16]

What Elton means by probability seems to be the plausibility of an explanation in terms of one's intimate acquaintance with the documents—a nice "fit" between hypothesis and evidence. He is not troubled that the evidence warranting the hypothesis is also the subject of explanation; nor would his standards of probability be recognized by colleagues in the social or natural sciences.

"Asking right questions," the second half of the formula, means framing heuristics that illuminate the evidence and yield new approaches to it. Elton does not extend this meaning to include new hypotheses regarding causal or noncausal explanation. He assumes that, although the framing of new "right questions" is the most difficult task the historian can face, it is "reassuring to know that it is a task not often imposed on him."[17]

Elton treats the question of causality in a similarly cavalier fashion:

> To suppose that causal relationships are the main content of history is an error, for they form but a particular case of the general principle that history deals in a movement from state *a* to state *b*. If *a* can be said to have caused *b* the relationship happens to be causal; but it is none the less properly historical if *a* and *b* are linked by coincidence, coexistence, or mere temporal sequence, all relations very often encountered in history, however less intellectually satisfying they may be.[18]

This kind of muddled thinking is inevitable whenever historians dismiss philosophical questions as impediments to their craft, and avoid the task of framing "new right questions." It would be a more serious matter if historians tried to apply such thinking to their writing. But that is seldom the case. Elton's chapters on writing, in which he affirms the utility of ordinary language, are clearly isolated from the problems of truth, judgment, or causality discussed in other chapters.

Separation of questions on methodology and theory from those on composition is a peculiarity of most such manuals on history. Whether the writers have a "scientific" orientation like that of Louis Gottschalk[19] and E. H. Carr,[20] who takes seriously the search for hypotheses about causal regularity, or an "antiscientific" bias like that of Isaiah Berlin[21] or of Marc Bloch,[22] it is hard to discover just how theory affects practice. Perhaps it doesn't: as Hexter remarks, theoretical commitments in this discipline are "so vague, inconsistent, and contradictory as to hamper but little in the pursuit of his historical rounds the historian who professes them."[23]

Hexter admits that historians "have not paid systematic attention to the relation between their concern with historical rhetoric and their concern with historical truth."[24] His own corrective, *The History Primer*, is a characteristically forthright exposé of recent arguments on causality and an impassioned plea for a kind of historical writing that widens the reader's moral sensibilities. Hexter's book is one of the very few that wrestles with the philosophical critics on their own ground (if not always in their own terms) and tries to bridge the gap between theory and practice by examining actual examples of narrative. However, time and again Hexter draws back from the novel perspectives implied by his investigation of rhetoric. His use of the term "processive" to describe historical explanation is promising, but after stalking his idea to the point of clear definition, he gives up:

> because I doubt both the feasibility and the fruitfulness of such an enterprise, I have not attempted to present a "model" of processive explanation.

And a few pages later:

> I doubt that the "adequate" or "satisfactory" form of processive explanation is abstractable from the rhetoric of historical discourse which is its vehicle. If it were abstractable, I doubt that it would be much more relevant to an account of viable historical explanation than the covering-law and narrative forms have turned out to be.[25]

And with that excuse, Hexter rejoins the ranks of historians who are, in his words, "not by temperament analytically inclined." In view of his emphasis on rhetoric as the primary component of historical explanation, his doubts are quite surprising. Not only does rhetoric have behind it a long and honorable analytic tradition, but Hexter himself demonstrates that it offers an intelligible alternative to the "scientific" model of explanation historians so strongly dislike. A model of the explanatory process derived from historians' rhetoric might help clear up the theoretical muddle among historians and the misunderstandings of their critics. In fact, a promising start has been made in this direction by Hayden White, whose work on nineteenth-century historians has provoked new interest in traditional categories.[26]

Reference has been made to the many manuals of historical method in order to show that the theory of explanation, which most writers perceive in terms of causal determinism, contradicts rather than complements the practice of constructing narrative accounts of events. And since many historians believe analytical theory is beyond their calling and irrelevant to their purpose, though somehow necessary to explanation, such theory continues to impede efforts at narrative intelligibility.

Enough has been said, however, to suggest that analysis and narrative serve different functions for the historian, and that they could support each other if those functions were delineated clearly. In particular, the function of analysis is to relate, usually by causal hypotheses, some significant characteristics of events in different temporal durations. These characteristics have to be abstracted from their concrete, particular contexts and defined in more general terms, so that the hypotheses can apply to more than one relationship. If the terms of a hypothesis remain too particular, then application is restricted and the hypothesis becomes merely a description of a single case.

For example, the table on which I am writing is rectangular. When I say "rectangular" I mean that I can project an image of rectangularity, abstracted from previous experiences, onto the table with a pretty good fit. Not perfect, of course: the table has rounded corners and is banged up around the edges. But the discrepancies are negligible enough that I can use the image for planning. I can predict, for instance, without having to haul the table all over the place, that it will fit into the corner of my (approximately) rectangular room.

By contrast, "the placing of an imperial crown on the head of Charlemagne, King of the Franks, by Pope Leo III on Christmas Day 800" is not much of an abstraction. It selectively groups a large numer of individual actions into a slightly more general configuration. But it hardly matches the degree of abstraction of a rectangle. Because of its particularity, it is neither very useful nor very meaningful as a term in a lawlike hypothesis. Even if one could demonstrate that such a particular act at such a particular time was predictable (which would be extremely difficult) one wouldn't have learned anything about other events. It is necessary for analysis, then, to describe the characteristics of events in more abstract terms than one normally uses for narrative description.

On the other hand, the examination of narratives has indicated that they involve both a structure and a dynamic process that are common enough to be generalized and abstracted for analysis, regardless of their specific content. The structure may be described as a pattern of emergence from a set of indeterminate conditions, full of possibility, to a realization of one concrete configuration, standing in contrast to what might have been. The one concrete configuration, called the event, provides a kind of focus in the middle of the structure, with the antecedent conditions ranged on one side, and the consequences ranged on the other. The quality of the narrative is judged in part on how coherent this structure is; in other words, on how elegantly the conditions and consequences relate to the focus. And such a judgment depends on comparison with other narratives at an abstract level.

Each of the two accounts of the coronation of Charlemagne discussed previously in this chapter has a characteristic structure. And in each account, the author steps back from the narrative from time to time to survey that structure. In doing so, the author helps readers anticipate the emergence of the whole temporal pattern and reflect upon the conditions from which it is emerging. Werner Ohnsorge appears to do a better job of structuring than Louis Halphen, if only because Ohnsorge's description of the antecedent conditions depends more heavily on his assessment of events subsequent to the coronation. In Halphen's account, the subsequent events tend to conflict with motives and plans previously delineated. Such a conflict may reflect Halphen's belief that the actors in the drama did not, in fact, anticipate clearly what might happen—that they did not see the more significant possibilities of their situation. Whether Halphen or Ohnsorge provides the more intelligible account is a question that can be decided by reviewing the documentary evidence; but the question cannot properly be asked until one makes the structural contrast illustrated above.

The anticipations and reflections provoked by the gradual emergence of the temporal structure, and guided from time to time by the author, are part of the dynamic process inherent in the narrative form itself. The narrative "explains" an event by casting up a number of plausible alternative lines of development and then realizing one of them (or a new combination of several). In this sense, the quality of narrative is judged by how plausibly the pattern finally realized relates to the patterns previously anticipated. For example, Ohnsorge shows that the hostility of the Byzantine emperors to Charlemagne's coronation, a hostility which is one of the coronation's significant aspects, might have been anticipated from a study of previous events. He estimates that Byzantine hostility toward the Franks had been growing since the fifth century and was a possible element in every event involving the Franks and the Byzantine court for some four hundred years. That there *was* a hostile reaction to the coronation of 800 and that this reaction gives the coronation part of its historical significance, becomes plausible in relation to what was anticipated. Halphen's account, by comparison, is less satisfying because it does not give the reader much cause to anticipate the Byzantine reaction, nor Charlemagne's subsequent responses to it.

This does not mean that the resolution of an event must exactly fit some anticipated pattern. In many cases, later developments cause the reader to reflect upon what happened earlier, and to reassess the relative significance of this or that antecedent. There is a striking example of this power to evoke reflection in the mysterious observation of Einhard, in his account of the coronation, that Charlemagne was at first so opposed to the ceremony that "he would not have entered the church that day if he had known in advance the plan of the pope."[27] Since no such plan is outlined in previous accounts, the historian is forced to review all the events previous to the coronation in order to ferret out some indication of the pope's design. And the question of whether Charlemagne knew about the ceremony in advance, or intended a different role for the pope, continues to stir controversy.

Now, the object of anticipation and reflection in the narrative is the formulation of possible patterns of development covering the whole temporal duration of the event. And these hypothetical patterns have several levels of abstraction. If one anticipates that Charlemagne will incur the hostility of the Byzantine rulers, one imagines a pattern of development involving individuals, groups, institutions, and ideas, held together by economic, religious, political, or other relationships. Some of these elements are more abstract than others, in the sense that they are also involved, in similar ways, in many other events. For example, the papacy as an institution is a more abstract element than Pope Leo III as an individual.

In short, anticipation and reflection are subjective correlates to prediction and retrodiction, using the same processes of reasoning to generate abstract configurations which are then tested against empirical data. The details of a narrative may be too particularized to use as terms in an analytical argument; but the configurations evoked by the dynamics of narrative are amenable to analysis and criticism, especially at the higher levels of abstraction. In particular, one can compare the configurations of one event with those of related events to see if they have elements in common, thus opening the way for a lawlike hypothesis of regularity.

It has been argued that narrative explanation performs an analogical function, namely, to evoke in readers an experience analogous to that enjoyed by participants in a historical event. To the extent that this is true, the anticipations and reflections derived from the narrative ought to be similar to those involved in the event itself. This judgment of analogical validity will be based on the documentary evidence that is available to provide an empirical warrant for the explanation. One duty of the historian is to construct a narrative account that evokes empirically warranted configurations in the minds of readers; and this is done by a careful selection and definition of particular terms, a process J. H. Hexter describes as "bracketing":

> When he uses a word much trafficked in, it is very hard for a historian to be sure that his readers will actually have in mind at the start what they need to have in mind to follow his pursuit of those moving targets with which history must so often concern itself. This is why some of the best history ever written by some of the greatest historians . . . takes the reader through the process by which they initially have bracketed their targets. That is, they take their readers with them in their effort to discover what the people of the times they are writing about had in mind when they talked of a fief, or seisin, or a free man, or a villein, or a serf.[28]

The medieval terms mentioned by Hexter are a reminder that the empirical warrant for a narrative is not just a matter of reconciling data from the past with present habits of thought. It is more often the historian's task to evoke configurations that are quite foreign to the reader's own culture, and to show how plausible those configurations are in terms of actual past events. Most graduate students in history are made aware of the need to do this. But a close examination of published historical narratives shows that the evocation process verges on irrationality; and that, in consequence, the relationships among events in a narrative may appear capricious or contrived.

The problem of analogical validity, like the problem of structural coherence, can be solved by a judicious application of analytical criticism. Such criticism will have to be separated from the narrative itself; but its purpose is always to clarify and improve the narrative explanation. In this way the two modes of explanation can function in a complementary, rather than contradictory, fashion, bringing theory and craft into a more harmonious relationship.

For such criticism to work, the analytical model of explanation must first be reexamined. As presently formulated, that model involves assumptions about the nature of historical events, and about the aims of explanation, that narrative-writing historians find quite irrelevant and unacceptable.

2. Analytical Explanation

Intuitively or traditionally, historians have engaged in operations that fit poorly the conception of knowing and explaining most widely current among the historians themselves, a conception which is itself a vague and clumsy version of the natural science model.

J. H. Hexter, *The History Primer*

The historian who ventures to investigate the theoretical roots of his discipline is faced immediately with a dilemma. People who do historical research are noted for their relative lack of interest in theory, and have written little about it. When they have written, they have often shown a cavalier attitude toward the work of analytical philosophers. On the other hand, the volumes of philosophical analysis produced during the past quarter-century often deal with theoretical questions that seem irrelevant to the practical difficulties of the working historian. To both groups, the questions of a theoretically minded historian may appear misdirected. The problem of finding a vocabulary of explanation acceptable to historians and their critics may be distorted from the start by their long-standing prejudices toward each other.

It is precisely because historians do feel out of place in the world of philosophical analysis that, in this chapter, I will avoid the usual approaches to the subject. I will not attempt a systematic review of the literature from the past thirty years, nor will I offer any breakthrough in analytical theory. Instead, I will merely review some basic arguments developed by the analytical school and its critics, and comment on them from the point of view of the historian as craftsman, as a writer of narrative. My intention is to show that some kind of analysis is required for the refinement of historical explanation, but that the mode of analysis suggested by positivist critics is unsuitable for that purpose.

This approach seems justified by the variety of arguments offered by philosophical analysts. Some have demanded a logical purity that virtually denies the importance of historical details, while others have attempted to accommodate traditional categories of explanation to the uncertain needs of historians. In part, these approaches reflect the state of the historical profession itself. As indicated in the previous chapter, historical explanations have rather paradoxical characteristics. They make frequent use of the terminology of cause and effect but constantly frustrate causal analysis. They claim a kind of scientific status but are cast in narrative form and embellished with imagery, irony, and inference. They seem to imply the existence of laws, norms, and levels of probability which are seldom stated and hard to abstract from the particular terms of descriptive accounts.

In *The Structure of Scientific Revolutions,* which applies to intellectual developments outside science as well, Thomas Kuhn described such a state of affairs as a "pre-paradigm" stage, in which there is no clearly accepted model of explanation to provide a coherent base for research.[1] The paradigm includes both theory and applications in a single striking example of successful inquiry. Such a situation existed during the seventeenth century prior to Newton's formulation of the law of gravitation, and during the last part of the nineteenth century prior to Einstein's development of his theories of relativity. Until a new paradigm is developed, there is a gap between doctrines of explanation (which may be at war among themselves) and the work done by researchers. The latter survive uneasily on the remnants of outworn models whose assumptions are either forgotten or constantly questioned. A great deal of hostility is generated by the lack of a generally accepted conceptual framework that would allow constructive criticism and response between researchers (in this case, historians) and theorists. This gap will only be overcome by the appearance of a new paradigmatic narrative which clearly embodies an effective and theoretically justifiable model of explanation. Neither philosophical criticism in itself nor an increased supply of traditional historical accounts will do the trick.

Kuhn suggests that clues to the character of a new paradigm may be found among those aspects of a discipline that have tended to be neglected in recent practice. And as I have indicated, one of the most neglected aspects of historical explanation is the structure of narrative discourse itself. Though historians are not ignorant of the meanings of words, they do not attach any definite meanings to particular terms in a systematic way. It should not be surprising, then, that the most significant challenge to the logic of historical explanation should come from philosophers of science, for whom each utterance must have a precise and constant empirical reference. Their attempts to force historians into the scientific mold have been both strenuous and controversial.

If the analysis of historical discourse involved no more than a clearer definition of terms, one might think of extending Hexter's practice of "bracketing" into a general method of comparing the meaning of terms as they appear in various accounts of a given period. There are, in fact, a number of monographs that attempt to bracket, for general use, concepts such as "feudalism" or "romanticism." But most of these proceed by illustrating the subject with particular cases in the historical record rather than by comparing historians' accounts. The latter procedure, through which one could arrive at a standard definition, is fairly common to the sciences but is limited in history to the introductory pages of textbook surveys.

But historical discourse involves much more than the use of a set of terms which might be more clearly defined. It also involves assumptions about the direction and dynamics of the historical process that, in most cases, are developed by experience or by immersion in the documentary sources rather than by obedience to a formal precept. As Arthur Danto comments,

> I should like to suppose that children begin with a temporally neutral language, and then, at the same time, so to speak, acquire together the use of past-referring terminology, a concept of causality, and a concept of the past, all three achievements being inter-dependent. It would only be natural, then, that any attack on our concept of the past would at once involve an attack on the concept of causality and upon our use of past-referring terms.[2]

Danto's observation might be turned around to say that any criticism of the terminology used by historians will automatically bring into question their half-formulated assumptions about the historical process and its explanation. Such a consequence is, in fact, the ground of contention between historians and their analytical critics. Thus the general question pursued through the following commentary is whether the notions of "the past" and of causality implicit in philosophical analyses of historical explanation are, or can be made, commensurate with the needs and perceptions of narrative historians.

One might also ask, of course, to what extent historians must change their habits of thinking and writing to conform to a philosophically justifiable model of explanation. This is the question raised by Carl Hempel in 1942 in his well-known article, "The Function of General Laws in History." Reflecting a century-old ideal drawn from the physical sciences, Hempel places historians squarely on the defensive:

> It is a rather widely held opinion that history, in contradistinction to the so-called physical sciences, is concerned with the description of particular events of the past rather than with the search for general laws which might govern these events. As a characterization of the type of problem in which some historians are mainly interested, this view probably can not be denied; as a statement of the theoretical function of general laws in scientific historical research, it is certainly unacceptable.[3]

What Hempel appeared to want was a confession by historians that they did make use of general laws ("universal hypotheses"), or statements implying general laws, when they wrote explanatory narratives, and that their use of such laws was arbitrary and incoherent when compared with explanations in the physical sciences. As a relatively immature discipline, history provides only "explanation sketches" at best, omitting much of the empirical warrant for its lawlike hypotheses and refusing, in many cases, to abstract a cause-effect relationship that would apply to cases other than the particular one under examination.

Hempel dismissed the claim that history is "ideographic" rather than "nomothetic" (that is, interested in the unique and nonrecurrent rather than the abstract and general). Despite the fact that historians do not regard it as part of their task to establish laws,[4] Hempel showed that they make constant use of them. It remained for analytical philosophers to guide historians toward more complete (scientific) explanations by elucidating the complex of general laws implicit in their narratives. Moreover, if the narrative form proved to be an impediment to the formulation of lawlike hypotheses because of its preoccupation with particular data and temporal development, then narrative ought to be given up.

The historian who writes, "Like Charles XII and Napoleon, Hitler fell victim to the treacherous Russian winter," implies the existence of one or more general laws which govern historical events. He implies, in other words, that there is some regular connection between the Russian winter and the defeat of invading forces. Most narratives, said Hempel, assert a regularity of the following type:

> In every case where an event of a specified kind C occurs at a certain place and time, an event of a specified kind E will occur at a place and time which is related in a specified manner to the place and time of the occurrence of the first event. (The symbols C and E have been chosen to suggest the terms "cause" and "effect," which are often, though by no means always, applied to events related by a law of the above kind.'[5]

In the example given above, there is an implied law regarding the fate of armies invading Russia late in the calendar year. Can this law be specified, and does it hold "in every case"? Most historians would answer with a horrified "No!" And Hempel would agree. But whereas historians would argue the difficulty, if not impossibility, of explicating a general law that held for all cases both past and future, Hempel simply took the difficulty as an indication of the relative immaturity of scientific history. Though he admitted the impossibility of explaining an individual event in the sense of accounting for all its properties by means of general laws, he claimed that explanations could and should be made ever more specific and comprehensive. There was no difference, in this respect, between the goals of history and of the more exact sciences.[6]

Hempel was clearly restating a doctrine laid down in the nineteenth century by John Stuart Mill: "Our conception of cause and effect is this: that given a definite configuration of wholly material things, there will always follow upon it the same observable event. If we repeat the configuration, we shall always get the same event following it."[7] The historian who offers a causal explanation for some event thus implies that there is a definite configuration of initial conditions that is related to the given event by an empirically warranted general law. A century ago, historians were confident that their empirical studies would eventually produce an edifice of detailed information that would, of itself, reveal the laws governing the relationships among its parts. A similar stage of information-gathering may be seen in the development of classical physics and Darwinian biology. But in the latter cases, the stage of information-gathering was eventually capped by a stage of sorting out lawful relationships to form a general paradigm for inquiry in each science. Given the remarkable achievements that such efforts promoted, Hempel appears quite correct in challenging historians to follow suit.

However, there are two reservations to be made to the type of challenge Hempel outlined. The first has to do with his abrupt dismissal of particular events as the focus of historical explanation. It is one thing to say that historians make use of general hypotheses, and that such hypotheses necessarily refer to types of events rather than to particular cases. It is quite another thing to say that the elucidation of types and of their lawful relationships constitutes the only legitimate purpose of historical investigation—that explanations of particular events are by definition nonsensical. In Chapter 1, I argued that historical understanding involves reciprocity between abstraction and particularization. The process of abstracting general types from particular events so as to study the connections between them constitutes one side of a dual approach. That one side remains meaningless without reference to the other, more particular, one. Hempel is probably right in concluding that historians have neglected the abstract for the concrete to the detriment of their discipline. But a simple reversal of focus will not solve that problem.

The second reservation centers on the deductive-law model that Hempel assumed was the standard model for scientific explanation. According to that model, a complete explanation should include (1) an empirically warranted description of the initial conditions; (2) a similar description of the event to be explained; and (3) and an empirically warranted general law stating the invariant relationship between the conditions and the event. But are causal explanations in the sciences always so rigorous? How general must a general law be, and how exactly must it fit the case? Must the relationship stated be absolutely invariant, or may it be probabilistic? Finally, how complete should be the description of initial conditions and of the event to be explained? These questions are not idle, for, as we have seen, the problem of explanation centers around relative degrees of abstraction, generalization, and complexity.

A number of scholars have worked with Hempel's model to criticize or to improve its applicability to traditional historical practice. A complete survey of these efforts is impossible, but the main arguments can be summarized as a means of highlighting issues relevant to the present study. It is well to remember that Hempel's model was offered as an ideal. The full development of deductive-law explanations for particular historical events would require unprecedented cooperation and mutual accommodation by historians and philosophers.

Are the laws of science so exact as Hempel's model implies? Michael Scriven argues that they are not; all are approximations with varying ranges of accuracy when applied to specific causal relations. They are laws about aggregates of identical units, not about individual events. Laws of this type, applied to historical incidents, can never demonstrate a fully invariant relationship.[8]

Scriven also argues that, to be complete, such an explanation would have to include not only the appropriate general law but also the empirical evidence for that law and references verifying the empirical evidence, the statement of initial conditions, and the description of the event whose cause is sought. Scientists obviously do not include these second- and third-order justifications in their research reports. They are understood to be implicated in any causal hypothesis, but their actual inclusion is not required by the context of the report. Historians operate on the same principle, argues Scriven, and in the context of an explanatory narrative a full statement of the relevant general law is not properly required.[9]

The deductive-law model, in fact, places a double burden on the historian. He has to demonstrate that the relation between event and initial conditions conforms to a general law, and to show that the law itself is empirically warranted. It is hard to see how one could fulfill the latter requirement without using, as evidence, the very events one is describing. This is the quandary examined previously with reference to Louis Halphen's account of the coronation of Charlemagne. To back up one's use of a general hypothesis, one should really offer accounts of several events that parallel, in appropriate ways, the event under study.

Morton White has offered an alternative method of justifying the use of general laws. Like Scriven, White believes that a law need not be explicitly stated in the narrative; but he agrees with Hempel that laws are implied and should be warranted by empirical evidence. One form of warrant is a demonstration that no other relationship could have existed between the given event and its antecedent conditions than the one implied as a general law. For such a demonstration, the historian need only add evidence to his description of events until there is nothing left to support an alternative:

> If "*a* is P always leads to *a* is Q" is not shown, then add another property to *a* such as "R"; the resulting law may still not be proved but may be

more probable; then add other properties to *a* such that each makes the implied law more probable, until the law "all P's are Q", while not proven, is reasonably acceptable.[10]

In other words, one can show that Q was caused by P in two ways. One can give evidence that all "type P" events are followed by "type Q" events; or, following White, one can give evidence that no other relationship could have existed than that between P and Q. For example, if the statement "Hitler's invading forces were devastated by the Russian winter" does not in itself prove the existence of a law—the law that all invading forces will be devastated by the Russian winter—then the historian must provide other information about the event (such as the logistical support for the invading forces, the time of year, the traditions of Russian defense, and the peculiar severity of the weather). Each additional piece of information helps articulate the general law while reducing the probability that any other relationship existed.

Now, if White's argument has been rendered correctly, most historians can breathe a sigh of relief. It seems that the conditions White outlined for meeting the demands of the deductive-law model are already met by traditional historical method. That is, in order to show that their explanations are valid, historians typically produce more and more evidence of a corroborating sort, so that the general law implied by the basic description of cause and effect is backed up by other statements. The historian who writes about the devastation of Hitler's forces in Russia knows that "winter" is not a sufficient explanation. So he goes on to write about the disposition of Hitler's forces, the weather, and so forth. Thus he arrives at an explanation which, while not proving the general law, makes its existence reasonably probable.

The fact that working historians appear to satisfy White's amendments to the deductive-law model, however, does not mean that the modification is valid. Instead, White has revealed one of the major difficulties of the analytical approach to history. As more and more properties are added to the event to be explained, and to the description of its antecedent conditions, the general law implied by the explanation becomes more and more complex. "A declaration of war followed the invasion" implies a general law of low complexity with many possible instances, the kind of regularity discussed, for instance, by Crane Brinton in *The Anatomy of Revolution.* "Britain declared war on August 4, 1914, following the German invasion of Belgium, whose neutrality had been guaranteed by the British since 1839" implies a far more complex law, or set of laws, with only one instance. And a law with a single instance is no law at all.[11]

As a historian begins to sort out the causes for some event, he is invariably forced to discard simple explanations, implying general laws with many instances, in favor of more complex explanations. If asked to articulate the particular relationship between a given cause and its effect, he would be led to construct a detailed narrative. The "law" is contained within the complex temporal pattern of that narrative.

But the articulation of a cause-effect relationship for a particular set of events does not demonstrate a general law. To do that, one must abstract certain significant properties from the events and show that *their* relationship holds in all similar cases. This is what Hempel himself did when giving an example of a deductive argument, one concerning a car radiator that burst during a freezing night. Though Hempel presented his argument in narrative form, he did not set it in a historical framework. Instead, he described *any* car with *any* radiator on *any* freezing night. The general laws he mentioned pertained to a class of events, not to a particular event that did in fact occur.[12]

Morton White's revision of the deductive-law model thus raises a dilemma: the full articulation of a relationship between particular causes and effects in their historical context precludes the kind of generalization needed for the formulation of a law. But anything less than a full articulation renders the argument nonhistorical. A general law pertaining to certain types of events cannot explain why a particular event happened just the way it did and not otherwise. White's formula for adding properties to an event until the existence of a law is demonstrated is thus self-defeating.[13]

There is another difficulty about deriving a general law from a full statement of a historical relationship. Aside from the fact that a full knowledge of antecedent conditions is impossible,[14] those conditions are also the antecedents for all other events contemporary with the event to be explained. For instance, if a historian were able to describe all conditions present in 1789, even in France alone, he would still not be able to show that the revolutionary actions of the Third Estate were the necessary outcome. All sorts of other outcomes occurred as well, stemming from the same background.

The solution to this difficulty is well known: the initial conditions are not equally significant to all subsequent events. When a historian describes the state of affairs in France in 1789, he states the relative significance of each condition for the events he intends to explain. And that significance, or weight, may change depending upon the particular event he is discussing. In addition, because many conditions are too insignificant to mention, the historian is not bound to articulate the state of the whole antecedent world in order to give a reasonable explanation.

The key to the deductive-law model of explanation, therefore, lies in the way one describes historical events. Only by looking at that description can one ascertain whether the statement of initial conditions is adequate, and whether the implied law is relevant. Also, the empirical evidence for the law will depend upon appropriate descriptions of other historical events with similar relationships. Hempel's challenge to historians, then, involves a very basic question: *What is a historical event?*

It is the answer to this question which separates Hempelians from their critics, and from the majority of historians as well. As Arthur Danto puts it:

> Historical events differ from "scientific" events in that they are not homogeneous members of a class of events covered by a general description. Hence the deductive-model of Hempel, though it works for science, does not work for history.[15]

The particularity and uniqueness of historical events, evident in much of the previous discussion, is a function of their nonrecurrence, both in the past and in the future. To define such events as members of a homogeneous class of recurring events would be contradictory, for then they would not be historical. This argument represents an article of faith among historians, precluding their acceptance of the deductive-law model, whatever its other modifications.

However, there is a sense in which historians have mistakenly accepted the definition of events assumed by Hempel. They tend to talk about them as discrete objects with specific properties, or in John Stuart Mill's words, "definite configurations of wholly material things." It is not too much to say that all discussions of the analytical approach to explanation have been confused by the transposition of the terms "object" and "event." The former denotes something substantial with discrete characteristics. The latter refers to the dynamic relationship between a state of affairs and its antecedents in a given duration. The former term is spatial; the latter is temporal.

Consider Morton White's argument, previously quoted:

> If "*a* is P always leads to *a* is Q" is not shown, then add another property to *a* such as "R". . . . then add other properties to *a* such that each makes the implied law more probable.

This formulation treats a set of initial conditions (P, R) as properties of an object and ignores the dynamic quality of their relationships to both *a* and Q. It also implies that the relationship "leads to" does not include either set of properties. By thus objectifying a historical event, the model fails to explain how the event happened. Hempel's original definition of a general law reveals the same problem:

> In every case where an event of a specified kind *C* occurs at a certain place and time, an event of a specified kind *E* will occur at a place and time which is related in a specified manner to the place and time of the occurrence of the first event.[16]

Again, cause and effect are considered as distinct entities located at separate points in time. They are related, not by what happens between them, not by their involvement with each other, but by their coincidental relationship to a system of time and space coordinates (which, in effect, are further properties). The historical interaction between them that allows us to call one a "cause" and the other its "effect" cannot be explained by considering events this way. Arthur Danto and Maurice Mandelbaum have criticized Hempel at length for this error. "The events in question," Danto argues, "are connected as end points of a temporally extended change—as the beginning and end of a temporal whole—and it is the change thus indicated for which a cause is sought." In other words, what Hempel regarded as the initial conditions are really part of the event to be explained.[17]

A definition of historical events as dynamic relationships between, and inclusive of, causes and effects helps focus attention on the process of historical change rather than on static arrangements abstracted from that process. The former appears to be the traditional concern of historians. Nevertheless, it does not preclude the kind of classification that leads to analysis of regularity. As shown in the previous chapter, it is quite possible to specify types of temporal development according to their structural characteristics and to compare the structures of different events. For example, the term "Renaissance" defines a transactional relationship between certain elements of various events. The transaction has an identifiable structure, as many historians have demonstrated, and the various elements have identifiable functions within that structure. Classification of the structural and functional regularities does not detract from the particularity of a given event. Indeed, it allows one to show how an event such as the Florentine Renaissance became what it was, and not something else. It permits an analysis of uniqueness and novelty.

In his criticism of the deductive-law model of explanation, Arthur Danto emphasized the question of novelty, and suggested that regularity hypotheses could account for the emergence of new configurations in history:

> The laws, then, which may be said to be implicit, according to Hempel's account, in typical historical explanations, are peculiarly loose, in the sense that they can accommodate any number of qualitatively different instances. They indeed permit creative opportunities, for the class of events they cover is open, in the sense that we can in principle always imagine an instance, covered by them, which need not in any obvious way resemble past instances. It is this sort of situation, for example, which allows us to class, as works of art, things which do not necessarily resemble objects already classed as such, and which permits artists to pursue novelty.[18]

In other words, one can perceive a regular pattern if one looks at the process by which a novel art object is created, and the context in which it appears, rather than at the object itself. Similarly, the historian can perceive in the destruction of the English monasteries a process of decision-making or a pattern of behavior that can be compared with other patterns exhibited by Henry VIII, or even by other monarchs of the same or different periods. The structural similarities of different event-processes are akin to the rules of composition in art: there are some basic principles that apply to most cases, and some intermediate principles that characterize one period or school more than others. Knowledge of the principles does not allow one to predict a particular novel occurrence or work of art. But it does allow one to appreciate the novelty, and to account for its emergence by the use of retrodictive reasoning. Thus a historian can show that the destruction of the English monasteries was an intelligible incident not because it followed necessarily from some set of initial conditions but because *the whole temporal process of which it was a part exhibits an intelligible structure.*

Now, to suggest that historical events are characterized primarily by the emergence of novelty is to challenge the main feature of the deductive-law model of explanation. For Hempel clearly stated that explanations correctly based on general laws "might as well have functioned as predictions." That is, any statement that a set of initial conditions is invariably followed by a given effect means that, given knowledge of an identical set, one could predict the effect, even without benefit of historical hindsight. None of the implications of Hempel's model have been so controversial as this. Even historians sympathetic to the need for scientific rigor have balked at the idea that past events could have been predicted, or that the historian's task is to define laws of cause and effect that could serve to anticipate the future configuration of events. Underlying the bulk of historical inquiries is the desire to explain the unpredictability of human affairs, to show how things did *not* turn out the way people thought or hoped they would.

Because the predictability criterion underlies Hempel's whole notion of scientific history, it is worth examining in some detail. By prediction, Hempel does not mean an assessment of probability. The model requires the demonstration, by deductive reasoning, of an invariant relationship between cause and effect. It is not enough to say, for example, that the German invasion of Belgium in 1914 made British intervention extremely probable. One must show, by an adequate description of initial conditions and the citation of the relevant law, that British intervention *had* to occur at a specified time and place. The reluctance of historians to subscribe to such a criterion is understandable; but there have been several challenges to it by philosophers as well.

In the first place, as Arthur Danto and Haskell Fain have pointed out, the predictability criterion violates Hume's principle that causes do not logically entail their effects. Hume argued, says Danto,

> that from a description of the manifest properties of one thing, we could not logically *deduce* what effects it would have, nor, from an exhaustive description of another thing, could we deduce what its causes must have

been. Our causal concept is built up out of certain associations with respect to what has *in fact* happened, but there is nothing compelling, logically at least, about such association, and the presence of a given thing is logically compatible with having had different causes than it in fact had, or, for that matter, with its having had *no* causes at all.[19]

The fact that two events are associated in a sequence a great number of times does not mean that one causes the other. It simply means that they are associated. Causation is a kind of fiction that we attribute to the association to make it intelligible for the purpose of controlling our environment. The fiction helps explain what has in fact happened, but that fact is not a proof of what *must* happen of logical necessity. Hume's argument thus denies the possibility of predicting invariant relationships on the basis of historical evidence.

In the second place, Danto claimed that a statement that serves as a prediction must be a statement about the future. In fact, all scientific hypotheses are essentially future-oriented, as Jacob Bronowski pointed out:

it is a mistake to suppose that the basic process in thought is looking back at what is known; and that looking forward to the future is to be justified from this. This is a reversal of the process of life. Anticipating the future is the fundamental activity; babies do it before they are born. Analysing the past and the present is a subsidiary process, whose purpose is still that we shall learn to recognize and interpret signals for the future. It is absurd to ask why the future should turn out to chime with our knowledge of the past. This puts the question upside down, and makes nonsense out of it. What we have learned from the past is knowledge only because the future proves it to be true.[20]

Bronowski's argument indicates that no historical explanation could satisfy a criterion of predictability, because a prediction necessarily implies that one does not know the outcome of the process. Similarly, the empirical data used to validate a general law cannot be the same data used to generate its hypothesis: they must be data from future events. Since the function of historical explanations is to account for what did in fact happen, it is impossible that they should serve as predictions.[21]

It was argued previously that historians choose to explain events because of their significance, and that their significance is a function of the contrast between what happened and what might have happened. It is also a function of what happened *after* the event in question: the judgment of significance depends upon hindsight. Arthur Danto rebuked the relativist historians for complaining that one cannot know the past as contemporaries knew it, without foresight: "The whole point of history is *not* to know about actions as witnesses might, but as historians do, in connection with later events and as parts of temporal wholes."[22] Predictions, by definition, preclude hindsight, and therefore preclude any assessment of significance. To give an explanation that might have served as a prediction is historically meaningless.

In the third place, Hempel himself acknowledged that predictions have a way of affecting the same human actions they are meant to explain. The formulation and verification of laws about history must have consequences for the verifier, and perhaps even for his human subjects, whereas the physicist has no such relation to the results of experiments with lifeless objects. It is true that, like historians, scientists may be biased in favor of their own hypotheses, that they operate in a human context, and that there are rewards for observing what one wants to observe. These are the dangers disciplines are supposed to guard against. But a law of gravitation does not change the action of gravitating bodies, whereas a "law" of revolutionary change may be known to one or more parties in a revolutionary situation and influence their behavior in ways that invalidate the law. One thinks of Lenin during the summer and fall of 1917, arguing vehemently with other Russian revolutionary leaders about the "proper" sequence of socialist development according to Marxist doctrine, or the long series of arguments against the welfare provisions of the English poor laws in the nineteenth century, based on the broad generalizations of Malthusian theory. In such cases, knowledge of a pattern of regularity may confuse a situation which is already more complex than the one the pattern was designed to deal with. That laws and norms are often confounded by human feelings about them (either a desire to fulfill or a desire to avoid what was predicted) is an underlying theme in much historical writing, and may account for the historians' opposition to the whole notion of general laws. A law that might have functioned as a prediction ceases to be a law and becomes part of the initial conditions of the event to be explained, if it can be shown that some actor in the period could have entertained such a hypothesis. And if no actor could have done so, then the law obviously contains information about subsequent events that would disqualify it as a prediction.

Finally, there is a problem in applying Hempel's rule that the effect must be related to the cause at specified times and places. It is one thing to say that a set of conditions such as the British victory in the Seven Years' War, the growing prosperity of colonial merchants, and the centralizing tendency of British imperial governments is sure to be followed by colonial demands for greater autonomy. But it is quite another thing to say when these demands will be made, or when specific actions will be taken. If the predicted action does not follow immediately upon the alleged causes, one must consider all intervening events which may have influenced that action. The logical difficulty involved has been summed up by J. H. Hexter: "any time interval between the presence of the factors and the occurrence of the event for which they are supposed to be the sufficient conditions simply demonstrates that, as they have been stated, they were *not* sufficient during the interval."[23]

If one includes the effect with the cause in a temporal duration, as was suggested previously, one can compare their relationship with the relationships of other events of similar durations. But predictions of the kind implied by Hempel's model of explanation do not specify durations. Their terms, abstracted from the chronological web of historical process, are discrete and timeless. They do not specify how long it will take for the causes to have their effect, or what will happen in between; unfortunately, these are the concerns that are most important to the actors in a historical event and to the historians who write about it.[24]

The arguments against Hempel's requirement of predictability have been rehearsed at some length because they concern the central notion of determinism on which the deductive-law model is based. Morton White commented that "so long as we do not abandon determinism, we may hold that a singular explanatory statement implies that strict laws exist."[25] But if determinism is not defensible with regard to historical events, then explanations by historians need not demonstrate lawful relationships. Their preoccupation with the new, the irregular, and the unexpected may be justified. In fact Karl Popper, whose name is sometimes associated with that of Hempel in the criticism of history, claimed that *"the main task of the theoretical social sciences is to trace the unintended social repercussions of intentional human actions."*[26] In other words, human history displays irregularities both *in spite of,* and *because of,* the ability of humans to derive hypotheses about the future from a study of the past.

Such hypotheses, deriving from concrete experience, are normative rather than deterministic. They anticipate some contrast between possibility and actuality, and allow the historian to investigate the uniqueness of events by comparing what did happen with what might have been expected. Although they lack the logical rigor of Hempel's model, they are nonetheless statements of regularity that can be empirically tested. Such normative (or "normic") hypotheses have been justified by Michael Scriven as intelligible alternatives to general laws.

For Scriven, the purpose of a historical experience is not to demonstrate the inevitability of an event, but to account for what does not meet one's expectations. The normative hypothesis can do this in three ways. First, it serves as a guide to the historian in his search for elements of continuity and change; it is an index of the variables one should consider when comparing an event with its antecedents. In this sense it is, as Hempel claimed, a kind of explanation "sketch." But instead of using the sketch to generate a more complete (and more abstract) deductive argument, the normative approach uses it to explain the relative importance of more specific incidents. "Castlereagh followed traditional British policy in trying to protect the Low Countries from the encroachments of Continental powers" is a statement that shows what was normally involved in a certain type of situation.

Its function in a narrative is to introduce the historian's more detailed account of Castlereagh's behavior. The account will reveal a contrast between what might plausibly have been anticipated and what actually happened; and that contrast, in turn, will provoke a reflective reassessment of the antecedent conditions. The normative hypothesis, then, looks very much like the anticipatory configurations generated by the structure of a narrative that were discussed in the previous chapter. As such, they are amenable to analysis, though not to the kind of analysis Hempel prefers.

The second function of a normative statement is to identify a subject's characteristic pattern of behavior as one of the initial conditions of an event in which that subject participates. To say that "Metternich's youthful exposure to the excesses of the French Revolution turned him into a lifelong reactionary" is not to claim a general law but to indicate, as a guide to understanding later events, what Metternich himself admitted was a factor in his development. Alan Donagan followed Gilbert Ryle in calling such statements "dispositional" in the sense that they account for the individual case by asserting an empirically verifiable regularity in the subject.[27] Thus one could explain some of Metternich's repressive actions against German dissenters in the post-Napoleonic period by reference to his reactionary disposition evidenced in previous events. One could not predict that Metternich would act in this "normal" fashion in every event, nor could one assert that Metternich must be involved in every instance of repression (that is, "without M, R would not have happened"). But for that very reason, the normative hypothesis allows one to deal with instances of abnormal behavior, by implying that there must have been exceptional circumstances involved, and that no explanation would be complete unless such circumstances were brought out.

The third function of normative statements is to identify patterns of behavior that seem strange to us because of differences in personal or cultural assumptions but that make perfectly good sense from the point of view of the historical subject. Historians are rightly criticized when they project contemporary ideas and standards onto past behavior; but in many cases, it is precisely the strange cultural assumptions of his subject that draws the researcher to it. The observation that we would not have followed such a course of action, or such a train of thought, prompts the quest for a normative hypothesis that will make the past intelligible. Did Henry VIII seek a divorce from Catherine of Aragon because he had lust in his heart for Anne Boleyn? That, one could understand readily enough. Or did he really feel the need for a legitimate male heir to prevent a recurrence of civil chaos? There is a reason requiring more knowledge of the times to understand. And what of his stated belief that the lack of male heirs was God's punishment for his marriage to a woman previously betrothed to his dead brother, a form of sacrilege that even the pope's dispensation could not atone for? Such an implied norm strains modern credulity, and prompts historians to investigate the possibility that Henry, if he was not hypocritical, faced circumstances quite different from those of our own time. The historian without a sense of the difference in cultural norms between one period and another is a historian without research problems; and the normative hypothesis is his chief reasearch tool.

In summary, the normic or normative hypotheses discussed by Scriven are different from the lawlike statements advocated by Hempel, not only in their degree of abstraction from concrete historical events but also (and more importantly) in their conception of meaning in historical explanations. Scientific laws always include an implicit normative qualification, "all other things being held constant." Historical hypotheses may be stated the same way, but historians know that "all other things" cannot be held constant as in a laboratory experiment. Their generalizations are applied as normative guides to find out *what* other things were involved in a particular case. In the sciences, events are described or arranged so as to minimize the number of variables. In history, it is the variables that matter most. As William Dray has remarked, science seeks control; but history seeks the acknowledgment and acceptance of contingency, for without contingency there is neither hope, nor tragedy, nor other human value in the past.

"Contingency" and "variable" are but different terms for the compositional elements of an emerging event and were discussed in the previous chapter. These elements, which express potential configurations in the process of development, can be abstracted from an event's concrete form, and analyzed in terms of their patterned relationships. But it appears impossible, even in theory, to demonstrate a deterministic causal connection between them. Strict adherence to the deductive-law model of explanation is self-defeating for historians, and one must agree with Morton White that "there is something wrong about a philosophical theory which forces us to say that virtually all explanatory statements that are made by historians are false."[28]

On the other hand, as White himself demonstrated, the risk of giving up rigorous standards of analysis is that one slides easily into descriptions of what historians already do, instead of prescribing remedies for their admitted deficiencies. Thus one should keep in mind the possibilities for abstraction and analysis, and the criticism of Hempel and his followers, when considering the arguments for narrative as a self-justifying mode of explanation.

3. Narrative Explanation

If a narrative form could be found which would enable the historian to offer real explanations of problems and to accommodate more than the traditional political story, the genre would again become respectable, especially if at the same time it could preserve its special distinction as literary art.

G. R. Elton, *The Practice of History*

In Chapter 2, historical events were tentatively described as temporal processes in which novel patterns of relationship emerge from particular antecedent conditions. These processes include both cause and effect considered together in a single duration, not separated as discrete entities. Particular historical events, defined this way, cannot be explained by logical deduction from initial conditions, nor can their individual occurrence be predicted according to strict scientific methods. However, statements about historical events do usually refer to some notion of regularity, without which novelty and uniqueness would remain incomprehensible. Notions of historical regularity, while not deterministic, are usually normic or normative, in the sense that they assert, from the perspective of the historian, what might have been expected to happen in given circumstances. They recognize the potential in a set of initial conditions and lead one to examine whether, and to what extent, that potential is fulfilled.

The concept that events develop some potential from their antecedent world is a genetic concept. Because history deals with change and continuity in an evolutionary framework, many critics regard genetic models of explanation as more appropriate for its study than models drawn from the physical sciences. Louis Gottschalk states the position directly: without judgments involving "development, rise, fall, growth, decay, fertility or sterility...historical writing cannot be good narrative or description, which is the essence of history."[1] Implicit in Gottschalk's argument is the notion that historical events themselves develop genetically and that narrative is the explanatory mode most analogous to that process. Haskell Fain, in supporting this notion, indicates the difficulty of combining narrative with nongenetic approaches:

> Narrative coherence between episodes depends, at bottom, upon showing how one episode leads to another, how one incident generates

another. Once one has taken on the positivistic philosophical style, though, one will strive to ensnare the concepts of growth, development, evolution in a "nomic nexus," to treat genesis as nothing but an archaic form of causal production. Since . . . the main purpose of narrative history is to trace genetic relationships between historical incidents, it is no surprise that positivists have failed to give an adequate account of history.[2]

It is obvious from these comments that the arguments between geneticists and deductive-law positivists begin from different assumptions about the nature of historical events and about the level of abstraction at which explanations of events have meaning. The difference between events defined as discrete, objectlike entities and those defined as temporal processes is metaphysically fundamental, and will have to be examined as a separate issue in the next chapter. I have looked at the question of abstraction in previous chapters, with the observation that explanatory meaning may be found at any level, and that an effective theory of historical explanation should include some means of allowing abstract analysis to complement narrative description rather than dismiss it as an impediment to understanding. By the same token, models of explanation based on the genetic aspects of narrative must provide a means of analyzing the genetic structure of events; for without such analysis, the understanding of narrative history becomes merely subjective, precluding critical discussion and disciplinary refinement. In this chapter, then, I will be reviewing the arguments of the genetic school for signs of a usable conceptual framework.

Walter B. Gallie, one of the pioneers of the genetic approach, asserts that historical explanations are essentially causal explanations of a special kind, akin to those used by many natural scientists. They can stand on their own, without external justification, if they meet the following conditions:

(1) A characteristically genetic explanation seeks to establish, or at least helps to indicate, some kind of continuity between one or a number of temporally prior conditions and a subsequent result.
(2) On the other hand, a characterically genetic explanation does not pretend to predictive power; the prior event is not taken, in conjunction with certain universal laws, to constitute a sufficient condition of the occurrence of the subsequent event.
(3) Moreover, a characteristically genetic explanation emphasizes the one-way passage of time—what came earlier explains, in the genetic sense, what came later, and not *vice versa*.[3]

The issue between Gallie and the Hempelians is whether there can be more than one valid form of scientific explanation. Whereas Morton White claims that physical, chemical, biological, and historical explanations are simply different kinds of causal explanation, which are more or less complete according to their adherence to the physical model,[4] Gallie contends that biological or genetic explanations are bona fide explanations on their own terms.[5]

When a biologist explains the evolution of a particular organism, such as a giraffe, he may give a fairly complete account of the conditions from which the species emerged, and may also indicate one or more general laws governing the process. But no biologist would argue the necessity of the giraffe, or agree that the giraffe could have been predicted. Fundamental to any genetic explanation is the notion of chance deviation or mutation as the mechanism of adaptation to a changing environment; and while there are regularity hypotheses involved, none of them are sufficient to explain the occurrence or responses of a particular organism. A genetic explanation in history, therefore, could give an adequate account of the conditions antecedent to a given event, and perhaps even identify the particular changes taking place, without being expected to conform to the requirements of the deductive-law model.

The notion of indeterminacy inherent in genetic explanations makes them especially adaptable to the dynamics of narrative form; and they have other features of interest to historical writers. In a genetic relationship, the "effect" may be said to grow out of the "cause" by a process which cannot be broken down into identical, discrete units. An oak tree emerges from an acorn through many stages of development, one of which includes the final effect. Yet the stages cannot be characterized as a chain of causes and effects, since the features of one stage may be merely vague potentials of a previous stage. Moreover, none of the potential features can be adequately assessed without inspection of the subsequent stages in which they are realized. This relationship recalls the argument that a historical event cannot be defined completely, for purposes of a deductive argument, without consideration of its future significance. It further illustrates the principle that an event expresses the relative significance of its antecedent conditions, insofar as they are elements in its constitution. Historians attempting to isolate the acorn from which the oak has grown are bound to be disappointed: the effect has internalized its cause.

The emergence of one event from its antecedents requires a minimum duration of time. It is impossible, therefore, to simply project an instantaneous set of properties labeled "causes" onto another instantaneous set labeled "effects." In order to explain the temporal relationship, it is necessary to focus on what happens between cause and effect, between acorn and oak. Even if one called the acorn the "primary cause" and the rest of the environment "secondary causes," one would still not be able to derive the full-grown tree directly, because the environmental conditions change during the process of growth. To do justice to such a genetic process with a deductive causal explanation, one would be led to construct an ever-expanding web of arguments that, in its ultimate complexity, would imitate the growth process itself. In other words, one would end up with a detailed narrative, for which the logical arguments would be merely explanation sketches.

The analogy between an event and an organism may be difficult to accept at first. And yet the difference in reasoning between an organic approach and a deductive-law argument makes the analogy appropriate, as John Tyler Bonner illustrates with reference to our conceptions of "time" and "events":

> We tend in our minds to think of individuals of a species as an object in an instant of time, and more than likely this thin slice of time is taken in the adult stage. That is, when we say "mouse," an image of a mature mouse is the most natural one to appear in our minds. But the logicians have often pointed out that "mouse" might more correctly refer to some longer segment of time, starting perhaps with a fertilized egg and ending with death from old age. Any organism is a living object that alters through the course of time by development, and the individual might be defined as the whole of these time-space events.[6]

If an effect emerges from, and gradually absorbs its causal antecedents through a process of internal development, then both cause and effect must be included in the definition of the event, as Arthur Danto has maintained. Haskell Fain appears to dispute this conclusion when he quotes Hume's argument regarding the arbitrariness of causal inferences, which begins with the statement that every effect is an event distant from its cause.[7] From this, Fain infers that no causal relationship can be genetic. But this inference is based on the tendency to treat events as mechanical objects, to which an objection was raised previously. If events are viewed as developmental processes, internalizing both cause and effect, the discrepancy between causal and genetic explanations vanishes. The causal significance of a given set of conditions then presupposes their genetic relationship to what follows.

Also, when the internal development of an event is complete, that event functions as a datum in the development of subsequent events. Viewed externally, the relationship between two events in a sequence may be defined as cause and effect, each event having a distinct form and constitution; viewed internally, they are related genetically by virtue of one's inclusion in the other's process of development. The acorn grew on the oak tree that grew from an acorn.

An example from history will perhaps show historians that the analogy is not spurious. There have been as many arguments about the "beginning" of the eighteenth-century revolution in France as about its causes and consequences. None of the arguments makes sense until the disputants attempt to define the event they are talking about, which often means deciding whether to include the activities of provincial parlements and the more ambitious nobility before 1788; the various political decisions made in 1788–89 before the Estates General were mobilized; and, on the other "end," the various changes wrought by the Directory and Napoleon. The point is that the "Revolution" refers to a pattern of development with no inherent gaps or temporal boundaries. Its definition, and thus the argument over its causes, can only be settled by an arbitrary (albeit reasonable) decision to regard some incidents as "internal" to the event and others as "external." The relationship of incidents regarded internally is not subject to causal analysis, because they belong to the same temporal duration and are thus contemporaries. As soon as one removes an incident from the internal context, however, and regards it as an event in itself, one is free to examine its causal relationships with other incidents similarly defined.

For instance, the flight of Louis XVI and his immediate family in June 1791, together with his capture and return to Paris, might be regarded as one element in that process of polarization that marked the period from 1790 to 1792 in the French Revolution. Historians seeking the causes of polarization would not attempt a causal analysis of the flight itself. Instead, their narratives would relate the flight, as one complex event, to antecedent conditions which are also events. On the other hand, if one wished to understand why Louis was caught, one would break down the flight into a series of discrete occurrences, related externally, and analyze the relationships between them: the absurdity of traveling "incognito" in a royal carriage, the two-hour lunch break around the traveling kitchen, and so forth. Causal analysis demands that one focus always on the external relationships of an event, ignoring the pattern of internal development, which is genetic. Trying to grasp both aspects simultaneously leads to fundamental logical difficulties. Many of the classic disputes among historians, and many of the problems associated with their narrative explanations, can be traced to a habit of confusing the internal and external relationships. And in regard to the present discussion, the argument between Hempelians and geneticists is an argument between those who focus on the outside of events and those who view from within.

In order to resolve this argument, which is basic to a theory of historical explanation, we need to clarify the terms of transition from external to internal that must characterize the initial stage of all historical events. In other words, it must be shown how an event in its final form becomes a potential element in the emerging structure of some subsequent event. Having accomplished this, one can examine the geneticists' description of internal development, to see if there is a way to analyze the interaction of a given set of elements derived from the past. For if analysis proves impossible, if the narrative of internal development is claimed to be so self-explanatory as to preclude logical operations, then the whole genetic approach must remain an empty excuse for avoiding methodological criticism.

Suppose one considers the flight and capture of Louis XVI as one complex event, with a pattern of development terminated by the king's return to Paris under heavy guard. Following Arthur Danto, one must remember that the full meaning of the flight is a function of the significance attributed to it by subsequent events. Yet, subsequent events are themselves conditioned by the fact of the flight, whose actual pattern of development cannot be altered or eliminated as an antecedent. The internal structure of the flight as one event, and its external interactions with related successors, are thus complementary.

The flight of Louis is included in subsequent events, such as the invasion of France by Austrian and Prussian forces early in 1792, as one of many conditional elements, whose objective form remains constant but whose relationship to other elements is merely potential. The Austrians could not eliminate the flight as an actual occurrence, nor could they change the structure of its internal development. But they could assess its significance relative to other antecedents. Their decision to invade France was influenced not only by the capture of the French king but also by the strength and disposition of their own army and the armies of France and Prussia, by the French exiles, by England, and by the liberal movements in various German principalities. All of these actual events were included as conditional elements in the initial phase of the new event, that is, the decision to invade France. In that sense, they may be regarded as necessary causes of the invasion.

At this point, the transition from external to internal relationships displays two features that characterize most genetic explanations. First, not everything happening in the world of the antecedent duration is included as a significant element in the emerging event. A peasant beating his llama in Peru, or a provincial samurai governing in Japan, might have been contemporary with the flight of Louis XVI. But so far as we know (and this is open to documentary verification), they were quite irrelevant to Austria's decision to invade France. They had no causal significance at all. At the same time, their irrelevance was not a property, nor a fixed feature of their occurrence. It was determined by the *perspective* (that is, the event) from which they were viewed. It is possible to imagine events in which both the beating of the llama and the activities of a Japanese samurai would be included as significant elements. In theory, any or all antecedents may be grouped together as a set of conditions for subsequent developments. But in practice the number of antecedents is reduced to manageable proportions by the attribution of relative causal significance as a function of the event being explained. Such attribution, of course, cannot be predicted before the event has occurred; and this is the basis for genetic explanations.

Ernest Nagel has argued that the notion of an internal structure for events means that all previous events must necessarily be included as conditions for any novel occasion.[8] In the sense that every occasion has a perspective on its entire past, Nagel is right. But, as shown above, the transition from external to internal relations involves the dismissal of many, if not most, previous events as relatively insignificant. Without such selectivity, all events occurring at the same time would be indistinguishable, because they would all incorporate the same "past." In order to emerge as a distinct event, the Austrian invasion of France has to be given a particular spatial and temporal perspective from which to assess the relative importance of its antecedents.

The second feature of the transition process is a change in the status of antecedents from actual to potential and from determinate to indeterminate. As actual events, the antecedents have a finished form and structure: their relationship to the past is fully decided. But when they enter into the constitution of an emerging new event, these same antecedents become potential elements for a different pattern of relationships; their meaning in that pattern remains indeterminate until its temporal process of development is complete. For example, if one regards the Austrian invasion of France as an extended event, starting with the initial shock of Louis's capture and extending through negotiations with Prussia to the actual mobilization of troops for invading France, then it should be obvious that the capture of Louis was a more important element in the earlier stages of development than in the later. In other words, the relative significance of the capture remained indeterminate until the whole temporal pattern of the event was complete.

This change of status may seem a rather esoteric notion unless it is realized that the historian's narrative account utilizes the same kind of transition to illustrate the dynamics of change. In a narrative sequence, earlier events are presented in their completed form, provoking anticipations of what might follow. Later events emerge in the story with reference to these anticipations, either by fulfilling them or by showing them to have been mistaken. In either case, the earlier events are present as elements of the later; and their importance as elements gradually emerges with the whole temporal pattern of a particular later event. Moreover, the earlier events are not reproduced in the later. They are perceived symbolically, as in human memory, so they lose that definite actuality they had as events in their own duration, becoming subject to changes in status and meaning.

When parents attempt to explain to themselves or others how one of their children came to be what he is (a common experience, one should say), they may examine the physical and psychological characteristics of the family tree, and also study the features of the child's environment. But it is impossible to say why certain characteristics, or environmental influences, should have predominated and what others should not have; nor is it certain that these influences will always work on the child in the same way. Central to genetic explanations is the notion that past conditions are indeterminate for the present subject until it is fully developed. In this sense the parallel between biological and historical explanations is very close.

The analogy of the child implies that the transition from external to internal relationships does not exhaust the genetic development of historical events. Somehow the various elements and their potential relations have to be sorted out and integrated into a pattern with definite coherence. Since this integrative process is emphasized in most genetic models of historical explanation, we can now reexamine them for signs of an analyzable structure.

W. B. Gallie and others have argued that bringing events together into a meaningful temporal pattern means telling a story, and that storytelling is best done in the narrative form. To demand that a certain type of deductive argument be abstracted from the narrative is to demand exclusion of the basic historical process and its understanding. Critics of the deductive-law model maintain that stories are the most basic and effective form of making sense out of our experience: anything else is derivative and shallow. They point out that Hempel himself, trying to give an example of analytical explanation, ended up with a narrative about a car radiator freezing during a cold night. And Haskell Fain, reviewing the positivist theme of F. J. Teggart's *Rome and China* (1939), showed that Teggart chose to write about the barbarian uprisings primarily because they played such a dramatic role in the story of Rome.[9] The tendency to embody explanations in narrative form is neither accidental nor unscientific, added Fain: geology, biology, and astronomy are all sciences that construct stories about the past.

Narrative stories also satisfy the need to account for the emergence of novelty in history, which deductive explanations cannot do. As Gallie comments:

> To be story-worthy, an action must be in a broad sense an adventure. Its circumstances and occasion must contain notable elements of surprise, accident, and the unforeseeable. In other words, it is non-routine and so cannot be judged for aptness or unaptness, for merited success or failure, by general criteria derived from previous similar instances.
> Routine and habitual actions may occupy ninety-nine point nine percent of life; but non-routine ventures, story-worthy actions, supply an essential test of the moral and intellectual vitality underlying our habits and routines.[10]

Confronted with novelty, the historian cannot turn to a deductive demonstration of its predictability (or lack of it). He needs, rather, a means of showing in retrospect that the novelty was intelligible, that its occurrence was not wholly incommensurate with its past. For Gallie, Fain, and others, the criterion of intelligibility is fulfilled by the dynamic story-lines of narrative explanations.[11]

What is a story, and how does it explain events? According to Gallie, a story is a sequence of actions and experiences of people in some situation where a predicament is developed and then resolved. The predicament may be a matter of overcoming some obstacle or a matter of conflicting intentions. People's responses to the predicament and the effects of their responses on others constitute a story-line. Of course, since people respond to each other more or less simultaneously, a simple sequence of cause and effect would not do justice to their experience. Thus the story-line requires a reader to hold some actions in mind as elements of other actions, while remaining aware of the difference in perspective. In addition, the characters in the story must be believable as real individuals, with real intentions, dispositions, and previous experiences, so that their actions become self-explanatory. In other words, it spoils the story if the author has to provide information after the fact which, had the reader known it beforehand, would have made a character's actions intelligible.[12]

Gallie's definition of a story means that the intelligibility of a sequence of events is gained by following the narrative with a degree of involvement, rather than subjecting it to logical analysis. Following is "a teleologically guided form of attention, with the peculiarity that the end towards which it is guided is essentially open." It requires patience to "wait and see" what pattern of meaning will emerge from a given set of contingencies.[13] In this view, a narrative represents a complex reconstruction of the past by the historian, which the reader is expected to use as a template for his or her own reconstruction.

Gallie asserts that a story-line is like a hypothesis: half-formulated before the account is written, it guides the researcher in the selection of data. It then provides a structure for his narrative, and it helps the reader comprehend all the various details.[14] It thus provides a foundation for the process of reflection and anticipation referred to earlier, which gives the narrative its overall coherence.

It may be evident now that the genetic approach can refer to each of the four aspects of historical inquiry: it describes the temporal emergence of events themselves, the process by which the historian comprehends those events, the dynamics of his narrative account, and the following of that account by the reader. Though one cannot say that the narrative is an exact reproduction of historical events, or that the reader reexperiences the past through the narrative, one can say that the four aspects of historical inquiry have analogous developmental patterns from the genetic point of view. Since the fact of analogy is important to my attempt to construct an analytical framework for genetic explanations, some further discussion seems in order.

Haskell Fain has made a useful distinction between the historian as story-teller and the historian as editor, faced with the task of reconciling many stories told by the participants in an event. In constructing a narrative, says Fain,

> you would tend to think of the players as having been engaged in writing that tale all along, though no one knew or intended the finished product at the time he made his contribution. The "internal logic" of the story would become the logic of your history, and the description of the con-tribution of each player would be prefigured by the role it played in that story.[15]

The problem for the historian is to preserve as much of the original stories (with their individual perspectives) as possible, while integrating them into an intelligible whole. Fain describes the resulting dilemma in an imaginary conversation:

> Suppose the historian-editor submits his improved version of the tale to the scrutiny of its authors, and some of them complain that certain of the lines they contributed were altered beyond recognition or omitted altogether. "But don't you see," the editor will retort, "some of the lines you wrote were not integrated into the story, were ignored by the other players, and were in fact so many lost opportunities? Should the historian deal with might-have-beens or with what actually happened?"[16]

The "editor" 's defense, however, is based on the misleading assumption that unrealized potential has no historical meaning. Both Fain and Gallie contend that the significance of what actually happened cannot be assessed without considering what might have been. "Assessing the various alter-natives open to the individual contributor at any given stage of the story's development in light of the particular one selected will provide the historian with insight into the individual mind of the contributor," argues Fain.[17] Lost opportunities and misguided intentions surround any historical inci-dent, giving it that dramatic intensity that makes it worth one's attention.

Still, there appears to be an unresolved tension among advocates of the genetic approach between the desire to re-create concrete past experiences and the requirements of narrative unity. On the one hand, R. G. Col-lingwood maintained that the task of the historian is to "think himself into" the action, "to discern the thought of the past."[18] Both Gallie and W. H. Walsh[19] have advocated similar positions, which are based on the belief that historical events are self-explanatory and that historical narrative merely replicates the experience of those events. As Michael Oakeshott says, "Change in history carries with it its own explanation: the course of events is one, so far integrated, so far filled in and complete, that no external cause or reason is looked for or required in order to account for any particular event."[20] From this point of view, reminiscent of nineteenth-century empiricism, narrative unity is automatically supplied by the unity of the historical process itself. All the historian need do is identify himself with the process and describe it in exact detail.

On the other hand, as Haskell Fain points out, reenactments of the past are usually based on a considerable amount of inference. It is one thing to identify the possibilities of a situation from the historian's advantage of hindsight and (possibly) superior information. It is quite another to certify the plans and intentions of historical agents as they experienced them:

> The ways in which men evaluate and understand their own actions often differ from the ways in which historians evaluate and understand those same actions. The historian, in working out the story-line of his history, views the incidents about which he writes with reference to that story-line. But the men whose activities or ideas provide the incidents of the story are not privy to *that* story. The historical significance of their own activities or ideas remains hidden to them.[21]

In short, history as a direct reenactment of past experience would be chaotic. It would read like a stream of consciousness novel, without the novelist's artistic form.

In creating an intelligible story-line, then, the historian risks losing the sense of immediacy enjoyed by his subjects for the sake of understanding the significance of their actions. Where documentary evidence of individual intentions and mistakes exists, the narrative may be enriched by its inclusion. Otherwise, the historian is left with inferences, and must be careful to distinguish his own reasoning from that of his subjects.

The tension between reenacting past experience and constructing a narrative account of it is not confined to the genetic approach. Implicit in deductive-law models of explanation is a belief that historical truth lies ultimately in an objective description of concrete events as they actually happened. The construction of narrative accounts is therefore bound to be judged an imperfect reflection of reality and to be approached with a different set of judgmental criteria. W. H. Walsh makes this distinction clear in his definition of history:

> It covers (a) the totality of past human actions, and (b) the narrative or account we construct of them now. This ambiguity is important because it opens up at once two possible fields for philosophy of history. That study might be concerned . . . with the actual course of historical events. It might, on the other hand, occupy itself with the processes of historical thinking, the means by which history in the second sense is arrived at. And clearly its content will be very different according to which of the two we choose.[22]

Now, it may be true that any narrative with pretensions to coherence could not possibly reflect the tangled skein of past experiences known to the many participants in an event. But it is also true, as previously argued, that historical events themselves have more or less coherent patterns of meaning for *their* pasts, from *their* perspectives. And though an event reflects past experience, it does not reproduce it, any more than the historian reproduces the complexity of the past in his narrative. For this reason Collingwood's ideal is quite misleading, and Walsh's argument quoted above needs serious questioning. There is no need for the "content" of history and of historical inquiry to be very different, if by "content" one means the process by which the past is given coherent form and significance. Both past events and narrative accounts, in that sense, have the same developmental structure.[23]

The analogy between historical events and narratives is recognized in literary theory, where a novel is often defined as a "temporally extended action." Though history differs from fiction in that it is a public account, subject to verification and agreement by other observers with access to the same data,[24] and though the historian may not sacrifice accuracy for coherence to the same degree as a novelist, both are centrally concerned with temporal development. It is the pattern of emergence, the integration of indeterminate elements into a temporal composition, that provides the true "content" of historical inquiry.

In a deductive explanation, the terms of the argument must remain constant throughout; they cannot undergo changes of meaning or form.[25] This requirement limits the application of deductive explanations to certain types of stories. As Morton White says, "the most typical narrative is one whose central subject has existed, or once did exist, for a reasonably long period of time, and the task of the typical narrator is to give a connected account of the development of that central subject."[26] That task is rather simple, rejoins Arthur Danto, when one is concerned with a physical object or person, such as the duke of Buckingham during the early seventeenth century. "But it is considerably more complex and metaphysically challenging when we are interested in such a change as, say, the break-up of feudalism, or the emergence of nationalism, or, for that matter, the progressive embellishment of the Christmas tree." In the latter cases, the "subject" simply did not exist as a constant until its various elements had been assimilated, integrated, and embodied in some enduring form. Its "history" could not be understood by reenacting or analyzing the experience of any one element involved. Nor would a sequence of such experiences reveal the pattern of integration displayed by the whole event. The only way to establish narrative unity with a "continuant subject," argues Danto, is to treat it as a temporal whole, inclusive of but different from its constituent elements.[27] In such a case, the subject is not the terminal incident in a sequence but the whole compositional form, which is considered to be implicated in every stage of the subject's emergence.

For example, a historian wishing to examine the origins of World War I might begin with an account of the French loss of Alsace-Lorraine during the Franco-Prussian war. The purpose of describing this event, however, is not primarily to reexperience the past. Nor is it to demonstrate a necessary cause of the war. There is, in fact, no reason to choose this event over another except that it has potential significance within a certain pattern of events leading to the war. The outbreak of the war is itself a phase of the pattern, and cannot illustrate the causal significance of the loss of Alsace-Lorraine without relating that loss to all other elements in the extended duration from 1870 through 1914. The narrative account, then, is unified neither by its terminal event nor by some continuing subject. It is unified by a temporal structure that emerges from potentiality to actuality.

But, one could argue, narrative unity is mostly a literary device, imposed upon an imaginary set of incidents or discovered after the fact. To what extent does the narrative historian likewise impose a unified pattern upon the development of his subject, a pattern not discoverable in the incidents themselves?[28] Was there, for instance, a World War I or a Renaissance or a French Revolution inherent in the web of events we associate with such labels, and did they have the emergent structure that is reflected in narrative accounts of them? In the genetic mode of explanation, the answer on both counts is a qualified "yes."

Like a DNA molecule inherited from one's parents, a historical event is definitely coded with respect to its antecedents. But this code is merely conditional with respect to its future transformations. The potential configurations that may emerge from its interaction with other molecules within the organic environment are almost unlimited, though some configurations obviously have more potential than others. Thus the pattern of interaction leading to World War I is already present, as potential, in the French loss of Alsace-Lorraine. And one can put the presence of that potential to an empirical test by examining the documentary evidence. Did Bismarck, or his French adversaries, express anticipation of future war as a result of the Alsace-Lorraine question? If so, then the war was already implicit in the earliest stages of its emergence, and its use as a unifying subject represents something more than a literary device.

The empirical test is not foolproof, of course. In the first place, documentary evidence that participants in an event anticipated future developments is not always available. In the second place, most participants are unable to foresee the precise pattern of the extended event. Most of the time their anticipations, biased by hope or despair, are inconclusive and contradictory. If they were not, if the singular pattern of future events was clearly present in a given set of intial conditions, then the deductive model of explanation would need no further justification.

But a lack of consistent empirical evidence does not disprove the existence of a potential pattern; the historian may discern what the actors cannot. The empirical test simply allows the historian to distinguish more explicitly between anticipations fostered by his own hindsight and those actually experienced by his subjects. It allows him to avoid illusions of reenacting past experience, and the fallacy of judging past behavior as if the pattern of future development should already have been known.

In summary, the desire for narrative unity need not impose a structure on events that was not really there. The constituent elements of any event are amenable to a great variety of transformations before their form and significance are finally determined in an overall scheme. It is the task of the historian to show, by empirical evidence and responsible inference, what those transformations might have been and what they actually were. The narrative account of the transformations is therefore comparable to and reflective of the actual past, though it is never the same as the past. And because history is a public inquiry (rather than private, as in fiction), the account can be judged and corrected by other historians.

I have tried to show, following Gallie, that the interplay of anticipation and reflection is characteristic of three aspects of history: the events themselves, the narrative explanation of them, and the "following" of the explanation by readers. If the theory is consistent, then one should also expect to find this interplay in the way historians think about the past. Proponents of the genetic approach maintain that, indeed, historians' prenarrative comprehension of past events involves the integration of symbolic elements into a temporal whole. Louis Mink called this process "synoptic judgment" and described it as follows:

> The minimal description of historical practice is that the historian deals with complex events in terms of the inter-relationship of their constituent elements (leaving open entirely the question whether there are "unit events" in history). Even supposing that all of the facts of the case are established, there is still the problem of comprehending them in an act of judgment. . . . It is not in any proper sense a "method"; it is neither a technique of proof nor an organon of discovery but a type of reflective judgment. And it is a kind of judgment, if I am not mistaken, for which the proto-science view cannot account—and does not wish to.[29]

The necessity and validity of synoptic judgment is supported also by Fain[30] and Michael Scriven[31] in separate essays on historical thinking. It is also reflected in Jacob Bronowski's conception of science, whose linguistic reference is interesting:

For science is a language, and like a language, it defines its parts by the way they make up a meaning. Every word in the sentence has some uncertainty of definition, and yet the sentence defines its own meaning and that of its words conclusively. It is the internal unity and coherence of science which gives it truth, and which makes it a better system of prediction than any less orderly language.[32]

In another place Bronowski says that the function of the historical process is "a synthesis, not an analysis." "When we speak of truth," he maintains, "we make a judgment between what matters and what does not, and we feel the unity of its different parts."[33]

In Louis Mink's view, synoptic judgment is "a single and self-contained act of understanding which does not *contain* temporal sequence" but can *refer* to temporal sequence. That is, the historian who arrives at a comprehension of some complex development does not relive its chronological emergence but tries to "hold together in thought events which, by the destructiveness of time, no one could experience together."[34] The historian knows, for instance, that the coming of World War I encompasses a great many incidents spread over a lengthy period; but in grasping a synoptic view of those incidents from the perspective of the war, he compresses the period of their occurrence into a single moment of thought–experience, with its own internal space-time dimensions. It is Bronowski's argument that science, because its understanding is also based upon language, arrives at its judgments in the same way. The meaning of the separate data is finally derived from their relation to the whole pattern, which is established in an act of synoptic imagination.

The fact that science and history make use of similar kinds of judgment does not, of course, prove that history is scientific. Benedetto Croce, in an essay written in 1893, suggested that the historian's activity should rather be compared to that of the artist.[35] And accounts left by painters, musicians, and creative thinkers do reflect Mink's notion of synoptic judgment. Mozart, for example, claimed that his compositions often appeared in his mind's ear fully articulated, with all the movements and instrumentation condensed into a single moment of incredibly complex sound. Reducing this "vision" to a conventional musical score was a fairly routine matter. Others have not been so precocious: their ideas appeared in fragments, which required extensive efforts at development, and the synoptic comprehension was not realized until a late stage of composition.[36] In every case, however, the synoptic judgment is described as an event whose internal development could not be analyzed chronologically or logically. This is not to say that analysis is impossible but that the process of integration proceeds without regard to external clocks or to the requirements of formal logic.

Louis Mink charges that the uses and advantages of synoptic judgments in historical thinking have been disregarded by critics because the historian has to express these judgments in narrative, sequential form. Especially if one views the narrative as merely a succession of objective terms, ignoring the dynamics of reflection and anticipation, it is almost impossible to appreciate an author's insight. As G. R. Elton laments:

> in a very real sense history cannot be correctly written. The processes to be analyzed and described occur on a broad front, simultaneously and interconnectedly; writing is a linear development quite unlike the matter to be written about. The human mind is perfectly capable of holding a variety of interacting events, personalities and influences in a well-ordered amalgam; for physical and technical reasons, the pen is vastly less well able to convey this true comprehension to another mind. People talk of straightforward narrative history and seem to think that complexity is introduced by the writer. But what can be straightforward about a narrative which has to hold an infinity of threads in a single skein? What can be simple about a process which demands constant selection and rejection, a permanent multiplicity of choices, an inescapable awareness of the matter left out, the arguments on the other side, and the unsufficiency of the activity engaged in?[37]

Yet one can go too far. The expression of synoptic judgments in narrative form need not be so labyrinthine as Elton suggests, and they are one part of the whole process of historical understanding. It may be, as Louis Mink suggests, that one cannot produce a guaranteed methodology by analyzing acts of creative judgment. But one can, by describing the process, move toward a more critical mode of explanation. We have already noticed that fiction writers pay much closer attention to the dynamics of narrative than historians normally do. Their work, and that of other creative people, has been subject to systematic study for a long time. It is therefore worth looking at the results to see the points of comparison with historical inquiry.

There are many descriptions of the creative process adaptable for this purpose.[38] Almost without exception, they assume an active process, temporally extended, with an internal pattern of development. The pattern is not fixed at the outset but unfolds in several phases, gradually realizing one of the many *potential* patterns implicit in its initial complement of elements. The final phase, in which the synoptic judgment appears, is not a separate event but part of the whole process.

The first phase involves the assimilation of data from the subject's antecedent world. For a historian, this is the research phase; for readers, it means receptive attention to the narrative. In the narrative itself, as in a drama, it is the initial exposition of characters and conditions. Selectivity is involved, because the data are assimilated from the subject's particular space-time perspective. But because the significance of the data is not yet fully determined, selection does not mean comprehension. In fact, every research historian knows (with regret) that his initial selection of materials may be incomplete, or misguided by faulty anticipation of the final pattern of events. Assimilation, then, is not a passive phase. It proceeds from a desire for the widest possible measure of intelligibility.

Studies of creativity sometimes stress the dual characteristics of assimilation. The data are perceived in terms of their objective forms (whether they are documentary statements or musical fragments or areas of color), which express their own identity. In other words, the data are facts. One can sense the objectivity of data when one is, say, making a record of the weekly price changes on the West Indian sugar market in eighteenth-century London, or poking through family account books to see what people bought to wear and to eat. Unless one is contemplating a major revision in the subject, one tends to accept the information with little fuss, leaving its interpretation for another time. Even so, the objective form of the data may be accompanied by some subjective feeling, of higher or lower intensity: the feeling involved in the recognition of a particular pattern, in contrast to what might have been expected, and in relation to other things in its context. The term "feeling" denotes no special sense of human value or consciousness. It could be embodied in something as inanimate as Thomas Jefferson's eyeglasses, or as mundane as a business-ledger entry showing that one Captain Bligh had arrived in the West Indies with a shipload of breadfruit trees on consignment from the Pacific. Clearly, the intensity of feeling embodied by a datum bears some relationship to its objective form; but it is also a function of its context. Since there are many intelligible contexts for any piece of information, depending upon one's perspective, its subjective feeling is expressed as a range of overtones rather than as definite fact.

For the historian studying a document, or for the reader pursuing a narrative, the juxtaposition of objective form and subjective feeling is automatic. One looks at a word, which is the datum; it has a form, which one considers more important than its parts (that is, one reads "power" or "Lincoln," not the individual letters); and it evokes an indeterminate, subjective response within one. Its more exact meaning awaits colligation with other words in the sentence, and with other sentences and paragraphs. Similarly, a musical note has a certain resonance, based on its frequency, or pitch, and on the timbre of the instrument used to produce it. One may identify the note objectively, and feel it subjectively, even while anticipating the emergence of some meaning in its relationship to notes which will follow.

It is the ability to appreciate the subjective intensity of events that separates the trained historian from his lay audience, and that makes historians despair over the latter's often-repeated disdain for "mere" dates and kings. As Mink says, there is no explicit methodology that can teach a person to feel this way; it grows, perhaps, in the process of being immersed in the raw documentary materials of the past, but only if the mind is ready. However, it may be that historians block the growth of feeling by treating events as mechanical objects, to be maneuvered and dissected. If they began from the premise that events, and the words that describe them, are expressive forms with subjective intensity, they would stand a better chance of making other people understand what history means to them.

Following assimilation, the creative process moves into a phase of symbolic transformation. In this phase, the forms and feelings of elements are sorted, contrasted, harmonized, and integrated to form ever more complex and comprehensive patterns of meaning. The historian labors to construct an intelligible account of his material and, if skillful enough, composes a narrative that leads the reader through an analogous process of mental composition.

Analyses of creative thinking often emphasize the relaxed, passive state of mind that seems to facilitate symbolic transformation. But the present theory is not limited to human consciousness and intention, and by avoiding a premature focus on those functions one can see more clearly the underlying activity, which (as in the incubation of an egg, for instance) is decidedly not passive. In historical narrative, there is an active formulation of potential configurations or gestalts,[39] characterized by changes of relative scale, by noncausal associations, and by the exploration of subjective feelings. The events represented as data at the beginning of the narrative tend to be related without precise regard for their chronological or geographical locations, or for their exact sequence. They are, to use a term favored by Alfred North Whitehead, brought into a variety of *contrasts* with one another, much as a painter might build up the composition of an oil painting, or a composer develop a set of musical fragments. As a historical example, take a barbarian king of the late eighth century who has pretensions to political, religious, and cultural leadership but who can't write his own name; place him in a religious sanctuary in the middle of an ancient imperial capital; and have him crowned by the vicar of God with a ceremony, title, and crown conferred heretofore on immeasurably more sophisticated rulers in another political and cultural center. The variety of contrasts involved in that situation has yet to be fully comprehended. A more concrete example occurs in Palmer and Colton's description of the outcome of the Franco-Prussian war:

> The chateau and gardens of Versailles, since Louis XVI's unceremonious departure in October, 1789, had been little more than a vacant monument to a society long since dead. Here, in the most sumptuous room of the palace, the resplendent Hall of Mirrors, where the Sun King had once received the deferential approaches of German Princes, Bismarck on January 18, 1871, caused the German Empire to be proclaimed.[40]

In this paragraph, situations almost a century apart are juxtaposed so that the reader can feel the symbolic nature of the occasion and the irony of the scene, which Bismarck no doubt relished. The references to Louis XVI are not included to establish a causal relationship. They distort the chronological dimensions of the proclamation ceremony in a meaningful way, evoking a variety of subjective associations in the reader's imagination. Some of those associations were probably present for actors in the event itself; others are products of historical perspective. The point is that they are symbolic associations, and they illustrate contrasts which cannot be reduced to causal regularity. Some can be linked to empirical evidence; if one investigates the documentary sources for 1871, one can find descriptions of how individuals felt about the situation, and these descriptions will display contrasts between what people thought was happening, had happened, and might happen in the future. Palmer and Colton's impression of the calculated irony with which Bismarck staged the proclamation of his empire was not a figment of their literary imagination. Nor, for that matter, do we lack evidence that contemporaries of Charlemagne conceived of his elevation to imperial status in terms of dissonance, resolution, or fulfillment—all types of contrast.

It is evident that the contrasts involved in symbolic transformation are not mere opposites. When one gets away from the limitations of the deductive approach, one realizes that human experience is full of relationships other than logical opposition or identity. What one does today is not quite the same as what one did yesterday, nor is it entirely different. The two sets of actions acquire significance as they are brought into contrast with one another, but the contrast may be a kind of augmentation or subordination or other complement.

Because of the nonlogical character of the transformations, they cannot be predicted from knowledge of initial conditions, although the historian immersed in a given context may be able to anticipate a good many of them. The abolition of the British slave trade, completed in 1807 after thirty years of argument, may serve as an illustration. The campaign was begun by evangelical reformers, but West Indian interests in Parliament and in commerce opposed a measure they claimed would ruin them and undermine the empire. One could expect, given these conditions, that some effort at compromise would emerge. In fact, there were several plans for gradual abolition proffered from different quarters. Each plan offered an alternative pattern of development for the emerging event we now call "abolition." What finally developed was the collapse of the West Indian economic and political strength, and the passing of a bill for total and immediate abolition with the grudging support of the planters themselves.[41] Many of the changes in this extended campaign could have been anticipated by a competent historian studying the initial period from about 1784 to 1788. But that abolition should be passed with an element of support from the very interests that opposed it for so long would have been a surprise. It was a novel transformation, the kind of unexpected yet retrospectively intelligible contrast that prompts the historian's inquiry.

Symbolic transformation will be discussed in more detail in Chapter 8; the sketch given here is intended only to indicate the indeterminate, non-logical character of the process, and to argue that this character is compatible with a valid descriptive analysis. One can talk about historical events, and about historical narratives, using terms at least as precise as "cause" and "effect"; historians do it all the time. The approach I have outlined has the advantage of providing such terms, without the problem of discrediting the historian's craft.

As contrasts among the various elements in an event are sorted out into ever more complex and comprehensive patterns, the tensions or "predicaments" mentioned by Gallie as features of a good story are resolved, and the relative significance of each antecedent is finally determined. The final form of the event is cast as a synoptic judgment, of the kind described by Louis Mink. In some cases, this form may be reflected in an actual document, such as the proclamation of the German Empire in 1871. In other cases, there may be a ceremony, an artifact, or a dramatic act to focus one's understanding. These terminal developments are used by historians as a kind of shorthand reference to the more complete process from which they emerged, as we saw in the example of Louis Halphen's account of Charlemagne. If that reference is ignored or forgotten, events become mere objects related by abstract properties, without temporal dimension.

The phase of formal resolution was called the "satisfaction" of the event by Alfred North Whitehead. But this term is misleading for historians, because it implies a degree of resolution that historical events often lack. World War I did break out: there is no denying the definiteness of that fact. Its outbreak relegates all alternative configurations to the realm of might-have-beens. And yet, the outbreak of the war is a very general image derived from the partial and often confused experiences of millions of people, over an extended period. It is hard for the historian to hold the image together in a narrative without him being haunted, as G. R. Elton suggests, by "the inescapable awareness of the matter left out." Moreover, the historian trying to grasp the whole temporal pattern in narrative form is acutely conscious that many events simply do not hang together at the end. There always seem to be loose ends that stick out (in Arthur Danto's image) like worms wriggling into the future. And as previously seen, the question of whether to let the loose ends hang out, or to snip them off in the interest of narrative unity, is hard to answer. One can hardly conclude an account of

World War I without either showing the tragic failures of the peace conference or hinting darkly at what the reader may already know: "Now it was up to the diplomats. . . . "

Regardless of this problem, however, every event displays a formal resolution of its compositional elements from some perspective and at some level of abstraction. The historian's task is to adopt a consistent perspective and level of abstraction, so that readers can follow his reconstruction of the past and so that other historians and philosophers can critically compare his account with others.

Articulation of the narrative account constitutes the fourth phase of the creative process. It is akin to the display of an artist's work or the performance of a composer's music. The event itself, the historian's synoptic conception of it, and his written account must all "go public" to be comprehended from other perspectives. This is the reverse of the transition from external to internal relations that characterizes the initial phase of events. The final form of the event or story, which has determined the relative significance of its antecedents, now becomes an antecedent for subsequent developments. Without such a transition to the external world of common space-time order, no event could be considered "historical"; and without a similar transition, no work of art could be considered finished.

It is important to remember that the phase of external articulation involves not only the objective form of an event but also the intensity of feeling generated by its formative process. The actual event stands in contrast to the many unrealized configurations that might have emerged from its antecedents and that remain as overtones of meaning. This contrast may be quite intense and dramatic, as in the "end" of World War I, or it may be relatively weak, as in the death of King William IV of England. But it is always a *felt* contrast, and the feeling enters the external world as a function of an event's objective form.

As previously shown, it makes a difference whether one approaches a narrative as a sequence of discrete events or as a single, temporally extended action: the former involves causal relationships, the latter does not. But it was also shown that the dynamics of narrative constantly shift one's perspective, so that one's experience of earlier episodes is objectified in later ones. For instance, one can follow subjectively the turbulent action which results in a head wound for a young Civil War soldier, and grasp the meaning of that wound in terms of that action. But its meaning is qualified when, in a later situation, it becomes a "Red Badge of Courage." One feels then that the "badge" was not a symbol of courage originally and that its subsequent meaning is ironic. But at the same time, one may reflect that the contrast between fear and courage is not just a feature of the later situation, that it was present after all, in a different guise, in the earlier action. This interplay between what the event means for itself, and what it comes to mean as an element in subsequent events, is the "genetic" aspect of narrative that carries the story forward.

For the purpose of outlining the creative process, its four phases—assimilation, symbolic transformation, formal resolution, and articulation—have been presented in sequence. Experience indicates, however, that the sequence may be disrupted. The historian composing a narrative may arrive at new insights, necessitating assimilation of other data. The reader grasping an idea which previously eluded him may retrace its development through earlier passages. In such cases, a new perspective is called for. But changing one's perspective does not change the basic process. The test of the value of a perspective, in fact, is to see how coherently and comprehensively it elucidates the process, which is assumed to be the same for all events. The test is both empirical (does it account for all the data?) and logical (are its terms consistent with those of other processes?). It is the same test given to all scientific hypotheses.

The four-stage process outlined above provides a descriptive analysis of the genetic approach to historical explanation discussed at the outset of this chapter. That approach tended to justify narrative accounts as self-explanatory, needing no further analysis to provide a full understanding of historical events. And in one sense the geneticists are correct: as an analogue to the events it describes, the narrative "explains" itself by gradually bringing into one complex configuration the indeterminate elements derived from its antecedent world. It finally determines the significance of each element from its particular perspective on the past, in a way that could not have been predicted

But this sense of explanation is focused entirely on the internal development of an event or narrative. As our discussion showed, the internal development must be articulated externally, or it remains as nonhistorical as a deductive-law syllogism. The two perspectives must complement one another to be fully explanatory.

The analytical scheme outlined here provides three types of "external" explanation, that is, explanation by comparison of relatively objective features. First, one can compare the temporal structure of an event with the structures of other events. Although each structure will display four phases, the development of one or another phase may differ among several events, and the differences can be classified and studied in relation to typical models.

Second, one can explain an event in terms of the contrast between its final configuration and the configurations remaining unrealized in its developmental process. The latter are assumed to be plausible in terms of the event's antecedents, and their contrast with what actually occurred is a measure of historical significance for both the event and its antecedents. For example, the abdication of Edward VIII of England, so he could marry a divorced American woman, was surrounded by alternative possibilities whose implications were considered by participants in that event and speculated upon by historians ever since. The actual abdication highlighted certain aspects of its antecedent world, but the possible alternatives highlighted other aspects. An explanation of this event would not be complete without considering both actual and potential elements, and both sets of highlighted antecedents.

The third type of external explanation is analogical. That is, the process of emergence illustrated in a narrative account is assumed to be an analogue to the process illustrated by the event(s) it covers. There is a further analogy between the narrative, the process of comprehension used by the historian in composing it, and the process of comprehension used by the reader in following it; each displays the same basic pattern of assimilation, symbolic transformation, formal resolution (or synoptic judgment) and articulation. This type of explanation starts with the narrative account as its primary datum and compares its structure, form, and internal dynamics with other narratives in critical fashion. Hayden White has attempted one such critical explanation, with interesting results.[42] More are sorely needed to counteract the widespread assumption, especially among historians, that historical accounts are all formally compatible with one another.

In expanding the genetic approach to history, I have suggested types of explanation which may be consistent with the general aims, if not the specific methods, of the deductive-law analysts. The question of compatibility will be taken up in later chapters. First, however, the suggested types of explanation imply a definition of events which, though it is based on human experience and on traditional historical practice, is contrary to the definition assumed to be "scientific" by analytical critics. This issue needs to be met by an examination of recent thinking in fields other than history; for no theory of explanation can succeed whose fundamental concepts are foreign to the general intellectual community.

4. Time and Events

. . . as so often happens when philosophers take up arms for science, the science that is being defended is long out of date.

Jacob Bronowski, *The Common Sense of Science*

Introducing a discussion of historical facts, the great historian Carl Becker observed that when one wants to know the meaning of words with which everyone is familiar, and which everyone seems to know perfectly well, the wise thing to do is to take a week off and think about them.[1] "Time" and "event" are words like that: the layman can be excused for believing that historians, who deal constantly with events in a time perspective, know exactly what time is, and what events are. But most historians, like most scientists, are not very interested in the precise definition or metaphysical significance of the general terms they use. Their notions of time and events are apt to be fuzzy and even contradictory, for they stem both from the craft of constructing narratives and from the remnants of nineteenth-century positivism, itself a derivative of classical science.

This chapter is an attempt to think about time and events in ways suggested by recent research and discussion in sciences other than history. It follows two suggestions made in the last chapter: that the genetic approach to historical explanation is based on a model of process that applies to many fields of study; and that the positivist, deductive-law approach is based on a conception of science that was already becoming outmoded when Carl Hempel challenged historians to follow it. The fact is, the scientific definition of "event" has taken on a genetic character as a result of a new appreciation for the dimension of time. Thus the arguments over historical explanation become part of a larger argument between advocates of a new paradigm for scientific inquiry and the defenders of the Newtonian tradition.

It is impossible to present here the mass of evidence for the new scientific notions generated during the twentieth century. Illustrations are given for most parts of the argument, but readers interested in more complete exposition will have to turn to the references provided. I have begun the argument with ideas from the physical sciences and then moved to the biological sciences, by way of a discussion of determinism and its alternatives. The purpose throughout is to show that time and events can be defined in an interdisciplinary way that makes the historian's practice scientifically respectable without requiring wholesale changes in his research and writing.

Until the end of the nineteenth century, the prevailing idea of science and of scientific explanation was based on the vividly successful paradigm developed by Newton and his seventeenth-century colleagues. This paradigm assumed that the entities to be explained had material substance, that they occupied infinitesimal points at simple locations of time and space, and that they interacted through a mechanism of cause and effect.[2] The Newtonian world was a triumph of systematic abstraction. It was held together by three articles of faith, which to this day cannot be proved empirically but which developed from logical necessity. First, time was conceived as absolute, unmoving, and continuous. Second, events were believed to occur at discrete, uniform intervals, or "moments," located at points on the temporal grid. They had none of the subjective qualities of variable duration and interconnectedness that make our personal experience of time so difficult to analyze. Third, although the material substances of the world were clearly separate from each other in their particular locations, they possessed objective properties which, connected by measurable relations of cause and effect, displayed a general pattern of continuity. Xeno had demonstrated the paradoxes involved in treating time as a series of discrete points. But this difficulty was disguised by the flat assertion of continuity as an essential quality of time, and by the use of the fictional mechanism of causation. In short, time was made subject to geometry, and for two hundred years science prospered under a spatialized conception of how things happened. The adequacy of this conception for explaining events was scarcely questioned until the work of Lyell and Darwin made the question of temporal development unavoidable.

It would have been difficult to describe the world in terms of matter, moments, and mechanism unless the classical philosophers had also disposed of mind. Cartesian dualism separated mind from matter, ensuring that our subjective experience of time and events would never interfere with the abstract, objective orderliness of physical entities. Causation took the place of perception as the fundamental activity. In the nineteenth century, mind was raised to the status of an autonomous realm by the theory of psychophysical parallelism. But dualism remained a basic principle in most systems of explanation.

In the same spirit, the seventeenth-century thinkers built a world system on the principle of order rather than organism. In an organic system, members do not necessarily form a homogeneous whole but are intrinsically related through their functions within the whole. Each member is to be defined in terms of its inclusion as an essential constituent of every other member. Since the organic metaphor was a favorite of medieval philosophers and theologians, it is understandable that early modern scientists rejected it. Needing a principle of mechanism unaffected by religious doctrine, the scientists defined entities as sharply separated objects related externally to other objects. Hence the order in the system was not intrinsic to the entities but constituted a "law" which they had to obey. Further, because the lawful order was derived through rigorous abstraction from everyday experience, it was simple enough to be expressed mathematically, elaborated logically, and applied to a wide range of observable data. From the seventeenth century to the twentieth, science has been largely an effort to elaborate and apply this lawful order, an effort to which historical inquiry itself bears witness.

The consequences of investigating a lawful order instead of a developing organic system were, however, not altogether beneficial for history. In the first place, the purpose of inquiry was shifted from humanistic (or religious) understanding toward the discovery of laws that would enable people to control the course of events. As a corollary, the significance of human subjects receded before the growing importance of trends, variables, dialectic, modes of production, underlying causes, and other abstractions. Such things are easier to deal with, remarked Marc Bloch, because they don't name themselves the way humans do. Planets suffer our labels, and molecules our descriptions, in silence; but Julius Caesar left an estimate of himself that inevitably influences our own judgment of him.

There is nothing wrong in such an approach provided one remembers the distinction between abstraction and concrete actuality. But the scientific fashion fostered in historical thinking what Alfred North Whitehead called the "fallacy of misplaced concreteness." This is the fallacy of regarding certain aspects of objects or events as the whole of that object or event, forgetting that, for purposes of inquiry, all other aspects have previously been ignored.[3] One can see the fallacy of misplaced concreteness operating in narratives that, for example, explain how "feudalism" prompted the actions of a provincial nobleman, or how the United States Constitution was determined by "economic interests." It is obviously necessary to concentrate on certain features of an event in order to make it intelligible and to keep the narrative within reasonable bounds. But the search for a lawful order constantly tempts historians to remain at an abstract level of inquiry, and to regard it as part of the concrete actual world. G. R. Elton, with this usual scorn for abstractions, cites another example:

> Wherever one turns in history today, one runs head-on into factors. There no longer are any causes of the Reformation: instead there are factors that made it possible. This is to go from the tolerably dubious to the quite abominable. A cause is something real: people do things in order

to produce results. A factor—outside mathematics and trading stations and Scottish estates—is a meaningless piece of tired jargon. . . . A word to be forgotten.[4]

The second consequence of viewing events as parts of a lawful order, rather than as parts of an organic system, is the tendency to isolate sections of the order for special analysis. So long as one ignores all but a few elements of an event, one can generate hypotheses that cover a great many instances, on the principle of "all other things being constant." "It is not going too far to assert," writes Elton, "that nearly all scientific study deals with specially prepared artificial derivatives from what naturally occurs."[5] And since the natural order is assumed to be inherently divisible, there is little impetus toward reintegration of its parts when study is complete. In the study of organic systems on the other hand, the researcher is constantly confronted with the complementary relationships that characterize every constituent member. It is impossible to forget that all other members of the system continue to function, even though their influence may temporarily be ignored.

The strength of scientific faith in an empirically warranted order was reflected in nineteenth-century historical positivism, expressed as the belief that isolated studies of select events would eventually produce enough concrete facts to constitute a self-evident body of knowledge (forgetting, of course, that it took a magnificent effort of imagination for Galileo and Kepler and Newton to bring an array of facts together and make their connections *appear* self-evident). It was this belief that led J. T. Bury to claim, as late as 1903, that history was a science, "no more and no less." Even the relativist historians who followed Bury, and ridiculed his presumption, based their arguments on a standard of science that history was bound to disappoint. They realized that the historian's perception was part of the whole process of explanation, and argued in traditional dualistic fashion that such a mixture was palpably unscientific.[6] The ideal of isolated, objective studies led not only to theoretical problems but also to the spate of specialized research, often unrelated to any wider conceptual framework, that has become the plague of the discipline today. The phrase "It's outside my field" which has become the Great Excuse for historical parochialism, is perpetuated by the habit of isolating subjects for investigation.

Even as some historians were refusing Bury's claims, however, science itself was undergoing a profound revolution. As E. H. Carr remarks:

Bury may have been more nearly right than we had supposed, though for the wrong reason. What Lyell did for geology and Darwin for biology has now been done for astronomy, which has become a science of how the universe came to be what it is; and modern physicists constantly tell us that what they investigate are not facts, but events. The historian has some excuse for feeling himself more at home in the world of science today than he could have done a hundred years ago.[7]

Unfortunately, the realization that scientific concepts had changed did not provoke a reexamination of related historical concepts. Instead, it was assumed that the subjective, developmental aspects of narrative history were at last free from "scientific" criticism and the quest for consistent theory. Marc Bloch set the pattern for this craft-oriented response in 1941:

> Our mental climate has changed. The kinetic theory of gases, Einstein's mechanics, and the quantum theory have profoundly altered that concept of science which, only yesterday, was unanimously accepted. . . . Hence, we are much better prepared to admit that a scholarly discipline may pretend to the dignity of a science without insisting upon Euclidean demonstrations or immutable laws of repetition. We find it easier to regard certainty and universality as questions of degree. We no long feel obliged to impose upon every subject of knowledge a uniform intellectual pattern, borrowed from natural science, since, even there, that pattern has ceased to be entirely applicable.[8]

Yet historians, more than other people, should know that paradigmatic changes in science do not mean the end of the search for uniform modes of inquiry. The fact that a new paradigm is not entirely applicable is always subordinate to the fact that it explains observed data more coherently, consistently, and comprehensively than previous paradigms. By the time Bloch wrote the above remarks, relativity, quantum mechanics, and the uncertainty principle had all been established as elements of modern physics. The definitions of time and of events had changed radically, and scientists close to the new research were exploring its implications for other fields of inquiry. There has now emerged a general set of hypotheses and a corpus of evidence sufficient to act as a new paradigm for the natural sciences. The links between physics and biology, thermodynamics and genetics are no longer so problematical.

The Newtonian conception of time as absolute, unmoving, and homogeneous is gone. In Einstein's theory of relativity, time is a dimension of interaction, measured differently by each of the interacting entities. Each entity is an observer, a focus of perceptual activity, not isolated and passive like Newton's objective points. In modern physics, events do not "happen" in a predefined space-time matrix. Instead, events create time as they emerge into actuality, and the actual units of time are defined by the duration of each emergent process.[9]

The relativistic notion of time is often hard to grasp because we are so used to clock time, which is homogeneous and atomic. Clock time is a technological abstraction, the result of the invention and proliferation of mechanical timekeepers since the seventeenth century. It is interesting to realize that clocks became refined enough to measure equal units of time just prior to the construction of classical scientific theories. Those doctrines rejected the notion that the earth was the center of the universe; but the idea of time they embodied was based exclusively on the earth's average motion relative to the sun. Since the seventeenth century we have learned that the earth moves in other time systems: the sidereal or star-based year is slightly different from the solar year, and the measurements of the cesium atomic clock, used for high-speed navigation and other precision systems, are different also. Thus, modern scientific time is subjective rather than objective; relative rather than absolute; and defined not as an a priori principle of order but as a characteristic of particular organic events.[10]

In the recent work of analytical philosophers of history, one can find discussions of statements in the form "C is X at time t_1 ... C is Y at time t_2 ...," as if temporal events consisted of points on a fixed grid, independent of any observer. It is not surprising that these critics find historical narratives ambiguous and incomplete. The critics are demanding deductive proofs of Newtonian relationships, while historians try to describe the temporal emergence of events relative to their antecedents. The dispute is not new: J. G. Herder fulminated against the tendency of Enlightenment philosophers to detemporalize history in their search for timeless "laws" of social order. In that period, scientific doctrine favored the philosophers. Now it favors the historians. Relativity defines time in historical terms.

Another significant change in scientific thinking was the development of quantum mechanics. In quantum theory, time as well as energy appears as chunks (quanta) of variable duration. Quanta cannot be divided up evenly into atomic slices because they define interactions between events, acts of reciprocal observation, requiring a minimum duration to become what they are. Every action takes place no faster than the velocity of light, and therefore must take time. An analogy on the human scale is the amount of viewing time one needs to be able to recognize an image. A motion picture image must be exposed a minimum number of frames before it is registered by the brain, even subliminally. And that takes time. Without the minimum temporal durations proposed by quantum theory, it is hard to imagine what an event would look like, or how historians would describe it. Duration gives events their characteristic form and the possibility of an internal structure that Newton's points could not have. Consider the unification of Germany. At what infinitesimal instant in time, or between what two instants, would one place that event? Historians usually think of the unification as a complex interaction with some minimum duration, and they might be able to describe it as such more intelligibly if they were not so encumbered by an obsolete doctrine of time.

The duration of an event is related directly to the idea of continuity between events. In the Newtonian system, continuity was either assumed as an essential characteristic of time, or it was assumed to be provided by the action of causes and effects. There was nothing inherent in material entities that would account for it. The problem of continuity outlined in Xeno's paradoxes was avoided simply by an a priori assertion of its logical necessity. In the modern view of time, such problems do not exist. The durations defined by emerging events are discontinuous with respect to their externally related, objective forms; but as each event incorporates aspects of its antecedents in the process of actualization, it creates continuity where none existed before. In place of causation, which was a fictional physical force, modern science has established perception as the ground of succession and continuity.

The perceptual bias of modern notions of time and space also informs the uncertainty principle, developed by Werner Heisenberg in the 1920s, which affirms that anything observed is affected by the act of observation. Whereas classical doctrines saw observation as a neutral activity, lying outside the range of natural phenomena to be investigated, the uncertainty principle sees it as a natural event that incorporates the observed object as an element of its own constitution. This principle is illustrated in historical theory by the relation between a set of indeterminate conditions and the significance attributed to them by some emerging event. The event observes its past, not as a neutral investigator, but as an agent of creative process: the past becomes *its* past. Also, the mere establishment of a new focus of interaction in some event means that the "world" to be observed is no longer the same world. It now contains at least one new entity, namely, the new event. The whole notion that one can describe an "objective" set of initial conditions from which to deduce exact consequences is thus brought into doubt.

When the uncertainty principle was first advanced, it was thought by nonscientists to make knowledge of the past impossible. If looked at from the historian's perspective, however, it appears to answer one of the basic epistemological questions raised by classical doctrines: how, from an inspection of a set of initial conditions, can one know that anything will happen next, let alone predict what will happen? By restoring perception to the natural world, the principles of uncertainty and relativity enabled the historian to say that the emergence of a new (percipient) event is by definition the "anything" and the "what" that follows from a set of antecedents. The very act of stating what features belong to a set of antecedent conditions constitutes one phase of the next occasion. For example, if a historian surveyed all the data available for A.D. 1491 (a physical impossibility), he would be unable to predict subsequent events unless he first isolated a coherent set of data, such as the activities of Christopher Columbus, Queen Isabella, the

European money market, and so on. But the principle by which such a set is selected for analysis is a principle of perceptual relativity, namely, that these data are important from the viewpoint of Columbus's voyage of 1492. Thus historical knowledge and the continuity of historical advance are mutually supporting propositions. The focal center from which the past is to be known creates the perceptual connections through which the past becomes part of the present.[11]

In the seventeenth century there was an urgent need for a principle of order that would encompass a mass of data regarding the motions of material bodies, without involving the kind of human judgment so perversely evident in religious confrontations of that period. It was sufficient that God be the sole observer, so long as he didn't interfere. The theories that answered this need did not suffer from logical contradictions. But, as Whitehead pointed out, they did suffer from inadequacy (a failure to apply to all elements of experience). The basic separation of mental from corporeal substance, following Descartes, was primarily responsible for these defects, even though at the time it may have been a necessary and useful step. For, aside from the obvious gain in simplification, there is no reason why there should not be a one-substance world, combining mind and matter. Descartes' separation of these elements led to similar separations of cause and effect and of actuality and knowledge. Whole segments of experience were excluded from the lawful order of science, and their place was taken by assumptions of absolute relationship.[12]

By the nineteenth century, it was evident that mental phenomena could no longer be regarded merely as manifestations of underlying corporeal interactions. Attempts to construct a "parallel" system of lawful relationships for the former were no more successful. Wolfgang Pauli, expert on quantum theory, sums up the twentieth-century position:

> The general problem of the relationship between mind and body, between the inward and the outward, cannot be said to have been solved by the concept of psycho-physical parallelism postulated in the last century. Modern science has perhaps brought us nearer to a more satisfactory understanding of this relationship, by introducing the concept of complementarity into physics itself. It would be the more satisfactory solution if mind and body could be interpreted as complementary aspects of the same reality.[13]

The principle of complementarity in physics is illustrated by the long-standing problem of light, which behaves as a particle phenomenon under some conditions and as a wave phenomenon under others. Though this may be a temporary difficulty, it is not the only instance of a breakdown in traditional distinctions. The transformations of energy and matter reveal the fundamental constituents of the universe to be complementary aspects of a unitary reality. "Atoms," wrote Werner Heisenberg, are not *things*. The electrons which form an atom's shells are no longer things in the sense of classical physics, things which could be unambiguously described by concepts like location, velocity, energy, size. When we get down to the atomic level, the objective world in space and time no longer exists, and the mathematical symbols of theoretical physics refer merely to possibilities, not to fact.[14]

It may be argued that the complementarity implied by relativity, quantum theory, and the uncertainty principle pertains only to microscopic or subatomic phenomena, and the macroscopic world which historians deal with is still explicable on the basis of traditional dualism. Indeed, in defense of the idiosyncracies of their craft many historians still claim that human events involve a thought dimension that physical events do not have. To some thinkers, such as R. G. Collingwood, this dimension *is* history. Recognizing that human actions display causal agency by intention, Collingwood assumed that electrons or planets could never act or observe as agents on their own behalf. Such a belief was plainly anthropomorphic, and anthropomorphism is a cardinal sin in science.

Yet one could argue that the projection of human experience into subjects of inquiry is the very foundation of science. Newton's model of causality ascribed to certain discrete points in absolute time the power to produce and determine subsequent arrangements of points. As Jacob Bronowski commented, that's very human![15] The classical model, in fact, recognized that physical and mental phenomena interacted, but it was not adequate to explain their reciprocal functions. It assumed a distinction between human and other events because it sought measurable laws of regularity, and it identified "agency" with "cause" in order to sustain the belief that the future is determined solely by the past. Modern science, having passed the limits of that model, is now considering the idea that "agency" is possessed by both causes and effects and is not restricted to either mental or physical events.

There is an ideal of unity in science according to which all its various branches should share a basic principle for explaining how things happen. Traditionally, that principle was determinism. Critics of disciplines as far apart as particle physics and social psychology have been united in the assumption that scientifically valid explanations must illustrate deterministic relationships and that any discipline that fails in this regard must be classified as immature. As I have shown, the analytical critics of history used determinism as the basis for their challenge to historical reasoning. Yet modern scientific researchers have become aware that the principle is no longer adequate, even for disciplines more "exact" than history. The unity of science now requires a principle of explanation consistent with the notions of complementarity and reciprocal agency.

Kenneth C. Denbigh, an expert in thermodynamics, has recently offered several alternative principles based on a wide range of recent research. His book *An Inventive Universe* emphasizes the temporal dimension of events that has long been obscured by classical concern for spatialized order.[16] It challenges the adequacy of determinism on several grounds and then provides a set of principles more conducive to the unity of science.

Determinism, says Denbigh, is a doctrine of faith rather than of empirical observation. It is a hypothesis that cannot be tested, because one has to assume determinism in the very process of testing. For example, if an experiment is made to discover an invariant relationship between certain phenomena, and a contrary result turns up, the difficulty can be explained by reference to forces or factors omitted from the initial experiment. If one finds that water does not always freeze at a temperature of 32 degrees Fahrenheit, then one tends to look for variables in the composition of the water, or the air pressure, or the containers; and so on. Morton White's procedure for explaining events, described in Chapter 2, works the same way: keep on adding properties to the formula until the results appear reasonably certain on the assumption that some finite set of properties must have determined the outcome. If alternative outcomes are still inferable, it only means that one has not yet adduced all the determining factors.

This mode of inquiry is impossible to invalidate on its own grounds because one cannot prove the nonexistence of those hypothetical factors which, if known, would supposedly determine the result. On the other hand, the procedure presupposes either the possibility of complete knowledge of the universe or a completely isolated system. The whole history of science shows the first to be an illusion; and the term "isolated" simply means that the investigator does not know of any force or factor that would change the results of experiments at the level on which he is working. Isolation itself is relative and cannot be rationalized without recourse to determinism.

Suppose a historian tried to demonstrate that the Lutheran reformation in Germany was determined by the economic and political ambitions of the German princes; the venality of the Roman church hierarchy as perceived by the more gothic German provinces; the ambivalence of the Holy Roman Emperor; the cultural differences between Mediterranean and Germanic regions; and the personal magnetism and anguish of Martin Luther. Any halfway clever student could imagine, given these factors and even a dozen more, other outcomes than those that actually occurred. Luther could have died in any number of ways consistent with the prevailing conditions, before launching his revolt; he might not have escaped the Diet of Worms; and so on. The advocate of determinism, however, can answer either that his investigation is intended to isolate certain types of factors (so that, for his purpose, all other factors remain constant) or that the possibility of alternative outcomes shows the need for further investigation. He can't lose.

The fact that determinism eludes testing does not make it a bad principle, says Denbigh. The first principles of all sciences are equally arbitrary. Their only qualification is that they generate more useful questions and account for more phenomena more systematically than other principles. However, determinism is becoming increasingly useless at the microscopic and sub-atomic levels of inquiry and is being replaced by statistical probability even at the macroscopic level. New principles of unity are needed.

For Denbigh, the unity of science involves a reductionist argument—that entities at any level of complexity are explicable in terms of the behavior of entities on the levels below. The levels are arranged as follows:

6. social groups
5. multi-cellular living things
4. cells
3. molecules
2. atoms
1. fundamental particles

Thus, the behavior of molecules is explained by atomic interactions, and the latter by the action of fundamental particles. As Carl Hempel himself wrote, "It is often felt that only the discovery of a micro-theory affords real scientific understanding of any type of phenomenon, because only it gives us insight into the inner mechanism of the phenomenon, so to speak."[17]

The preference for micro-theoretical or reductionist explanations accounts for the progressive discovery of the structures of cells, molecules, and atoms during the last two centuries. The principle of determinism accompanied each new step, until it was found inadequate. However, if one looks at the levels of inquiry listed by Denbigh, it is evident that the higher ones cannot be predicted, on deterministic grounds, from the lower ones. The existence of molecules does not entail the emergence of cells, for instance; the natural history of our world is a story of very long odds.[18] The idea that some level of phenomena might be determined presupposes its prior existence, which means it could not have been predicted. It is easy to be facetious about this, claiming that human beings are the last thing one would create if one were given the job of creating things. But, in fact, the existence of each one of us, with our individual circumstances and characteristics, is statistically less probable than the existence of the universe we live in.[19]

Denbigh offers three alternative principles to deal with the difficulties of determinism. First, the only principle consistent with the now widespread observation of statistical regularities among aggregate phenomena seems to be *in*determinacy. That is, the very necessity of statistical averages presupposes the impossibility of determining the precise properties of any particular event or entity—even its spatiotemporal location—from an examination of initial conditions. That one can estimate certain properties within a range of probability under isolated conditions is simply a demonstration of uncertainty at all levels of inquiry. In this respect, scientific explanations are as normative as historical ones.[20] They assert what may be expected to happen in a normal situation, given the normal behavior of the subjects. If historians were to offer hypotheses regarding the behavior of millions of people in a carefully defined situation, as chemists do with gaseous molecules, their predictions would likely prove equally accurate.[21] Such hypotheses are in fact borrowed by historians from other social disciplines and offered as truisms in developing a context for understanding more particular incidents. It is no more necessary for a historian to give the empirical evidence for these statements than it would be for a chemist to reconsider the evidence for the kinetic theory of gases when reporting the results of an experiment. The purpose of most research in chemistry and in history, after all, is not to create new laws but to refine those already proposed, by comparing the norm with the individual case. Indeterminacy is the principle most consistent with such activity.

For this principle to function as a unifying idea in science, one has to accept the notion that novel entities can come into existence that are not strictly entailed by the properties of their antecedents. This corollary Denbigh identifies as the principle of emergence. Since the appearance of novelty from sheer nothingness would reintroduce dicontinuities in the scheme of things, it must be assumed that novelty arises from the reorganization of what previously occurred. Here the idea of organizing (developing a network of reciprocal functions) triumphs over the idea of mere order. Organic systems display a temporal dimension lacking in orderliness, because of the need to synchronize activities. The temporal and spatial relationships among all members of an organic system have to be constantly adjusted to maintain the whole network, and the relationships of the network to other organisms have likewise to be regulated, in order for the organism to keep functioning. Constant change is required for continuity.

"Emergence" is the term for that process of organization through which each entity becomes temporally and spatially connected with its antecedent world, transforming those connections into elements of its own constitution. If such connections were predetermined, organization would be instantaneously given by its predecessor. In that case, the notion of time would be reduced to a logical absolute, as Newton realized. In the post-Newtonian scheme, indeterminacy is a necessary condition for the organizing process through which events emerge from the past, and through which the more complex levels of entities develop from the less complex. The principle of emergence accounts for both change and continuity in the scheme, without the need for additional postulates or fictions. Change is necessitated by the mere occurrence of events, which establish new relationships in the world; continuity is ensured by the fact that these new relationships derive from past conditions.

The relation of indeterminacy to emergence may be illustrated once again by the unification of Germany under Bismarck. It is doubtful that the pattern of relationships developed by 1871 could have been predicted with any assurance before 1859. Yet the German Empire proclaimed in the former year cannot be separated from the organizing activities that preceded it. Even the so-called lost opportunities—the revolutions of 1848, the Frankfort Assemby, the Germanic Confederation—became, through memory, regret, imitation, and rejection, elements in the pattern displayed in 1871. The empire was not produced; it emerged over a period of time. And it emerged precisely because its past was both conditional and indeterminate.

The appearance of novelty, and the evident increase in the richness and diversity of form in the universe, cannot be explained solely by the idea of organization. It also requires some kind of invention, which Denbigh proposes as his third fundamental principle. Invention connotes a purposeful activity of adaptation to increasingly complex environments. Each event in history creates, by its emergence, a new and richer environment, to which all subsequent events must respond. Given any initial state of the universe, the inventive process is self-sustaining. The continuous adjustment to changing circumstances requires not merely a reorganization of existing elements but the emergence of new levels of complexity and synchronization.

In previous chapters it was argued that the process of invention or creativity is common to historical events, to the historian's imaginative reconstruction of them, and to the dynamics of narrative explanation. It is also known to be characteristic of biological and social adaptation. But there is some difficulty in extending the idea of invention to the lower levels of inquiry, dealing with molecules, atoms, and fundamental particles. The anthropomorphic overtones of the idea are uncomfortable, and it seems to imply a teleological principle for the universe.

Teleology, or the belief that some final cause guides the development of a system, is indeed derived from human experience. And as a heuristic, it is no more useful to science than the search for a first cause. But teleology has been victimized by polemical arguments that throw out the baby of anticipation with the bathwater of destiny. For example, Ernest Nagel dismisses the question this way:

> Perhaps the chief reason why most contemporary natural sciences disown teleology, and are disturbed by the use of teleological language in the natural sciences, is that the notion is equated with the belief that future events are active agents in their own realization. Such a belief is undoubtedly a species of superstition. . . .[22]

—though no more superstitious, perhaps, than the belief that events are predetermined by the properties of a finite set of antecedent causes. Whenever one fastens the notion of agency onto one side or one part of a dynamic relationship, one is bound to ignore important aspects of the other. Nagel is as guilty of this prejudice as the subjects of his criticism.

Ernst Mayr, a practicing biologist, has offered a more useful approach to this problem. While teleology, in the sense of a preestablished harmony for the organic world, is not valid, he says, there are undoubtedly systems (particularly organic systems) operating on the basis of coded anticipation of future circumstances. These systems Mayr terms telenomic rather than teleologic. Telenomic systems are neither deterministic nor passive regarding their future. Rather, they establish rules for the adaptation of the system to contingencies within an expected range of conditions. All genetic codes are therefore telenomic. So is the course of evolution. The exact outcome may not be predictable, but the temporal development of the system is not random. It is subject, like the actions of fundamental particles, to the laws of probability.[23]

Arthur Koestler has broadened the idea of telenomic systems into a general theory of creative advance, pertaining to all levels of activity from subcellular biochemical reactions to human thought. Advance, says Koestler, is a matter of *biosociation,* or synthesis, between different matrices, each coded autonomously for flexible strategies of adaptation. When two or more organic entities interact (predator and victim, kidney and bladder) they exchange coded stimuli and equally coded selective patterns of response. The stimuli are usually given as whole patterns, in gestalt fashion. The responses are selective in terms of the state of the respondent and its environment. The basic activity, then, is neither mere stimulus–response (cause–effect) nor inclusion of submatrices into a larger matrix, but synthesis of stimuli from one matrix with states of the environment from the other.[24]

This picture of telenomic process is consistent with our earlier discussion of interactions among historical events. That is, an emerging event responds to its antecedent world not by incorporating other events in their entirety, as actual entities, but by selectively assimilating their relevant characteristics, which are stimuli coded with respect to their own temporal development. The process of emergence is characterized by the synthesis of the several codes presented by the antecedent world, guided by the novel event's anticipation of future circumstances. "Agency" is shared by all entities concerned in the transaction.

Invention, as part of a telenomic rather than teleological process, is easier to reconcile with the unity of science than the anthropomorphic overtones of classical causality. Without some notion of novelty guided by anticipation, events would emerge entirely at random, and historical continuity would be all but impossible to explain. This does not mean that invention is equally intense or apparent at all levels of inquiry; as a function of the need for organization, it will be most evident at levels of higher complexity. Denbigh says invention is articulated through chance, through selection, and through amplification (the phase of symbolic transformation referred to in Chapter 3, above). The unity of science displays a continuum from entities for whom chance is foremost, to entities for whom selection and amplification assume primary emphasis.

Since the seventeenth century at least, invention has been connected with human thought, and its use as a principle of explanation for nonhuman phenomena immediately raises the question of consciousness. Denbigh himself uses this term in discussing emergence: "Consciousness," he says, "is not a concept we can do without—in science any more than in everyday life. Therefore, the possibility of consciousness must be supposed to be explicable, and thus in some sense latent, at the very deepest level of the reductionist system, i.e. at the level of fundamental particles."[25] According to Arthur Koestler and others, matter cannot influence consciousness (as classical dualism maintained) without the reverse also being true.[26]

But though consciousness is apparent in human beings, and must be accounted for in any scheme of scientific inquiry, it need not be used as a principle of unity. Indeed, the term is misleading in the context of Denbigh's general argument. In his reductionist scheme, consciousness occupies the *highest* level of complexity, so it cannot be used as the starting point for explanation. Rather than call inventive activity on the lower levels "latent consciousness," as Denbigh has done, one ought to reverse the perspective and call consciousness a highly complex type of energy transformation. This would be consistent with the structure of events outlined in Chapter 3, where the term "symbolic transformation" was used to describe the reorganization and synthesis of elements after their initial assimilation from the past, without implying conscious mental operations.

Also in Chapter 3, the term "feeling," borrowed from Whitehead, was used to describe how events relate to each other, again without the assumption of consciousness. William James, from whom Whitehead gained many insights, wrote, "If there be such things as feelings at all, then so surely as relations between objects exist in *rerum natura,* so surely and more surely, do feelings exist to which these relations are known."[27]

The point of these references is that invention need not be limited to human activity. It exists below the level of consciousness and existed prior to the evolution of conscious thought. It is a complex type of feeling, a function of the organization of things. The more complex the organizing activity, the higher the level of invention. Misunderstanding of this aspect of events is due to the anthropocentric prejudice that creativity in any form presupposes a conscious mind in a single organic body.

That organizational invention need not be confined to a single organism has been illustrated by Lewis Thomas in his delightful book of essays *The Lives of a Cell*. Discussing the phenomenon of an anthill, Thomas pointed out that the individual ant has no brain to speak of, just a poor little scrap of molecular material. It is programmed to fetch and carry, but there is nothing in its genes to account for the wonderful, intricate architecture of the whole hill, or the specialized functions which the hill as an organization performs. How do these things get done? Thomas explains the hill as an organism in itself, with a level of intelligence commensurate with the network of information provided by its whole population. The individual ant functions like a cell in the human body. The hill is a highly complex body; it just isn't wrapped up in a skin like ours.[28]

Thomas goes on to show that the ecology of the whole earth may be thought of as an organic system. In fact, from the level of galaxies down through human societies to subatomic particles, the universe might be explained better by an organic reductionism than by a mechanical one. That is, it is more helpful to explain an anthill or a human body as a temporal organization anticipated by its specialized members than it is to explain it as the sum of its parts. The individual ant, without the hill, is nothing. It dies. Likewise, the physical structure of the anthill at any moment, frozen at a Newtonian point and dissected like a mechanism, ceases to function. Only if it is viewed as an organized development, growing and changing over sixty or more ant generations, does its full significance emerge.

Because the inventive activity associated with telenomic processes is evident at all levels of inquiry, the strict division between mind and matter bequeathed by the seventeenth-century philosophers is no longer appropriate as a ground of explanation. If consciousness is defined as a function of inventive activity at an extremely high level of organic complexity, rather than as "latent" in all nonconscious events, then all events—human or nonhuman, physical or historical—can be shown to have the same general form and structure.

The idea that consciousness was only the tip-end of a continuum of awareness that extended throughout nature was proposed over fifty years ago by Alfred North Whitehead. Whitehead, like Denbigh, saw awareness as the measure of an entity's response to its environment, and he argues that the level of awareness must increase with the level of complexity of organization. In short, responses must get organized over a period of time with some minimum duration. For a rock, the need for organization is minimal; the pattern of relationships assimilated from its past will be actualized with few significant changes. For humans, however, the need to synchronize various bodily processes with one another, and to adapt the bodily system to the environment, makes the developmental aspect all-important.

Evidence to support Whitehead's idea of a continuum has been ac-

cumulating in recent years in the laboratories of biologists trying to understand the rhythmic time-keeping processes of plants and animals. These
"chronobiologists" study synchronizing systems that regulate the behavior
of internal organs relative to periodic changes in the external environment.
The systems are called clocks, and they have been found in an amazing
number of species. For example, many types of birds navigate and feed
facing in certain directions, which they maintain through the day by making
allowance for the "motion" of the sun. Similarly, the elaborate dances of
honeybees, giving directions for getting to the nectar from the hive, must
include a time factor, because bees gather nectar on a fairly strict schedule.
Changes in the polarization of sunlight in the atmosphere during the day
provide clues for the bee's clock.[29]

Many plants and animals change their behavior in relation to environmental cycles of night and day. Plants open leaves in daylight and close
them at night. Animals migrate and mate and nest in specific seasons, often
with only a few hours difference from year to year. And they do it by telling
time, independently of cues such as local temperature. This is why ducks,
for instance, can start back north while it is warm in their southern winter-
ing grounds, and can sometimes arrive in the north before the ice thaws.
Their internal clocks are far more constant than the weather.

Humans have clocks, too, including the lunar cycle of female menstrua-
tion, the twenty-four hour cycle of temperature changes in the body, the
DNA-RNA replication cycle in cells, and familiar rhythms in physical and
mental illnesses. The evidence for such clocks is often missed due to our
prevailing concern for mechanical timekeeping. But if one keeps a diary,
recording things like periods of drowsiness, incidents of respiratory ail-
ments, desire for certain types of foods, one will find upon review a number
of cyclical patterns. If the body is healthy, these patterns will be fairly well
synchronized.[30]

These examples may seem like evidence for traditional determinism: if
biological clocks operate in direct response to environmental changes, then
their "time" is not relative to the observer. The need for organizational
inventiveness is reduced, and the continuum of inventive awareness proposed by Whitehead remains unwarranted. But, in fact, many if not most of
the time-regulating processes discovered so far are more or less autonomous
within the organism. Photoperiodism and other temporal rhythms have
been maintained in the absence of environmental cues for significant periods
in many experiments. As early as 1729 it was demonstrated that plants
which extend their leaves in daylight and fold them at night would continue
doing so, on schedule, even in constant darkness. More recently, it was
discovered that the rhythmic movements of plants and animals are only
approximately related to external cues. Some proceed through a "daily"
cycle of twenty-three hours, fifty-two minutes; others choose twenty-four

hours, seven minutes; and so on. Trees leaf out and animals migrate slightly early or slightly late by solar time, but always *on* time by their own internal clocks. The term "circadian" has been applied to those rhythms whose period approximates a day, the term "circannual" to those approximating a year. Such rhythms, though they may have originated in more direct response to the environment in the early stages of evolution, are now regulated by the organism itself.

Is it possible, however, that these rhythms are genetically predetermined, or that their synchronization with external cues is simply part of the complex but lawful order of the universe not yet fully mapped? Is there evidence for that integrating, developmental process associated with invention? The answer to both questions is a qualified "yes." The interactions between various parts of an organism, and between the organism and its environment, can be reduced to a quasi-mechanical system of complex coordination, and researchers have obtained often startling results by statistical correlations of separate rhythms.[31] But in this process, one undermines the deterministic argument that the mechanism is directed solely by the environment. There are two reasons for this.

First, a predetermined rhythm obviates the need for time regulation only if it is set exactly for twenty-four hours, or one year, or one lunar cycle, with no deviation. Otherwise the system will move out of phase and will malfunction. There is a species of swan in Russia that has fallen victim to this malady. It begins migrating south each spring before the wing feathers have developed enough for flight. The swans have to *walk* for ten days before their internal processes catch up to the solar clock. Easy prey for wolves, they are fast dying out. In organisms where the discrepancy is less drastic than this, periodic checks on the external environment help prevent increasing dissonance. The synchronization, or "resetting" of the systemic clock, is a selective response by the organism not determined by the external cycle. The latter does not explain the former.

Second, it seems unlikely that in a multicellular organism, or even in a complex cell, every member of the community must take its own periodic bearings on an external cycle. According to chronobiologists, there must be some "master clock" that not only synchronizes the variety of internal rhythms exhibited by the community but also synchronizes the whole system with the external environment in a semiautonomous way. The master clock acts like an orchestra conductor, making sure that each player's temporal pattern fits in with the whole, and seeing to it that the whole orchestra interacts properly with its audience. If this regulating function is not performed, the organism begins to malfunction despite the continuing influence of the environment. A vast number of carefully monitored experiments have shown that insects, plants, birds, and humans subjected to internal desynchronization succumb to stress-related illnesses, disease, and death.[32]

The precise location and character of master clocks remain obscure, though in some systems they have been associated with the periodic secretion of hormones. More than one biologist has concluded that they are best defined not as objects but as bioelectric wave-fields, pulsing through the whole system.[33] Such an electromagnetic phenomenon would account for the synchronization of energy transformations throughout such a complex system as the human body.

Also in humans, the "alpha" rhythm of the brain, which has become something of an occult subject, appears to coordinate the activities of a great variety of cells and organs in regard to the processing of information and to motor activity. The coordination is achieved by "entraining" the frequencies of individual cell rhythms by the stronger frequency of the alpha wave. This does not mean that they all have the same frequency but that their frequencies coincide at regular intervals. Electromagnetic frequencies have been monitored on every level of organic activity during the last few years. Even a freshly laid egg yields a slow but regular pulse. As organic complexity increases, the frequencies exhibited by the various members of a community need a more sophisticated master clock to enable them to remain synchronized with each other and with the external environment. It is virtually impossible to explain the operation of master clocks by a traditional cause-effect argument; the causal agency is shared by every party to the transaction.

If one considers that electromagnetic frequencies are now used to explain the behavior of phenomena at both subatomic and cosmic levels of inquiry, one can see that they form a basis for the unity of science, and for that continuum of inventive activity proposed by Whitehead and Denbigh. Instead of looking at the universe as a system of mechanisms within mechanisms within mechanisms, all obeying universal laws of order, scientists are coming to look at it as a system of rhythmic processes within rhythmic processes, synchronized organically.

Biological clocks have been discussed at some length because the relevant research indicates strongly that inventive processes operate at all levels of complexity, without requiring consciousness for their explanation, and because the indeterminate and emergent character of organic activity can be extended to inorganic activity as well as to human thought. Although the difference between "life" and "nonlife" is still extremely important, it can be seen as a quantum step in a fundamentally unified scheme. The steps from atoms to molecules and from nonconscious to conscious awareness are not different in that respect.

The three principles proposed by Denbigh—indeterminacy, emergence, and invention—provide a ground for the explanation of temporal events that is consistent with the most recent research in several fields of science and with the general scientific paradigm that has emerged in the twentieth century. Time is no longer absolute, unmoving and universal. It is a dimension of interaction between emerging events. Its units are not homogeneous. Their duration varies with the amount of organizational invention required by a given entity to create a determinate pattern of relationships from the indeterminate conditions of its antecedent world. Time is *derived* from events. In the metaphysical sense, the notion of events is thus more fundamental than the notions of time or of space.[34]

The definitions arrived at by modern science make it unnecessary to base either historical explanation or its criticism on the classical or neopositivist model of deterministic causality. As an ideal model for deductive analysis this has become an anachronism; as a working method of explanation it has exhausted its adequacy. The terms "cause" and "effect," with all the euphemisms for them created by generations of frustrated historians, need to be redefined and relegated to a subordinate status in historical theory. In their place, I will now propose an analytical scheme emphasizing the complementary nature of transactions between an event, its past, and its future.

5. The Historical Event

What is called realism . . . consists precisely in the placing of what occurred (or might occur) in the context of what could have happened (or could happen), and in the demarcation of this from what could not; and this is all . . . that the sense of history, in the end, comes to.

Isaiah Berlin, "Determinism, Relativism, and Historical Judgments"

In the previous chapters, arguments about the proper approach to historical explanation were reviewed with an eye toward identifying the salient points of disagreement and confusion. Samples of historical writing showed that traditional explanations had a dual purpose and a dual character: one part analogy, one part analysis. Arguments about explanation tend to favor one part over another, ignoring the possibilities of complementarity.

Most historical narratives reflect a belief in some model of analysis derived from classical science. However, it was suggested that the historians' inept application of this model was due, not to their own immaturity, but to the inappropriateness of the model itself. By rigorous abstraction from the flux of experience, the classical model presents a spatialized picture of reality that is incapable of dealing with temporal development. Hence its use in a narrative is counterproductive.

The genetic approach to explanation, discussed in Chapter 3, was found to be more consistent with historians' understanding of past events. But this approach, pervaded by a belief in the self-explanatory qualities of narrative, provided few analytical categories upon which critical revision and theoretical advance might be based. To show that such categories were neither impossible nor irrelevant, I sketched a pattern of creative process, drawn from studies of creative thinking and the arts. This pattern reflected the *temporal* aspect of events.

The main difficulty uncovered so far is that the kind of explanation suggested by traditional historical narratives is badly in need of clarification, but that clarification cannot be achieved through the model proposed by positivistic philosophers, even though many historians are resigned to it because of its "scientific" reputation. Chapter 4 was meant to show that the meaning of temporal events has shifted radically in the twentieth century. Any model or theory claiming to be scientific must come to terms with that shift before offering itself as a basis for explanation. As an exponent of the new approach remarks,

> when discussing and analyzing the human condition we have not integrated adequately into the language of description and response the shift from a metaphysics of substance, thing, and place to one of process, relations, and field. Nor have we absorbed significantly the evolution of the meaning of inquiry from primarily that [of] "looking at" to primarily that of "constituting."[1]

From this perspective, an event is defined as a temporal process, constituting a definite pattern of relationships with respect to its antecedents. The antecedent world is presented as a set of conditional data, each with a subjective intensity derived from its own formative experience. These data and feelings are assimilated as elements in the emerging pattern of the novel event. They undergo transformation and integration to a degree consistent with the event's organizational complexity. The final, integrated pattern represents a decision by the event to be what it is and not anything else, a decision implying a range of alternatives that were not realized on this occasion.

Explanations of historical events thus require analysis of the temporal process through which antecedent conditions are transformed into a new actual pattern, and analysis of the relations between elements in the final pattern and elements in other events, past and future. The two modes of analysis are complementary: every pattern presupposes a constitutive process, and every process presupposes the existence of a set of elements derived from the past.

It should be added immediately, for the benefit of historical writers, that such analysis is not a substitute for narrative accounts of the past. Narrative, being an analogue to the constitutive process, is the most appropriate vehicle for understanding past events. But as I argued in Chapter 1, the anticipation and reassessment of potential patterns of elements that characterize narratives (and events) must be raised to conscious levels and studied systematically if historians are to create intelligible explanations. "Following" the narrative is useful only if the narrative makes sense.

For similar reasons it may be awkward to analyze the structure of the temporal process, or the logical and aesthetic relationships among elements of events, within the typical narrative. This is a task of clarification best left to separate studies, or to introductions. But the task still needs doing before historians can be confident of their explanations. In the present chapter I will suggest an analytical scheme pertaining to all historical events, and indicate some of its applications.

Before I outline the scheme itself, it would be helpful to review the subject of analysis, namely, historical events as presented in narrative accounts; and the purpose of analysis, which is to show relationships between different events and between different narrative accounts.

The first information given in most narratives is a brief identification of the event(s) to be explained. Sometimes this information is merely assumed, as if the title of the account alone provided sufficient direction for the reader. In the positivist tradition of explanation, this approach makes sense because it is believed that the event to be explained has no real shape prior to the full analysis of its antecedents. Paradoxically, however, it is also assumed that events, being things, have a fixed identity which is encompassed by their labels. So it is only necessary to give the label for everyone to know what is being examined. For example, George Lefebvre began his *The Coming of the French Revolution* with the sentence "The ultimate cause of the French Revolution of 1789 goes deep into the history of France and of the Western world."[2] This is to assume that the dimensions of the subject—its geographical area, temporal duration, and future significance—are already given. But if one does not know those dimensions in fairly exact terms, either from some previous analytical work or from a prefatory statement by the author, then the search for antecedents and their causal significance becomes arbitrary. One has to take it on faith that the author is guided by a valid definition of the event, and that this definition will be revealed in the course of his narrative. The validity of the explanation then rests upon the closeness of the "fit" between the initial conditions and the final definition; in other words, on the internal coherence of the narrative itself. Objective criteria for judging the critical worth of the explanation remain uselessly vague. One doesn't really know what has been explained. In response to the question, "What does it mean?" one is told, in effect, "Read it again!" Thus there is no *historians'* French Revolution to compare with Lefebvre's, except a generalized and constantly shifting image of a multiplicity of names, dates, and actions.

Lefebvre's work itself is not mistaken. Events in a narrative must emerge into clear definition through interaction with other elements, analogously to the historical process itself. But such accounts can be justified only by presupposing an explanatory scheme in which events are clearly defined according to their temporal structure and constituent elements. Such a scheme does not yet exist for history. If it did, one would know what Lefebvre meant by "French Revolution" as surely and completely as a biologist knows the meaning of *Rhizopus nigricans* (common bread mold). The absence of a method of critical comparison is the chief reason why history is considered scientifically immature.

The development of a comparative method should proceed from analyses of the most well-known events, and from those whose elements are most widely agreed upon. This may pose difficulties, for the most famous events are often those whose elements excite investigators by their very exclusiveness and complexity, and about which there are strongly divergent opinions. Yet the work can be done if one proceeds as in the sciences, from areas of relative certainty to areas of relative uncertainty.

The "elements" that make up the final form of an event, that constitute its meaning for other events, are not physical properties. Rather, they are the patterns of experience brought into focuse by individuals, groups, institutions, and ideas involved in the event's organization. One may identify these patterns and compare them with each other or with the patterns of other events. Obviously, the patterns represented by different individuals or groups will stand in *contrast* to one another. The process historian will try to identify the salient contrasts within an event and to show how they are resolved as the analysis moves from a field of general potentiality toward specific actuality. In theory, every historical event displays the same developmental structure; only the constituent elements and contrasts change.

In keeping with my desire not to separate theory from practice, the proposed model will be illustrated by a typical historical event. The Reform Bill of 1832 in England is useful for this purpose because its passage had a fairly clear terminal phase, and it involved a good mix of personalities, groups, institutions, and ideas. It is also well known. I have no intention of digging up new evidence about this event, or of offering a new interpretation of the available data. The discussion relies primarily on the anthology of accounts edited by William Henry Maehl, Jr., under the title *The Reform Bill of 1832: Why Not Revolution?*[3]

The passage of the Reform Bill may be defined in a shorthand way as the procedure of voting by Parliament, and approval by King William IV, of a law changing the qualifications for voting in British elections and redistributing the seats in the House of Commons. By a modest extension of the duration of that procedure, one can consider also the complex of parliamentary elections, political maneuvering, and economic changes that accompanied the bill's emergence from 1830 to 1832. This extended duration is what historians usually have in mind when they speak of the "passage" of the Reform Bill. Incidents in this duration are explicitly or implicitly present as constituent elements in the final form of the "passage" as a complex occasion.

For analytical purposes, the geographical dimensions of an event may also be extended. The Reform Bill was passed at Westminster but involved activities throughout the British Isles. There is also a question of the importance of the French and Belgian revolutions of 1830 in the constitution of the bill's passage. Whatever the answer, these and perhaps other parts of Europe need to be considered in the definition of the event.

Finally, one has to look at the event according to its future consequences—what it meant for subsequent events. The historian does this because he senses that the significance of an event depends upon hindsight: it is really determined by what happened later. By looking at subsequent events, the historian can more readily identify constituent elements that will repay special attention. From the theoretical standpoint, subsequent events have to be assessed because they are anticipated by the emerging event itself, as a means of guiding the formation of its synoptic judgment. This anticipation is grounded upon data from the antecedent world, which make some future environments appear more likely than others. In its selective assimilation of antecedents, the emerging event makes a prediction about its own future. The historian reverses the process, using retrodiction to explain the event's emergence from the past.

Passage of the Reform Bill of 1832 was followed in England by other reform bills which gradually extended the franchise to most adult subjects. It was also followed by an extension of empire, development of capital industry, and the rise to prominence of the bourgeoisie and its cultural habits, relative to the prominence enjoyed previously by the aristocracy. It was not followed by revolutionary action of the type experienced on the Continent. These events represent some of the hypothetical consequences of the passage of the bill, and therefore the reasons for studying it in the first place. They indicate which elements of the bill's passage are likely to repay closer study, and which features of its antecedent world will be most relevant to an explanation of its emergence. Analysis guided by hypothetical consequences is not, after all, a matter of uncritical subjectivity, as Beard, Becker, and other relativist historians believed. It is the procedure followed by most scientists. Historians simply need to be more explicit about the consequences they think are significant, so that their readers have a better idea of what is being explained.

From this brief survey of subsequent events, one can note that passage of the Reform Bill of 1832 involved at least the following elements: parliamentary action; the relations between members and leaders of both houses; the king's behavior; industrial development; bourgeois and working-class activity; and differing ideas about the preferred pattern of interaction among all of these. The tensions, contrasts, and potential combinations of these and many other elements were more or less resolved by the passage of the bill, and many of them are mentioned explicitly in the legislative records.

The historian's task is to explain how the pattern of elements displayed by the final form of the event emerged from the indeterminate conditions displayed by its antecedent world. To do this, it is first necessary to construct a hierarchy of elements, according to their respective levels of abstraction. Lord Grey's warning to King William IV about possible adverse reaction of popular reform groups to his planned dismissal of Parliament is on a different scale altogether from the concept of "virtual representation." If one is to analyze the relation of these two elements to each other, and to the antecedents from which they derived, one needs to be clear about their respective levels of abstraction.

The hierarchy is constructed by abstraction from the most complex particular elements to the simplest, most widely applicable ones. For example, in geometry, points are abstracted from lines, lines from planes, planes from definite volumes and volumes from the recurring complex experience of spatial extension. In history, the field of "zero" abstraction is merely a multiplicity of subjective interactions with indefinite spatial and temporal dimensions—the "experience of becoming" described in Chapter 1 and connoted by Heraclitus's statement, "all things flow."[4] It is the one actual "History" to which all "histories" refer, and in itself is impervious to analysis.

The first level of abstraction is the level of synoptic judgment, in which the objective form of the whole event overrides the particular relationships within it. One extracts from the seamless web of experience *this* event, with its temporal and geographical dimensions. There are of course many other events which one might have delineated on similar grounds, which could include elements ascribed to the Reform Bill: passage of the Factory Act of 1833, for instance, or abolition of West Indian slavery. But though many events may incorporate a given element, only one displays the whole pattern of elements implied by its definition.

Some historians will argue that the "whole event" is a generalization belonging to the highest level of abstraction rather than the lowest. Such writers tend to begin their explanations by identifying antecedent conditions. The overall form of the event then emerges last, in hindsight as it were, and appears to be a generalized view of what happened. As an analogue to the historical process this view is probably correct. But as a method of inquiry it is backward. It is clear from studies of perception that one's initial knowledge of an event is gained by reaction to its form, not to its parts. Analysis of parts comes later. Also, the actual event must be more complex and particular than a concept such as "political reform" or even a group such as "the Whigs," because such elements may be constituents of more than one event, while the reverse is impossible. The defined event includes aspects of each element in a pattern of great complexity, but the elements themselves belong to classes of entities with many instances. Thus the whole event is less abstract than its elements.

The epistemological question of whether this and other levels of abstraction are actually present in events, or are the constructs of the historian's mind, must be reserved for later discussion. In the mode of explanation proposed here, the levels of abstraction are constructs based on the use of terms in typical historical narratives and monographs. The test of their validity is pragmatic. Historians may not always agree on the level of abstraction to which a particular element should be assigned, or on which elements belong within an event's definition. But such disagreements point to a belief in an "ideal" configuration for each event, in the sense developed by Max Weber and others. The ideal configuration is a heuristic, constantly refined and amended by each generation according to its needs. In science, terms such as "the universe" and "atom" serve the same purpose.

The historian viewing an event from the special perspective of one of its elements is not offering a description of the whole complex configuration, and this ought to be made clear at the start of every such account (as G. D. H. Cole does, for instance, in his account of the Reform Bill).[5] Nor is a "general survey" of an event's development necessarily an account of the ideal configuration, since many surveys are constructed around a conceptual theme, a perspective of high abstraction. A critical treatment of an actual event, in terms of its ideal configuration, must reflect the character of the event itself: a synoptic view of the relationships among all significant elements, and of the pattern of contrasts between their perspectives. In historians' language, such a treatment involves a narrative, together with a critical review and effort toward reconciliation of the interpretations offered by various historians. The anthology used as a source for this chapter goes only part way toward that goal—it includes many partial accounts but does not attempt a critical comparison and synthesis.

Abstractions at the first level (whole events) may be compared and classified in terms of geographical extension, temporal duration, and future significance. This is commonly done when one refers to "the French Revolution of 1789" or "the War of the Roses." One can compare events whose dimensions are roughly equivalent, even though their locations in time and space are quite different. But it is a mistake to try explaining some event by reference to another of quite disparate dimensions, because the significance of each from the standpoint of the other will be distorted. The fact that Henry VIII got the title "Defender of the Faith" from the pope for publishing a virulent attack upon Martin Luther may be ironic in view of Henry's later career, but neither element in the contrast is an adequate explanation of the other because they have different dimensions as events.

An event at the first level of abstraction is a distillation and a synthesis of the potential configurations brought into focus by elements at higher levels. Those levels, in ascending hierarchical order, are: the individual, the group, the institutional, the conceptual, and the field. Each level will be discussed in turn, with appropriate examples.

The second, or individual, level expresses the view of events brought into focus by individual people. Each person, as he or she interacts with other individuals, groups, institutions, and concepts, brings into focus one configuration representing his or her experience of what actually happened. This configuration is made up of aspects of other elements, that is, the features of elements that are significant from this person's point of view. For example, Francis Place experienced the passage of the Reform Bill from a position as organizer of working-class demonstrations. He had close connections with other organizers, with working-class individuals and groups, and with certain individuals among the Whigs and Radicals in Parliament and in the Cabinet. His connections and perceptions with respect to the urban political magnates, the gentry, and the king were less direct and complete. Then there were some aspects of the situation, such as the duke of Wellington's dealings with the king's household, which Place didn't perceive strongly at all, or perceived as irrelevant.

The level of individual elements is the level of biography, with all its wealth of detail, its perceptual bias, and its psychological insight. Biography has always been slightly suspect among historians, for the relationships among individuals and other elements of an event are, for the most part, too complex and irregular to fit into explanations based on causal determinism. Biography tends to be organized in temporal patterns, where development of the character changes the meaning of explanatory terms from one period to the next.

The biographical approach is not "wrong" however, because it allows the historian to substantiate or amend his definitions of elements at the group, institutional, or conceptual levels. One understands the eighteenth-century Enlightenment more precisely by looking at its expression in the life of Diderot or of Jefferson, just as one clarifies the meaning of a group by studying the feelings of its members. Care must be taken, of course, that no single individual be represented as the full expression of any other element in the hierarchy. The individual perceives aspects, not wholes, just as the actual event incorporates only aspects of that individual's experience.

At the individual level ones sees most vividly the contrast between what actually happened and what might have been. The plans and hopes of people are often recorded in detail, and their reflections on actual events are informed with deep feeling. One can read Francis Place's despairing letters about the apathy of workingmen, and his warnings to government about working-class excitement, during the reform agitation; and one can read his reflections on the bill's exclusion of working-class interests afterward.[6] These contrasts add to the dynamic intensity of the passage of the bill as an actual event, and they function as dynamic elements in a narrative.

The third level of abstraction is focused on groups. At this level, individual psychology is replaced by group dynamics. The historian who analyzes an event from the perspective of some group, or by the contrast between two groups, may illustrate his arguments by referring to individuals. But the argument itself concerns the functions of the group in its institutional and conceptual environment. Norman Gash, for instance, disputes Halévy's contention that the French Revolution of 1830 was a decisive conceptual influence in the passage of the Reform Bill. Gash reached his conclusions by close study of several groups, including the ultraradicals and the ultra-Tories. He looked at significant individuals in each group, and these are mentioned in his work; but his conclusions refer to group perceptions, and it is on this level that he refines the general account of the actual event.[7]

Whether a collection of people is treated as a group or as an institution depends on the purpose of the account. The Birmingham Political Union may be treated as a group if one is considering the function of political unions as collective institutions. Similarly, one may investigate the House of Lords as a group within the context of the House of Lords as an institution. It is even possible that a highly significant individual, like Queen Victoria or the Marquis de Sade, might be represented by name at the institutional level. The purpose of these remarks is to indicate a level of analysis, not to nail down members of each category. Accordingly, one could *suggest* the following group-level elements for passage of the Reform Bill: parliamentary factions such as ultra-Tory, Ministerial (Wellington) Tory, independent Tory, conservative and liberal Whigs, Canningites, Benthamite Radicals, working-class Radicals; extraparliamentary political unions; the Rotunda group; the trade unions; Owenites. This list is of course not complete.

The pattern of relationships between a specific group and other elements in any event may be analyzed so as to clarify the significance of the other elements. For example, the ultra-Tories show important responses to working-class activism, to the idea of revolution expressed in France, to the church and the monarchy as institutions, and to the duke of Wellington as an individual. Such an analysis would reveal what the various elements meant to this group regarding this event. Analyses of other groups' viewpoints would supplement and refine the first, until one had constructed a multiperspective description of each element in the event's configuration.

The pattern of relationships for a group may also be compared with the group's pattern in another event, to see where changes have occurred. Thus it is instructive to compare the ultra-Tories' behavior during the Reform Bill passage with their behavior prior to and during the previous controversy over Catholic emancipation.

Because the Reform Bill proceedings centered on Parliament, there is a tendency to look at them from the institutional perspective, restricting one's survey of groups to those directly related to parliamentary concerns. But if one focused on an individual in the same duration, one would have to consider other types of groups to which he might belong: a church congregation, a family, an investment venture, a scientific society. Making a survey of all groups involved in an event, regardless of perspective, is a difficult but necessary step toward more comprehensive explanations.

The fourth level of abstraction is the institutional. It is often hard to decide whether or when a group becomes large enough, permanent enough, structured enough, or associated closely enough with certain physical structures or symbols to be called an "institution." In general, institutions emphasize order more than organization, while groups display more organic functions; it is a relative judgment. The historian studying the actions of Democrats in Congress in 1877 will be interested in their group features, while a historian working on the development of the Democratic party will emphasize structural, institutional elements.

The idea behind the hierarchy is that analyses of an event on one level should proceed from elements of the next highest level. Thus an individual experience can be examined by reference to certain aspects of groups to which that individual belongs. The groups function institutionally, and the institutions reflect aspects of prevailing concepts. To explain individual experiences solely on the basis of conceptual elements, without the intermediate group and institutional levels, would be a distortion of reasoning and of the historical process. It would leave a gap in explanation, because the conceptual elements related to many alternative individual experiences. Lord Grey's experience from 1830 to 1832 was certainly infused with the concept of parliamentary reform. But it illustrates only one aspect of that concept, seen from Lord Grey's particular perspective and filtered through the institutional and group contexts of his life. Parliamentary reform was important to many other people as well. Thus one cannot use the concept as a whole to explain the experience of any one person, saying in effect, "Lord Grey did this or that because he believed in parliamentary reform."

Since the aim of the hierarchy is to avoid leaps in reasoning from one level of abstraction to the next, the relation between institutional and group elements must be worked out on a relative scale appropriate to a particular inquiry. In general, very large groups such as "classes," "sectors," or nations can be analyzed on the institutional level, for their relations to other elements are most apt to be mediated through smaller groups. During the passage of the Reform Bill, the gentry, the political-union network, "industry," and the working classes related to other elements in this mediated way. Relations between the gentry and Parliament were not those of a group functioning within an institution, but rather those of two institutions interacting through groups. If a historian wants to find how parliamentary representatives of the gentry voted on the several motions regarding reform, he will consider them as a group, bringing into focus certain aspects of the gentry's relationship to other elements.

Conceptual elements make up the fifth level of abstraction. Ideas, principles, and doctrines serve as foci for patterns of meaning that involve many other elements. As in the previous case, there may be judgments of relative scope to work out. Depending upon one's research aims, one might define ideas within principles within doctrines. For the present, all three of these conceptual elements will be considered together as one level.

The conceptual elements of a given event are connected to each other in a variety of patterns; each pattern is articulated by an institution. Thus Parliament, during passage of the Reform Bill, responded to aspects of the concepts "constitution," "aristocracy," "democracy," "property rights," "revolution," and so on. Only certain aspects of a concept are involved, from the institution's perspective. "Property rights" is perceived by other institutions, and through them by various groups and individuals, that may have been irrelevant to the Reform Bill. A vigilante group shooting a lurking trespasser in northern Wales involves "property rights" but from an entirely different perspective. On the other hand, "property rights" is significant for the institutional experience of Parliament mostly in respect to its meaning for people who stood to gain or lose voting rights and control of boroughs and counties. The full complex meaning of the concept, illustrated perhaps in a thousand different incidents during the reform era, cannot be realized in any particular event, or in any potential configuration of an event.

Conceptual elements at the fifth level of abstraction are usually compound or complex: one speaks of "property rights," not of "property" or "rights"; "parliamentary reform," rather than just "reform." This distinction is made because single-term concepts are often linked to the notion of universals. Universals form the highest level of abstraction possible, and their place in the scheme of explanation needs separate treatment. At this point, it is useful to define a level of abstraction for those ideas, usually complex, that move people to act and to make sense from their experience in the everyday world. The compound labels are reminders of this level.

A concept such as "virtual representation" is articulated by a number of different institutions. The historian may study these articulations to clarify the full meaning of "virtual representation" for some event. Or he may study them to find out how the different institutions related to each other. Thus Bristol had one view of the concept, the gentry another, and urban industrial magnates a third. The contrasts between these views provided a dynamic force for parliamentary action: the Reform Bill of 1832 represents one of many possible resolutions for those contrasts. The differences between the bill's definition of "virtual representation" (written or implied) and the definitions intended by the gentry and by Bristol voters is a difference between actuality and potentiality.

In an explanatory narrative, conceptual elements are usually identified in association with their institutional, group, or individual expressions: "A storm on the nationalist issue was caused by the speech of Gustav Noske in the Reichstag on April 25, 1907, in connection with the vote on the budget."[8] But concepts may also be isolated as a means of developing a critical framework for explanations. For example, Justin McCarthy, talking about the Reform Bill from the perspective of later developments, identified three concepts of government established in 1832:

> They settled the principle that the House of Lords were never to carry resistance to any measure coming from the Commons beyond a certain point—beyond the time when it became unmistakably evident that the Commons were in earnest.
>
> . . . It became thereby settled that the personal will of the Sovereign was no longer to be a decisive authority in our scheme of Government. . . . the Sovereign always yields to the advice of the Ministers.
>
> . . . to establish in practical working order the principle that the House of Commons was a representative assembly, bearing due proportion in its numbers and in its arrangement to the numbers and interests of the constituents.[9]

From another viewpoint, E. P. Thompson maintains that the passing of the Reform Bill promoted the class consciousness of workingmen with regard to other classes.[10] Such statements imply that the conceptual element realized during the reform was also realized in subsequent events in more or less the same way. As will be shown later, the sequence of realizations of a given element or contrast in a series of events may be analyzed so as to clarify the relation of continuity and change over an extended period.

A sixth level of abstraction contains the "forces" or "factors" traditionally used by historians to indicate their field of inquiry: economic, political, technological, religious, philosophical, physical or physiological, geographical, aesthetic, psychological, social.[11] These categories are so ubiquitous that they demand inclusion in any scheme of abstraction that proposes to be of service to historians. There are of course subfields within, or between, each of the fields mentioned above, which belong to the same level of abstraction. Many accounts of historical events are, in fact, based on the interaction between two or more fields. In accounts of the Reform Bill, political and economic perspectives figure prominently; technological, religious, and philosophical concepts are subordinate. The ideal configuration of an event will show the relative importance of each of the fields. Such a configuration will be subject to dispute between historians who favor one field over another a priori. But if, for instance, one school of historians believes that economic elements are the ground of all events, and that political and religious behavior is merely the manifestation of economic conditions, it is still possible to say that this or that event expresses religious elements to a more significant degree than it does economic elements. The use of the economic field as a focus of relationships in an event merely brings out the economic aspects of the elements at lower levels of the hierarchy. The major contrasts between the economic view and the political or religious views ought to be clarified before one makes final judgments about contrasts at lower levels. This kind of problem need not preoccupy the writer of a narrative account with an economic bias, but it does belong in any analytical study that hopes to make narratives intelligible. For example, one could assume that the Reform Bill proceedings were tied to developments in the technology of manufactures, communications, and finance. Using the technological perspective, one would then select certain individuals, groups, institutions, and ideas to include in a narrative account. The narrative might be coherent, thorough, even witty, but its validity as an explanation of the Reform Bill passage would have to await collation with other accounts based on other perspectives—an analytical task.

The seventh level of abstraction is the level of universals. Such terms as "justic," "space," "reform," and "deference" belong at this level. As universals, they have potential to be included in any and all events. But their historical meaning is determined by how they are included in this or that particular event. The notion of "reform," for instance, has no definition outside of the actual events in which it functioned as an element.

Since universals may be mutually exclusive (whiteness and blackness) it is not possible for any one event to include all universals in its hierarchy of elements. Nor is it possible for any one event, from its limited perspective, to include all aspects of a universal. Thus, no event can realize the full potential in the world from which it emerges. Its decision to become *something* automatically leaves all other might-have-beens unfulfilled.

Several historians have shown the possibilities of tracing the adventures of universals such as "skepticism" or "progress,"[12] which are illustrated in many fields through many institutions, groups, and individuals. In addition, abstractions like "Enlightenment" or "romanticism" may be used to analyze a cultural period. When tied to a specific field ("romantic art") such terms become conceptual elements at the fifth level of abstraction; but when the historian begins to analyze their impact on other fields ("romantic nationalism") the perspective becomes more universal. This is not to say that the levels of abstraction are interchangeable. Rather, the level at which an element is placed for analysis depends on the degree of abstraction relative to other elements considered. If one intends to study just the technological features of the Industrial Revolution, then one begins on the fifth level of abstraction, with appropriate references to the wider field of technology and to the universal "revolution." But if one wishes to study the widespread influence of the Industrial Revolution in the fields of religion, art, social structure, and hygiene, one begins at the level of universals. All that is required is that the levels be arranged systematically.

Historians may wish to elucidate a contrast between certain universals, such as the tension between equality and justice, or between freedom and order. In such cases, one compares the configurations brought into focus at the seventh level by each universal, noting how each highlights or subordinates elements at lower levels in the hierarchy of some event. Each actual event determines one meaning of the contrast; a sequence of events would reveal its regular and irregular features.

The notion that universals have meaning only as they are included in actual historical events runs counter to the idealist view (e.g., of Hegel and Whitehead) that their meaning is given a priori, regardless of historical experience. It also counters the materialist view that universals are derived from actual events and are utterly passive in the actualization process. Neither view is adequate for a theory of historical explanation, and neither accords with the direct experience of reality. The idealist doctrine implies that events are formed by the combination and manifestation of universals without regard for antecedent occasions. An ideal such as "progress" seems to hover over history, entering this or that era on its own terms. Such a scheme completely obscures the physical continuity between events and makes causation a theological or metaphysical mystery. Materialism, on the other hand presupposes determinism, whose validity has already been questioned. Materialism's denial of conceptual influence in the formation of events contradicts human experience and forces one to deny the claims of historical agents that concepts, whether universal or not, played a significant part in their behavior. A theory of historical explanation demands the affirmation of conceptual elements with real potential for involvement in the emergence of actual events, elements whose meaning is derived from experience in the historical world.

The level of universals completes the hierarchy of abstraction proposed as a way of analyzing historical events. The seven levels of elements have been sketched in to reflect perspectives commonly employed by historians, though obviously amplification and correction will be needed for all the levels. Each level is to be analyzed in terms of the elements at the next highest level. Thus, the actual event embodies aspects of individual experience, which embodies aspects of group relationships, which have institutional functions, and so on. By proceeding step by step in the hierarchy, one avoids the fallacy of explaining a particular incident in terms so abstract that they could account for many other particulars as well.

As one moves up the hierarchy, one proceeds from the level of complex actuality toward levels of greater simplicity and greater potential for alternative applications. One also moves from an emphasis on organic function to an emphasis on orderly position, and from temporal activity toward spatial definition. Thus the higher levels of the hierarchy are amenable to logical analysis, the lower to narrative description. But these are relative distinctions. Even in a narrative, the perspective moves from the particular to the general and back again, as the writer tries to combine genetic and analytic explanations in a single form.

By analyzing the elements in an event's abstract hierarchy, one can see more clearly the contrasts between the event's actual configuration and the unrealized possibilities from which by comparison, it derives its significance. What "actually happened" in the Reform Bill passage from 1830 to 1832 would be meaningless without one's awareness and evaluation of what *might* have happened. In addition, the contrast between actual and potential configurations generates the intensity with which the event enters into and conditions subsequent processes.

If one compares the hierarchies of two or three events from the same general chronological period, one will discover that they have many elements and contrasts in common, especially at the higher levels of abstraction. This is only to be expected, because the hierarchies in such a case are all derived, indirectly, from the same general antecedent world. For example, the Reform Bill, the Factory Act, and the Bill to End Slavery in the West Indies differ in many respects at the individual and group levels. But at the institutional level their antecedents tend to be more alike, and to focus on Parliament. At the conceptual level they overlap still more, and at the field level quite extensively. The elements identified at the higher levels, just because they are so broadly defined, are easier to identify in antecedent events. If used as the focus of an account, they will tend to show continuity over a longer period than will elements at the lower levels of abstraction.

By the same token, a sequence of events considered to be a trend will feature certain elements or contrasts that reappear over and over again, with slightly varying significance. The concept "parliamentary reform" appears in the late eighteenth century, even linked to the figure of Lord Grey as a young man, and it reappears on other occasions prior to, and after, the passing of the Reform Bill in 1832.

Comparing the hierarchies of events in a sequence helps clarify the relative strength of the forces for continuity and change. An element nicely integrated with its associates in one event may become discordant in the next, opening the way for novel arrangements to emerge. But it is a mistake to follow one type of contrast through a sequence as though it were the "essence" or the "key" of historical change. For example, students tracing the origins of World War I are apt to place considerable blame on Bismarck's methods of unifying Germany. They overlook the fact that Bismarck believed the utility of war to be very low after 1871, and that the kaiser was not the only European ruler to continue thinking of war as a brief, dramatic march to victory. The "origin" of this element is a much more complex matter than a sequence at the conceptual level would indicate.

Before going further with questions of continuity and change, I must identify, for analytical purposes, the salient features of the "antecedent world," that is, the state of affairs that existed prior to the emergence of a given event. The antecedent world is made up of events also, and it can be described according to the same scheme of abstract elements sketched in this chapter.

6. The Antecedent World

Whenever a system is really complicated, as in the brain, or in an organized community, indeterminacy comes in . . . because to make a prediction, so many things must be known that the stray consequences of studying them will disturb the status quo, which can never therefore be discovered.

George Thompson, quoted in Ronald Clark, *Einstein*

When an event has been properly defined for the purpose of explanation, it is ready to be compared with that part of the historical world that constitutes its past. The question is, shall "the past" be defined as a set of discrete events whose shape and substance are given, or as a set of indeterminate elements involved in a pattern of emergence? The framework presented in this chapter is based, like that of the previous chapter, on the idea that the question involves different perspectives on the same subject. Both of its parts, therefore, can be answered affirmatively if one keeps the perspective clear.

A model of an antecedent world must be derived from a model of an actual event, so that the terms of one are commensurate with those of the other. In this chapter, the antecedent world is described in terms of the same constituent elements, arranged in hierarchical fashion, that characterize all events in their final, synoptic phase of development. Instead of one hierarchy, there are many. Obviously, at the higher levels of abstraction, the elements of many hierarchies will overlap. A great number of events just prior to 1940, for instance, were conditioned by Germany's drive for European hegemony. The great variety of *individual* experiences related to this period was unified by the inclusion of the German drive as one aspect common to all.

Thus, the antecedent world of a given event contains three features accessible to the historian's analysis: configurations of elements represented by the individual events of the past; contrasts within each event and between events, regarding what happened and what might have happened; and patterns of order, especially at higher levels of abstraction, made up from elements held in common by an array of past events. By studying types of contrasts and patterns of order, one can begin to classify events as though they had common properties and to discover probabilistic or relatively invariant relationships among them. But by emphasizing individual configurations and contrasts, one can also create an account of the past complex enough to show its relative indeterminacy with regard to the emergence of a subsequent event. The same model can serve both purposes if the historian is clear about the levels of abstraction he is using.

The term "antecedent" refers to that portion of the past perceived from the standpoint of some subsequent event. The event itself is an assertion about the relative significance of events prior to it. Thus, whatever the metaphysical standing of a concept such as "the historical past," the actual past studied by historians is always defined by the unique perspective of some actual event. This is analogous to the idea that the historian always selects his data with regard to some fixed or emerging story line, the final episode of which guides the arrangement of the whole. The "final episode" may in fact be an event in the historian's present, which is used as a touchstone to draw out the significance of the past for the historian's generation.

By comparing the elements making up an event with those making up its antecedents, the historian can get a sense of the changes in scope and intensity that characterize the transition from past to present. Some elements, which seem very important in the antecedent world, become relatively remote and insignificant in later periods. Other elements, dramatically emphasized in the hierarchy of a later event, will have been prefigured only vaguely, or by some minute aspect, in the past. The historian has to make decisions about the treatment of such changes from obscurity into prominence, which parallel the "forward" movement of history. But one could just as well investigate why some aspect declined in importance, and by doing so throw into relief the real novelty of the emerging event.

Whatever the decision, the antecedent world will be analyzed from the perspective of a later event, and the array of antecedent conditions will be sorted out by criteria of importance, of relevance, and of logical compatibility. Whitehead grouped such criteria into a general principle of intensive relevance, meaning that the adoption of any particular perspective upon the past automatically intensifies the relationships among certain events and weakens others.[1] For example, seen from the German or even American position around 1925, the events leading up to World War I seemed to be characterized by a calculated greed and cavalier use of secret diplomacy by France, England, and other European states. Seen from the position of England in 1941, the same events would be highlighted in quite a different way. Furthermore (as was shown earlier) all events prior to August 1914 are colored by one's awareness that the First World War happened. Some relationships thus become more intense than others.

The principle of intensive relevance explains why all events are not alike, even though, in theory, they all share the same antecedent world. While the objective form of the shared antecedents may be the same for all subsequent events, their relative importance can only be judged from a particular viewpoint, so each subsequent event will have, in effect, a different set of antecedents. Each grows out of its own past. Historians understand this principle almost intuitively because they use it when selecting some items for emphasis in their narrative accounts. Such a selection process is analogous to that used by historical events, as has been remarked previously.

Most models of historical explanation consider the antecedent world to be that portion of the past immediately prior to a given event, and roughly equal to it in duration. This is done so that the terms of explanation will be roughly commensurate with the terms of the subject being explained, and the relations between event and antecedent will not be distorted. Thus the antecedent world of the Reform Bill passage, 1830–32, would be the period of British and European history from about 1828 to 1830. In comparison, if one took the period 1750–1830 as the antecedent world of the Reform Bill of 1832, one would be forced to entertain elements such as the reign of George III or the American Revolution, and groups such as the Clapham Sect and individuals such as William Pitt as being of equal explanatory value with the economic slump of 1829, the issue of Catholic Emancipation, and the July Revolution in France. Or one would be tempted to attribute the Reform Bill to some general trend covering eighty or a hundred years, such as the geometric growth of urban population, without showing how that trend was articulated through the institutions, groups, and individuals involved more directly in the reform agitation. The practice of identifying a distant change or a long-term trend as the immediate cause of a given event, without specifying its particular relevance from the event's unique perspective, is one of the most common errors in historical explanation. It can be avoided if one takes the trouble to delineate the antecedent duration. What one really wants to know about the American Revolution or the personality of George III, from the standpoint of the Reform Bill, is their immediate significance in the period 1828–30, just before the emergence of the bill's passage.[2]

The precise dates of the antecedent world are a matter of judgment for the historian, depending partly on the perspective used and partly on what happened in the immediate past. If a complex concept such as "Florentine Renaissance" is to be the focal point of the account, then the historian will look for an event or pattern of events in which that concept was previously embodied. If there are no obvious events delimiting the period, one must consider the level of abstraction, and look for contrasting or corollary concepts embodied in events of a related kind, which may have been assimilated by the event in question. Thus, for the Reform Bill passage, the institution of Parliament is a primary focus, while a prevailing contrast in its emergence is the opposition to Whig reforms by the duke of Wellington and the Tories. It would seem logical to define the antecedent world of the Reform Bill by events incorporating these elements.

Several authorities agree that the parliamentary elections of July–August 1830 (necessitated by the death of George IV) did not bring reform into special focus.[3] However, between the first of August and the last of October, when the new Parliament met, great expectations of reform had been aroused all over the kingdom. The new Parliament gathered, in the words of Wellington's biographer, "in a state of excitement contrasting sharply with the comparative apathy of the election."[4] Retrenchment (economic reform) and antislavery seem to have been the chief topics for candidates, although William Cobbett had created a stir by riding around the counties in August, urging parliamentary reform and leaving social disturbances in his wake.

It was during August 1830 that revolutionary events in France gained public attention in England, and though the precise influence of these (and of revolts in Poland, Germany, Belgium, and elsewhere) is a matter of some dispute,[5] it would be useful to include them in the antecedent world, rather than in the duration of the Reform Bill. If any event is included in the latter duration, it cannot then be treated as cause or condition. Revolutionary action on the Continent is different enough from the reform agitation in England that most historians treat it as a condition. If it were included within the duration of reform (that is, if the line dividing reform from its antecedents were drawn at the first of August rather than in September 1830), then it would have to be treated as one element in the event to be explained. This could be done legitimately if the historian were trying to explain, say, the phenomenon of political agitation in Europe from 1828 to 1832; but in the present case it seems best to separate Continental from British agitation.

The Reform Bill proceedings in Parliament are a fairly clear example of the line between event and antecedent, perhaps clearer than most. When the new session opened on October 26, 1830, the king's speech read by Wellington made no mention of reform at all. In reply to Lord Grey's immediate question, the duke replied that the unreformed system possessed "the full and entire confidence of the country" and that he would resist any measure of reform so long as he was head of the government. Two weeks later his government was voted out of office. The principle of reform, the institution, the opposition groups, and the central individuals for the drama were all established in that short period.[6]

The beginning of the antecedent duration is less sharply defined than its end. If one were to speculate on the difference George Canning might have made, as leader of the "liberal" Tories and a gentlemanly opponent of Wellington,[7] one would look to the date of his death, August 8, 1827.

Between then and March 1828, when Wellington assumed the head of a new ministry, there is little to focus upon from the perspective of reform. But in April 1828, several boroughs were disenfranchised for blatant corruption. When Wellington refused to reassign their seats to a large industrial area, Huskisson and the other Canningites resigned from government and went into opposition.[8] Thus the beginning of 1828 seems a promising base from which to start analyzing the antecedent world of the Reform Bill.

The analysis consists of identifying the principal events related to reform and sorting out their hierarchies of elements. The more abstract elements are apt to be held in common by many different events, while the group and individual elements are less orderly. However, by comparing events in this duration one can see which individuals and groups are involved most intensely or most often in those situations that condition the novel event. These individuals and groups are most likely to serve as foci for elements being assimilated into the emerging event; through them, posssibilities for future change and continuity are expressed. One cannot always assume this hypothesis, of course: the duke of Wellington is at the center of parliamentary action in the period 1828–30 but then fades as the Whigs take over, while Lord Grey suddenly emerges from obscurity to become the primary focus of reform legislation. But because the analysis begins with the event to be explained, rather than with the antecedent world, one is not taken by surprise by such developments. One knows better than to ignore Grey's activity in the antecedent world.

At first glance the analysis of a whole field of hierarchical elements seems hopelessly complicated. It multiplies many times over the analysis of elements in one event. Even elements that become insignificant for the new event have to be dealt with, because the historian must explain their significance in the antecedent world, and account for their change of status. However, in most explanations the bulk of antecedent elements is tacitly dismissed, and the reader knows that it is probably irrelevant. Only where some question arises about the change in significance from what might have been expected, must the historian deal with such items. Thus Elie Halévy and other historians assumed that the revolutionary events in France during July and August 1830 must have influenced the outcome of the British elections held during the same period. But Norman Gash, reviewing the election dates and the number of uncontested seats, concluded that the cross-Channel influence was generally negligible.[9] One historian analyzed the revolutionary impact because he thought it mattered; the other analyzed it because its impact was not evident in the available data. If one were talking about another event, say the opening of the Liverpool and Manchester Railway, or the start of construction on the National Road in the United States, perhaps no explanation of its lack of importance to reform would be necessary. But one of the chief occupations of historians is the review of events or elements that have been neglected in previous accounts, with the object of calling attention to their real relevance for subsequent occasions. In this way, critical models of antecedent worlds can be constructed and refined in accord with models of the events that they condition.

The other feature of the antecedent world that simplifies its analysis is the overlap of elements among many hierarchies, especially at the higher levels of abstraction. This sharing of elements makes up a principle of order that conditions the arrangement of subsequent events. For instance, the concept of "Catholic Emancipation" runs through a number of events in the period 1828–30, from the election of Daniel O'Connell for County Clare to the signing of the Emancipation Bill by a reluctant George IV. Individuals such as Wellington and groups such as the Whigs also appear as elements in a number of events, although the manner of their appearance varies more than that of concepts. It is unnecessary, therefore, for the historian to elaborate the full hierarchies of all events in the antecedent period. It is enough to indicate the salient principles of order among common elements, and to account for irregular elements on an individual basis.

Continuing with the example of the passage of the Reform Bill, one can identify certain events in its antecedent world that are more significant than others. For instance, between March and May 1828, Wellington formed a government from the remnants of the Liverpool administration, but immediately precipitated the resignation of the Canningites over the issue of reassigning rotten borough seats to new urban industrial areas. This episode includes individual elements relevant to the Reform Bill passage, namely, the men involved. It also includes groups (Canningites, the cabinet, urban constituencies), institutions (Parliament, the cities, the cabinet again), and complex concepts (parliamentary reform). Defining these elements from the perspective of the Reform Bill passage, one provides the reasons for their status as antecedents.

Other important events were the passage of Catholic Emancipation; the death of George IV (and of George Canning and the duke of York, who would have succeeded George IV); the formation of the Birmingham Political Union in May 1830; incidents of economic distress; and more generally, the growth of urban industrial power and population. And then, of course, there was the French Revolution.

The difference between Elie Halévy's estimate of French revolutionary influence on reform and Norman Gash's revision has already been mentioned. It is now thought that the reactions of the British people were more indirect and muted than Halévy believed. But Gash's argument is more useful in any case because he points out what aspects of the Revolution were being perceived and reacted to by different groups of British subjects. Whether one considers an event as "effect" (as in the previous chapter) or "cause" (as in this one), one can't grasp its real character unless one looks at its constituent elements, and those of events related to it. No British subject perceived the July Revolution in its entirety. Some perceived its violent aspects, others its relative moderation. Some drew analogies with England in 1830, others thought smugly that the French were finally "catching up to 1688." The reaction to certain aspects of an event is what constitutes an element in the hierarchy of another. When discussing the French experience as an item in the world antecedent to the Reform Bill, one wants to know how that experience was perceived and assimilated by the individuals, groups, institutions, and concepts involved in the reform.

In addition to relationships realized in the events of the antecedent world, one should investigate those that remain merely potential, that is relationships that did not fully develop but are still meaningful in contrast to what actually happened. They are also part of the field of conditions from which subsequent events emerge. For example, Charles X, Polignac, Lafayette, Louis Philippe, and Talleyrand appear as individual elements in the French Revolution. Among actual group elements one could include the French republicans, the *pays legal,* democratic radicals, and reactionaries. Institutions include the monarchy, the army, the National Guard, and the Chamber of Deputies. The July Ordinance and the Constitutional Order of 1814 express representative concepts. These are all actual conditions assimilated by subsequent events as real elements of their constitutions. But they were also elements of unrealized potentials. Consider, for example, the attempt at a coup d'etat by Charles X and Polignac in July 1830 when the French army and navy were occupied in an attack on Algeria, unable to defend the king from revolutionary violence or to defend France from a British invasion. The French popular response stimulated uprisings all over Europe: the Belgians revolted against their Dutch rulers, asserted their independence, and asked Louis Philippe's son to be their king. Left-wing revolutionaries in the French Chamber, recalling the glory days of the First Republic, welcomed the return of Belgium. All this would have unsettled Wellington across the Channel, for the old soldier wanted at all costs to avoid a repetition of his earlier international wars. But in addition, Czar Nicholas convinced himself that it was imperative to send the Russian army across Europe to put down the Belgians and uphold the principle of legitimacy.

Now if one looks at these elements from the viewpoint of the duke of Wellington, leader of His Majesty's government, commander-in-chief of the armed forces, and veteran of the Napoleonic wars, a host of potential developments rises up, as they did before him. If Wellington intervened on the Continent with British troops to maintain order and prevent another international conflagration, he would most certainly be branded a repressive reactionary by the British middle and lower classes, who were agitated enough to take advantage of the absence of British troops to imitate their French counterparts. Also, the presence of British troops might spark rather than quell other disturbances on the Continent. On the other hand, if Wellington did *not* intervene, the French might go the way of 1792, the Belgians would join them, and the czar's army would wreak havoc across Europe.

In fact, Wellington was spared from dealing with the alternatives listed above. The Poles mounted enough of a rebellion to tie down the Russian troops until the Belgian situation was straightened out. The duke convinced Louis Philippe that he stood to lose more than he would gain by placing his son on the Belgian throne. And the moderate monarchists in France got the ship of state refloated with a minimum of carnage. There is little evidence that Wellington considered an actual invasion of France, and in the end he decided not to intervene at all.[10]

Of course, Wellington was not the only British subject to react to events across the Channel. Cobbett the radical orator drew appropriate analogies between the revolt of the French and the plight of the English working classes. John Stuart Mill and some other young reforming types visited France, talked with Louis Philippe, and applauded the Revolution. These are only the more obvious instances.

Reactions on the group and institutional levels must be defined in more general terms. The three main attitudes displayed in England were different from what might have been predicted by an observer of the earlier revolutionary era. (This is why Halévy's interpretation, which is more deductive than inductive, required amendment by later researchers). Radical-left opinion was divided between those who thought the French experience was a prelude to political and economic reform in England and those who viewed it as a pretext for repression by Wellington. The latter fear grew from the fact that Wellington had been a close acquaintance of Polignac and had relatives among the European diplomats who urged him to intervene on the side of royalty. There was also some doubt that William IV, who had been on the throne only a month, could prevent the duke from attempting a Polignac-style coup.[11]

The two chief ministers were linked most vividly in the minds of ultra-Tories, however. One would not expect such archconservatives to champion revolutionary action. But the ultras were still smarting over their defeat on Catholic Emancipation, and they saw in French anticlericalism a welcome relief from the rising tide of popery. They accused Wellington of direct complicity in Polignac's July Ordinances, which had taken away civil liberties. As Norman Gash comments, "scarcely a person of consequence was found to believe in the charge."[12] But the accusation is indicative of the curious configurations that can be derived from the antecedent world and made relevant to an emerging event. That the French Revolution should have had some influence on the passage of the Reform Bill seems obvious enough. But that one aspect of its influence should be the vengeance of ultra-Tories against Wellington for his role in Catholic Emancipation, defies logical prediction.

Between the ultras and the radicals, the great body of British subjects gathered in various meetings to congratulate the revolutionaries in France and to collect funds for the relief of victims of the fighting. But on the whole, far from applying the French principles to a movement for parliamentary reform in any direct fashion, most of the orators and editors took pride in the fact that the British had established the same principles back in 1688.[13]

Thus an examination of the ways the July Revolution was perceived by the British in 1830 reveals few precise clues to the emergence of the reform agitation after that date. What it does provide is a number of carefully appraised conditions that either became elements in the actual pattern of the Reform Bill passage or remained as potential elements in its hierarchy, giving the actual event its compliment of contrasting values. One contrast between the potential of the antecedent world and the actual event is expressed by the title of Maehl's anthology, *The Reform Bill of 1832: Why Not Revolution?*

Antecedent conditions need not be positive, of course. Individuals important to a given event may have been obscure in the preceding duration, and the significance of what happened may be heightened by one's awareness of alternatives foreclosed by the disappearance or failure of a key individual. During the period previous to reform, for example, Lord Grey was conspicuous by the muted quality of his political performance. He was involved in the antecedent world, but from the perspective of 1832 his presence was curiously unremarked. In a less important but no less ironic way, one could note the self-imposed silence of Mrs. Fitzherbert, a Roman Catholic secretly married to George IV when he was Prince of Wales, and since abandoned. She was naturally concerned about Catholic Emancipation in the period 1828–30 but resolved not to speak about it lest she embarrass the king. Her behavior is worth mentioning because, in the months following the death of George, she became a voluble agitator against reform.

The absence of certain people after 1830 closed out potential alternatives which, being remembered, served to accentuate the meaning of the reform legislation. Thus the passing in 1827 of Lord Liverpool, the duke of York, and George Canning helped bring Wellington into office and removed the influence of the "Protestant Champion" (York) from the coterie around George IV, whom Wellington then persuaded to sign the bill for emancipation. It also broke the back of the Liberal-Tory coalition that had governed England for so many years and that would most probably have carried a far more moderate Reform Bill than the one passed in 1832. The death of York also ensured the succession of William IV. Historians traditionally disdain speculation about such might-have-beens, except for obvious cases. Yet the proceedings of the reform legislation are everywhere highlighted by such lost potentials. Wellington worried that when the new Parliament convened in October 1830, his government would suffer from a lack of good speakers to present its case: they were either dead or among the Canningites in opposition. And if one compares the duke's speech against reform that session with the magnificent oration of Lord John Ruseell later on, one can see just how serious the absence of speakers was.

A few of the events most involved in the emergence of the Reform Bill have been discussed in order to show the levels of abstraction and types of elements that should be considered when analyzing the duration antecedent to a given event. It should be evident from the examples that some elements are relatively more intense or more comprehensive than others, in terms of bringing into focus a pattern of relationships characteristic of an event or set of events. Such elements are not always the most obvious. For instance, it might be useful for a historian to use Mrs. Fitzherbert as the focus for analyzing one set of relationships, if through this perspective he can explain what happened to other people, groups, and institutions in the most coherent way. It is not Mrs. Fitzherbert, after all, who is important. It is the pattern of meanings attributed by her to other elements that helps one understand why the period 1830–32 developed the way it did. In another case, one might use Francis Place, organizer of political unions and liaison between the agitators and members of the Whig Cabinet, as a focus for discussing the tensions and ironies that he himself had to cope with. Narrative historical accounts are usually written from the "omniscient" point of view of their authors. It might be more enlightening, in the explanatory sense, to present accounts from several viewpoints and to discuss the contrasts between them.

By mentioning the deaths of Liverpool and Canning just prior to the start of the antecedent world. I have touched upon the problem of the more extended past, so far as it is involved in the event to be explained. In my proposed model of explanation, the rule is that an event in the distant past enters into the account only as it has been incorporated as an element in the immediate antecedent world. There is not direct long-range influence. This problem is dealt with more thoroughly in Chapter 9; here the only caveat is that a past event never means the same thing, or is present in the same form, after its original period of emergence. In all subsequent periods, it will be present as one element in a web of relationships.

The contrast between "distant past" and "antecedent world" may be illustrated by the case of Queen Caroline. As a princess, Caroline had led a wandering and scandalous life on the Continent. When her husband became King George IV, however, she determined to return to England and enjoy the perquisites of queen consort. George began divorce proceedings, and his opponents immediately took up Caroline's defense on behalf of all victims of government "tyrany." G. D. H. Cole believes that the Queen Caroline affair was important in solidifying working-class support behind the case of parliamentary reform. By his account, the popular antigovernment followings built up by Cobbett in 1820, and by O'Connell in Ireland after 1823, were turned in favor of reform after the original issues dissolved.[14]

Cole's hypothesis is attractive to liberal historians. But having seen how disjointed the cause of reform was in the period 1828–30, one must ask what evidence there is that the Queen Caroline case was in fact an element in the events of that duration? One may grant the probability of working-class support for reform, but was it derived in a demonstratable way from the events of 1820? Did it mean the same thing and have the same form? Or was the situation in 1830 quite different from that perceived by Cole for the earlier period? It is important to ask such questions, not to create more research problems, but to guard against the common assumption that past events retain their original form and meaning in all subsequent occasions. Historians may be aware of all the changes intervening between 1820 and 1828, but will readers appreciate them when they see the two dates so close together on the printed page?

Besides looking for evidence that people had Queen Caroline's case in mind during the 1828–30 period, there is another way to measure the impact of the case in the antecedent world of reform. One can ask whether any aspect of the case is evident in the passage of the Reform Bill itself, that is, in the structure of the new event. If it is present, the historian has reason to look for it in the antecedent world; if not, he may ignore it until some signs of its importance appear. As in other parts of this model of explanation, a comparison of the novel event with its antecedent world should resolve most questions. If some aspect of Queen Caroline's case is not found in one of the two durations, it should be considered irrelevant.

The same rule applies to other past events that seem to be involved in the immediate antecedent world. When Wellington entered the Irish House of Commons as a young man, his maiden speech called for immediate Catholic emancipation and a permanent injunction against parliamentary reform. He badgered Pitt about emancipation during the 1790s while an equally young Lord Grey was introducing reform bills into Commons.[15] By 1829, however, Wellington's zeal must have been tempered by thirty years of military and political turmoil, and we have to compare it with his loyalty to the monarchy, whoever the monarch might be.[16] Those qualities came together in the duke's decision to carry Catholic Emancipation despite the hypocritical appeal of George IV to his anachronistic title "Defender of the Faith." In retrospect, it was a characteristic incident. While Wellington bluntly took it upon himself to save the throne from the embarrassment of its occupant, he also amended the Emancipation Bill to raise voting qualifications in the boroughs, thus producing the only restriction on the franchise in the long campaign for parliamentary reform. Here his maiden speech, half a century earlier, has some direct application.

The Reform Bill is not, in fact, a particularly good example of the diminished status of the distant past in a new event. It was not just Wellington who remained constant through the years. Lord Grey was also a relic, with a record of fifty years of failure at reform, and less than two years of administrative experience to his credit.[17] Yet, upon the fall of Wellington's ministry in 1830, no one else was considered to lead the new government. It was as if the debates of 1792 were revived intact in the persons of the two old campaigners. But there is a lesson even here, for if the principle of reform espoused by Grey remained essentially unchanged from half a century before, the other elements in the emerging event had changed considerably. Both Wellington and Grey were caught by surprise in this respect. The Reform Bill drafted by Grey's younger colleagues was far more radical than the other Whigs, heirs of the moderate past, expected. It was even more traumatic for the Tories. But it did not go far enough to suit the working classes, who defined reform in terms of the economic problems of 1830 and who had no timeworn illusions about the degree of change required. Thus, if one analyzes the elements in the antecedent field at the fifth level of abstraction, one discovers that the principle of "reform," inherited virtually intact from a past focused on Grey or Wellington, stood in contrast to another principle of "reform" held by the younger Whigs and Canningites, and to yet another brought into focus by the popular radical leaders and workingmen.

In a narrative, the historian offers events in a sequence designed to evoke the contrasts mentioned above, with the expectation that the reader will hold them together in a continuing synoptic pattern. By the time a narrative reaches the year 1830, the field of conditional elements should be fairly well constituted. However, the historian can afford to be suggestively vague about the relative intensity of these elements, because the average reader will have been making that kind of judgment for himself as the narrative proceeds. In other words, the evaluation of antecedent conditions with respect to their importance for the emerging event is carried out privately.

In an analytical explanation, which refines and justifies the narrative, the antecedent elements must be examined publicly and their relative intensity made explicit, so that other historians can make an intelligible critique of a given account. Moreover, the analysis must extend beyond the most obvious antecedents. In discussing the Reform Bill, I have concentrated on political events surrounding the institution of Parliament. But the activities of the king and his associates, of workingmen and rural laborers, of factory owners and philosophical radicals, of French republicans and English bishops—all must be considered on the individual, group, institutional, and conceptual levels if one is to make a full account of the conditions antecedent to this event.

This is not to say that analysis precludes narrative. The relative intensity of antecedent elements is derived from their inclusion in actual events; to appreciate the intensity, one has to follow an account of the events. It is worthless to attribute causal significance to the Yorkshire voters or the Benthamite radicals without showing what they did in the antecedent duration. On the other hand, too much narrative tends to break up the duration into a sequence of unrelated stories, undermining the logical treatment of its overall pattern. The answer is to use just enough narrative to establish the character of a sequence of incidents, and then treat the whole sequence as one event.

For example, the founding of the Birmingham Political Union in December 1829, was imitated by political organizers in other cities, and by July 1830 there were more than ten large unions and scores of lesser ones dedicated to putting pressure on Parliament for some kind of reform.[18] The development of this united strength was important to the emergence of the Reform Bill and should be characterized in a short narrative. But the purpose in mentioning the development is not to trace its own internal composition but to assess its intensity and form relative to other elements in the antecedent world. The best way to do this is to look at the last significant incident in the sequence, and analyze its abstract hierarchy as one would the hierarchy of any other event. It will show the relative significance of the other incidents by implication. In the example of the Birmingham Political Union, it is not the founding of the union that matters most, but the fact that it was imitated successfully elsewhere in England by 1830. Even the rapidity of its development can be mentioned as one element characterizing the whole duration. Similarly, if the historian considers a sequence showing the decline of an element's importance during the antecedent period (such as the disintegration of the Tory coalition that had governed England since 1820), it is the overall fact of decline, not the details in the temporal sequence, that figure in the analysis.

By a judicious use of narrative, then, one can arrive at terms of analysis that are commensurate with those of the event to be explained. They will have the same time duration, the same levels of abstraction, and comparable patterns of relative intensity. These antecedent terms "explain" a given event only in the sense of providing the conditions from which it emerged. The conditions are necessary, as any historian knows, to make the given event appear intelligible. But they are not sufficient to explain why that particular event should have occurred rather than some other. In fact, there are at least five features of the antecedent world that preclude the demonstration of invariant, lawful relationships between an event and its past. Each of the features is on the other hand an argument for indeterminacy, and each provides a reason why history, under a principle of indeterminacy, should continue its advance.

First, while the antecedent world does establish finite conditions to which subsequent events must conform, it is indeterminate with regard to any particular event in its concrete actuality. The paradox is that the most particular elements, such as individual experiences, are too irregular to support lawful statements. And elements that do show regularity are those abstract elements, common to many events in a period, that are incapable of demonstrating why any particular event should occur just the way it did. In other words, one can say "this class of events usually results in that class of effects"; and one can say "this event followed that one." But one cannot say, "this particular event usually follows from that class of events." That would be nonsense: the particular event occurs only once, not "usually."

This is not to say that regularity hypotheses are impossible. From the information presented so far on the Reform Bill passage, one could derive the following: Whenever a principle such as "parliamentary reform" is found in the antecedent world as a primary element in a set of contrasts among (a) ultraconservative reaction, (b) moderate revival of an old ideal, (c) anticipation of radical change, and (d) a vehicle for ambitious young politicians, the principle in form (d) will be the primary focus for the event to be explained. Now, this is neither so rigorous nor so barren as the kind of statements preferred by advocates of deductive-law explanations. But it is abstract enough to be applied to other events in a class, either to predict what will be found in the future or (retrodictively) to tell the historian what might be discovered in the past.

The second feature of the antecedent world that shows why history should continue its indeterminate advance is the incompleteness of antecedent events. No single event, in its finite constitution, from its limited perspective, can possibly incorporate all the elements of the universe. And the array of antecedents is further bound by the perspective of the event to be explained. For example, it was pointed out that events in Japan and in Peru in 1792 were probably insignificant from the point of view of the royalist invasion of France. They were not part of *its* past. By the same token, the flight of Louis XVI, which did seem relatively important, was highly selective with regard to its own antecedents. The incompleteness of events is not just a matter of historians' ineptness or laziness in reporting the past. It is a reflection of the fact, noted in Chapter 4, that the restoration of perceptual relativity to the universe by Einstein and others makes it necessary to redefine the nature of events. In this case, they have to be defined as incomplete statements about the past. And that means that they cannot completely determine the future.

The third feature of the antecedent world is much like the second. Because of their finite actuality, events cannot resolve all the contrasts and conflicts among the elements they derive from the past. As has been shown in the previous chapter, there are always logical and aesthetic choices to be made. An event cannot incorporate both roundness and nonroundness, for instance, or both the duke of Wellington as a supporter of reform and as an opponent of reform, in the same terms. Such contradictions may be thrown up by the antecedent world, but they must be resolved if the new event is to have an actual form.

Aesthetic choices refer to elements that are not logically contradictory but have to be subordinated one to another. Thus, the Reform Bill passed its final reading in the House of Lords in 1832 due to the absence of about a hundred peers who had formerly opposed it. These peers could have absented themselves at any time, but they chose to wait until the king promised to create enough new peers to carry reform in spite of their opposition. By way of contrast (which Grey might have recalled), when the abolition of the slave trade had been held up in 1807 by the formation of a conservative ministry, the abolitionists were told that no opposition would be given to their bill because it was obviously supported by a majority in Parliament. The two situations are comparable, but the principles involved are neither identical nor opposite. The contrast between them is an aesthetic one, and they could coexist in the same event, one as a primary element, the other as a secondary one.

The fact that no single event is capable of resolving all the contradictions and tensions in its antecedent world, and that no event can bring into one concrete synthesis all the potential relationships offered by the past, means that the world is never complete, never in a state of equilibrium. Because events in the universe emerge only in relation to other events, the process of forming new relationships is continuous. That is historical advance.

We are thus brought to the fourth feature of the antecedent world. Because of the indeterminacy of its past, each event must create for itself a new pattern of relationships. This process, of necessity, introduces something new to the universe. For example, the outbreak of World War I determined the relative significance of the various conditions in its antecedent world. This determination (the "synoptic judgment" of this event) characterizes the outbreak of World War I as a new event, transcending the very past which it defines. It is as if all events were statements about history: every time one says, *This is what happened in history, so far as I perceive it,* then something new has happened, and history has changed. Thus the process of history, like the process of explaining history, is self-perpetuating.

The final feature of the antecedent world, which explains both its indeterminacy and its propensity for advance toward the future, is its polychronicity. This is obviously a different sort of feature than those previously noted, and requires some illustration. Polychronicity is a term, borrowed from anthropologist Edward T. Hall, that refers to the habit in some cultures of using time in a variety of ways simultaneously.[19] In Mexico, for example, store clerks and government officials may wait on several people at once, dealing with them with scant regard for who arrived first. Also it is not uncommon to witness a religious service, a boxing match, a bus arrival, a market, and a street-band performance occurring at the same time in the same area. Americans tend to find the first practice infuriating, and the second absurd, both being (for them) interruptions of a natural sequence as orderly as the minutes on a clock. The Mexicans see it as a natural way to organize time, which for them is a web, not a sequence.

When applied to history, polychronicity means that several events could be emerging at the same time but with different individual time boundaries. One could select a cross section of the universe at a particular moment and find a great many events happening, but each event has its own duration. Some durations are longer than others. The composite duration one selects for the "antecedent world" of an event to be analyzed is not the real historical world. One decides upon important features, such as the death of George Canning or the parliamentary elections of 1830, to mark off manageable boundaries; but in doing so, one arbitrarily ignores the many events included within those boundaries whose periods of emergence extend into the past or the future. For example, during the antecedent period 1828–30 the Birmingham Political Union began to function, while the strictures against Catholics, in force since the 1550s, were eliminated in law. Viewed as separate events, these elements had durations quite different from that of the world antecedent to the Reform Bill. The Catholic restrictions had a duration of some 280 years, while the political union lasted less than a decade. If one drew a diagram of such an antecedent world, the various events involved would stick out at both ends like worms (as Arthur Danto envisions such events), wriggling into the past and future.[20]

Polychronic time is a notion that for cultural reasons most Anglo-American and northern European historians have a hard time grasping. Yet, the notion makes sense of the historians' intuition that the sequential structure of narrative does not quite reflect the reality of events. Although one may feel that a good sequence means a good explanation, one also has to be aware that things don't follow simply one after another the way words do on a page. But if polychronicity is not reflected in the structure of narrative, it can be appreciated through the dynamics of narrative, as discussed in Chapter 3. The way a good narrative evokes anticipations and reflections in the reader's mind is closer to the polychronic aspects of the historical process than are the definite terms of an analytical deduction.

The significance of polychronicity is this: if one assumes that history moves from one momentary state to another, then one cannot explain how to get from the "end" of one moment to the "beginning" of the next. As Xeno argued, there is no feature inherent in such a world that would account for the transition. Newton covered the problem with the flat assertion that time was absolute, unmoving and continuous. However, if one assumes that history moves from one event into another, each event assimilating its antecedents and each having a minimum (but not uniform) duration, then the difficulty of accounting for historical advance disappears. Continuity is assured both by the fact that events never "end" all at the same moment (and according to the theory of relativity, no moment is the same for all events anyway), and by the fact that each event creates continuity with its past in the very process of its emergence.

If the world is polychronic, it is also indeterminate, for in the historical process one could never find a moment when there was a fully determined set of conditions, from which the next set could be derived or predicted. Indeterminism is inherent in the antecedent world of any historical event, for all the reasons discussed above; and for the same reasons, the historical process is bound to press forward toward the determination of actual events, limited by their singular perspectives on the past.

The framework for analyzing the antecedent world presented in this chapter is consistent with the previously illustrated framework for analyzing a single event. Each requires the historian to define temporal boundaries and levels of abstraction for his terms of explanation, and each provides a procedure for sorting out the various constituent elements, the configurations they represent, and the contrasts between actual and potential configurations. All this work is necessary to make historical explanation and its criticism systematic and efficacious. On the other hand, this work is only a systemization of what many historians already do without benefit of analytical framework or theoretical justification.

The antecedent world has some other features, not shared with new events, that require special consideration. One such feature is the inclusion of events from the distant past as elements in antecedent hierarchies. Another is the sharing of some elements, especially at higher levels of abstraction, among many antecedents, so as to form patterns of order. And there are a number of features that, together, reveal the indeterminacy of the antecedent world with regard to the final form of subsequent events.

When one compares a fully analyzed event with its fully analyzed antecedent world, one will be able to appreciate, in a critical way, the continuities and changes that connect one to the other. At the higher levels of abstraction there will be considerable continuity but less of a grasp on the particular. At the lower levels there will be a greater impression of change within a smaller arena. The comparison of event with antecedent allows the historian to make hypotheses about regular relationships that approach the rigorous requirements of deductive-law models of explanation. But they are always accompanied by the realization that such hypotheses do not explain the emergence of the particular event. For that kind of explanation, for showing how *this* event, with its singular structure, intensity, and perspective, emerged from *that* set of conditions, a narrative is required. Thus the whole thrust of the analysis, with its definitions, categories, and comparisons, is toward the justification and improvement of narrative explanations.

7. Assimilation

History is neither determined nor random. At any moment, it moves forward into an area whose general shape is known, but whose boundaries are uncertain in a calculable way.

Jacob Bronowski, *The Common Sense of Science*

The first phase in the emergence of new events involves the assimilation of elements from their antecedent worlds. Assimilation is guided by certain conditions inherent in the past and is brought into focus by certain elements highlighted by the perspective of the new event. Because traditional historical theory does not recognize the temporal pattern of events, it is hard to offer explicit examples of the assimilation phase from previously published narratives. Also one has to consider some theoretical questions about the origin and nature of the assimilation process. This chapter, therefore, will be less craft-oriented than the others. On the other hand it will show, from a different angle, why narrative explanations are so appropriate for historical events. And it will answer a question that, stripped of its philosophical terminology, has bothered historians and other people for a long time: Why should an event be related to its predecessors at all, and why should it be related in a particular way rather than some other way?

The focal elements in the assimilation process are really aspects of the antecedent world which bring into focus one potential configuration of elements. Many configurations may be derived from the richness of the antecedent world. One may prove to be the final configuration of the new event, but it is more likely that some combination and modification will take place before the event is fully developed. In any case, each potential arrangement of elements has one focal element which the analyst will identify as having a particular perspective upon the past, at a particular level of abstraction. For example, in October 1830 a set of potential elements converged on the duke of Wellington, in Parliament, regarding a concept of blocking reform. If one were working at the individual level of abstraction, the focus of the set would be Wellington; if at the institutional level, it would be Parliament. The narrative historian uses such elements as a composer uses a motif of notes, or a painter a color key: as a focus for the arrangement of the whole set that gives it continuity and shape. Similarly, historical events take shape by adopting particular perspectives upon the past, which are focal points for their emerging configuration. The Reform Bill in England developed the way it did because its antecedents were assimilated from the point of view of Lord Grey and Wellington and the king, and of Parliament and the Birmingham Political Union, and of "political reform" and "industrial growth." Different points of view, such as that of the contemporary French painter Eugene Delacroix, would have yielded quite different configurations than these.

There are two major ways of explaining why certain focal elements are more likely to appear in the initial stages of an event, or will appear to be more prominent, than others. The idealist approach centers on certain ideals or universals that are claimed to be inherent, a priori, in the historical process. These ideals, such as "progress" or "freedom," are usually divinely inspired. They enter into events of every period, guiding the emergence of elements at more concrete levels. The ultimate explanation for history, therefore, is metaphysical or theological.

Historians have been reluctant to accept idealist approaches in their work because the search for universals contradicts the empirical tradition of modern science. Moreover, universals by their very nature are ahistorical: they attempt to account for change by removing the very temporal features that make change interesting. Yet idealists like Hegel have provided the most famous and vigorous answers to the question, How do events develop in relation to the past? Historians have been hard put to discuss the question without falling back into an unacceptable frame of reference.

However, there is an empirical approach to explaining the appearance of certain focal elements in the initial stage of events, that refers to actual features of the antecedent world rather than to abstract ideals. These features are amenable to observation and description by narrative historians.

Polychronicity is one feature of the past that helps account for the establishment of certain elements. As discussed in Chapter 6, it means that the developmental durations of many events overlap, and that the elements of the antecedent world may extend into the temporal zone of a new event. If such antecedents are regarded as constituent elements of the new event, they will tend to become foci for potential configurations. Robert Peel, for example, had an individual role in the antecedent world of the Reform Bill, and that role developed during and after the period 1830–32. The duration of his career overlaps the duration of the Reform Bill proceedings. And because Peel already had a strong position in government, his individual role became the focus for a potential configuration regarding reform.

Another reason for the prominence of some elements is the fact that, through a series of events, they may build up relationships of high intensity, which give them a kind of momentum in the transition to an emerging event. A "high intensity" relationship results when an element stands in strong contrast to another (Wellington vs. Grey), or holds contrasting aspects of other elements together in an increasingly complex synthesis. For example, Wellington had built up momentum as a focus for Reform Bill activity prior to 1830, by the long record of his experience and the steadiness of his principles, and by the intensity of the opposition he had created. It is sometimes said that such people are "full of energy," "magnetiç," or "always at the center of things." These physical metaphors are quite correct. Mere repetition of innocuous behavior will not generate such intensity. Only actions that organize the very tensions they create result in the kind of momentum that Wellington brought to the passage of the Reform Bill. By comparison, Lord Goderich, who was asked to form a government in August 1827 upon the death of George Canning was a nullity. He could not put the conflicting elements together into a viable synthesis.

It is interesting to compare the kind of focus provided by Wellington with that provided by Lord Grey. Wellington was the soldier, blunt and outspoken, a leader of men who was often intolerant of ambiguity or dissension in the ranks. He had much administrative experience but was not skilled in the kind of political etiquette needed for compromise and conciliation. In 1829 he fought a duel against a man whose denunciation of Catholic Emancipation offended the duke's honor.[1] Grey, on the other hand, had only two years of administrative experience, back in 1806–7. He was titular head of a group of Whigs who had not held important office since that time. A country aristocrat, Grey became the focus for reform advocates only after Wellington announced his opposition, and he was made head of the new government largely because he was well-known for his lifelong advocacy of reform. Wellington gives a highly intense focus for elements that became increasingly discordant in the overall constitution of the event, while Grey presents just the kind of soft focus that enabled people of many persuasions to forge a new party for reform.

The third reason why some elements become foci in the development of their successors, is that every event emerges from its past in anticipation of a future environment derived from that same past. In other words, an event such as Catholic Emancipation is formed out of a set of conditions which hold for many contemporary incidents, and still hold to a degree for the immediate future. Thus Catholic Emancipation developed the way it did partly because its elements were already oriented toward Parliament, Wellington, the king, the religious situation in England, and the relation between Irish and English politics.

The note on anticipation seems to run counter to the emphasis of this book, which has generally been on innovative processes. Anticipation is conservative, in that it tends toward continuity of form and function. If, however, one combines this principle with that of intensive relevance, discussed in the previous chapter, it can be seen how a generally conservative process could build up certain configurations that anticipate their future

more comprehensively and more dynamically than others. The elements of
these configurations would be the foci of potential configurations in subsequent events. The general movement for reform in England, which began
in the eighteenth century, is one such configuration. Waxing and waning
over a period of more than a century, it reached a relative intensity in 1830
that guaranteed it a place in many subsequent events until its potential was
almost fulfilled in the twentieth century.

The fourth source of focal elements is almost the antithesis of the third. It
is the fact that no event in the antecedent world can resolve all the tension
and potential of its own past, and no set of events can resolve all the
contrasts inherent in the process of emergence. This fact yields new contrasts, new configurations, and of necessity new elements with the dynamic
quality needed to be foci for development in some future event. For example, prior to World War I military defensive experts were organizing the use
of barbed wire and machine-gun nests, which had not been used in the
Franco-Prussian war, while the offensive generals were planning cavalry
charges to break through the enemy lines. This combination of old and new
resulted in a change of focus for the European war theater. The configuration of events after August 1914 had as a principal element the new defensive tactics and technology. Similarly, events in England between 1828 and
1830 generated the possibility of a new government coalition with Grey, the
Canningites and Radicals, the reforming Whigs and a few Tories. This
arrangement was not predetermined: Trevelyan says that the majority of
M.P.'s came to Parliament in late October 1830 not knowing whether they
were Whig or Tory—whether Grey or Wellington would give them the
moderate Reform Bill they wanted.[2] In retrospect, one could say, "It was
already decided." But in retrospect, no such statement can be proved. That
Grey should emerge as the nucleus of a new government reform group was
a new possibility thrown up by the inability of the antecedent world to
resolve its inherited conflicts.

One can usefully extend the idea of focal elements to the idea of elements
that fade from importance after the initial phase of assimilation. There are
often some rallying elements, individuals or groups or institutions, whose
importance in the past gives them an initial advantage in the early stages of a
new event, until the fact of changed circumstances demonstrates their impotence. Some of the generals who were pulled out of retirement to lead
armies at the start of World War I are obvious examples of the type. But the
reaction of the British to the French Revolution of 1830 is also illustrative.
The local insurgent committees that sprang up in France had their more
moderate counterparts in the political unions of England. This comparison
was appreciated not only by their organizers but by government leaders
too. There were unauthorized training sessions for local militia during
1830–31, and some radical leaders called for a "run on the banks" to break

government authority and force financial reform.[3] In other words, passage of a Reform Bill in Parliament was not the only focus for development to be derived from the antecedent world. There were others that many people though equally viable. These nuclei may fade from importance as the event emerges, but they remain as contrasting elements in its temporal constitution, giving overtones of value to the primary configurations.

Thus there is in the antecedent world sufficient impetus for the establishment of certain focal elements for development in a new event. These elements—individuals, groups, institutions, and ideas—are derived from the past according to the principles discussed above. One can explain their origins and appearance by reference to their antecedents, with traditional empirical arguments. However, the explanation remains indefinite, because the antecedent world is so rich with potential that the emergence of any particular element or any particular event, to the exclusion of others, cannot be predicted.

Thus the phase of assimilation that initiates the emergence of historical events appears as a creative response to the potential of the past. The individuals, groups, and ideas that emerge as nuclei in the assimilation process are the same elements that the narrative historian uses to bring his account of events into focus, and the creative response organized around these nuclei is the narrative that must be followed through to be understood.

The initial phase of the passage of the Reform Bill, which has been located in England beginning about October 1830, reveals a set of potential elements that can be accounted for by derivation from the antecedent world. There were possibilities for the realization of "justice," "compromise," "revolution," "opposition," and so on. So far as is known, the potential for "sepuku" (Japanese ritual suicide) or of "machismo" (in its Mexican sense) was not present. These abstractions represent the general orientation of the new event, and thus explain why it had the antecedent it did. The assimilation of antecedent conditions as elements for the emerging event is guided by such an orientation, just as the participants in the Reform Bill controversy saw *their* past in terms of reform or revolution or opposition.

Historical events have a lengthy enough duration that information about the initial, assimilation phase is usually available (for microscopic events the initial phases are more often merely postulated). One can read the minutes of debates during the first week of November, 1830, and extract from the various speeches many of the general categories through which the past would be perceived. When Wellington told Parliament that the system of representation "possesses the full and entire confidence of the country," he was making a statement about the past that reflected part of the set of potentials for the passage of reform. Other parts can be reconstructed from other data, until the whole set is delineated; then its accuracy can be checked by referring to the potentials generated by the antecedent world.

The purpose of looking for the most general forms of potentiality in the initial phase of an event is threefold. First, it is necessary for the analysis of relationships between events that one clarify the general categories that they have in common. "Revolution" is a category shared by the passage of reform and many of its antecedents, both as potential and, in some cases, as reality. Second, the potential forms express the intensive relevance of antecedent conditions from the singular perspective of the new event. Identifying the potentials is a way of gauging the significance of the past. Third, the difference between the set of potential elements in the initial stage, the actual elements in the final stage, and the possible elements offered by the past is the primary justification for the construction of narratives. The array of potential elements shows that the past has special possibilities from this perspective that could not be predicted prior to its emergence, and it shows that the final form of the event was not derived directly from the past but indirectly through a process of combination and synthesis. The unpredictability and indirectness of these processes are, as previously argued, best explained through narrative.

The search for potential forms can be justified by an ontological principle: the existence of any entity is proof of the prior existence of its potential. In other words, if it happened, then it must have been possible. This is not the same as saying that, if it happened, then it must have been predetermined. The ontological principle is indeterminate, in the sense that the conditions of the past can only be assessed in relation to subsequent events that are already given. It is retrodictive principle, not a predictive one. The historian cannot know what the past is capable of before he sees what happened next.

Several qualifications are necessary before historians can employ the ontological principle effectively. First, there is sometimes not enough evidence for a rigorous ontological argument in the initial phases of events. One would like to find documents that refer clearly to the elements derived from the past, so that one could demonstrate how important they were, and where they orginated. But people don't usually refer to the more abstract concepts of their society or physical environment, because such concepts are rarely called into question. Unless a radical change is taking place in economic, religious, military, or social patterns, there may be few attempts to identify the concepts in the extant sources. In fact one could say, along with Thomas Kuhn, that the degree of change involved with any event is indicated by the level of abstraction mentioned in its documents.[4]

Nevertheless, a tentative description of potential elements can be inferred from the antecedent conditions and also from the hierarchies of more "radical" events in the same general time period. For example, in the period 1828–32 one could find mention of quite fundamental institutions, concepts, and field perspectives in sources for the Catholic Emancipation Act, the Factory Acts, and the debates on the abolition of slavery in the British

Empire. During the agitation for reform, which itself concerned a basic change, there were references to the "historical constitution" of England, to "revolution," and to "injustice." Some references, of course, were the common hyperbole of political rhetoric, and the historian is always faced with the task of separating illusion from reality. In general, however, the set of potential elements constructed by a historian can be empirically justified, so far as the evidence permits.

The second qualification of the ontological principle, as used by historians, is that the initial perspective of an emerging event is rarely drawn directly and solely from the most abstract level of pure potentiality. Instead, the actual event is guided by intermediate elements, often in combinations. Such combinations are fragments of configurations that may become central to the development of the event. They might include two or three individuals, a group, one or two institutions, a few concepts, and a "field" orientation, in some tentative arrangement. In the arts, such fragments are known as "ideas," and are credited with initiating the creative process. A musician may come upon a melodic line, or a chord progression, or even a feeling for silence; the "idea" is carried around, played with, tried out in a few compositions, and finally (perhaps) developed in full along with other ideas. Historical narratives are created the same way, and if they are well written they reflect what actually occurs. An event such as reform begins with several fragmentary packages: Wellington and the Tories; William IV and Queen Adelaide; Parliament and some of the gentry; the idea of the "constitution" opposed to the idea of "reform"; a religious backlash from Catholic Emancipation—these are fragments representing, in a tentative way, the potential configuration of the complete event.

The ontological principle serves to remind the historian that such fragments exist as potential in the antecedent world. Historians know this intuitively and typically ask whether a given set of elements, evident in the event they are trying to explain, is also evident in the past, combined in the same way. When did Wellington come under attack by the ultra-Tories? How long before World War I was Italy's defection from the Triple Alliance indicated as a possibility? Did Franklin Roosevelt espouse "New Deal" sentiments prior to 1932? Such questions illustrate the ontological principle used as a guide to historical explanation.

By raising the question of why do some events emerge and not others, we have been able to draw a contrast between four types of historical explanation. The positivist type answers the question by saying that events are determined by previous conditions; no alternative to what actually happened was ever possible. The teleological or idealist argument is that every new event determines its own emergence in keeping with some final or ultimate cause, an equally deterministic argument. Whitehead, although an idealist in many respects, suggested a middle ground: that events emerge as a creative response to the conditioned potential of the past. The response is guided by the perspective of the event, which in turn is manifested in its hierarchy of elements. The question "Why this event?" is answered by looking at the elements. More fundamental answers are given by the more abstract elements, and the most abstract, God, gives the ultimate reason.[5]

I have presented a fourth type of explanation, which adapts Whitehead's doctrine of assimilation as a guided transaction between event and antecedent, without his emphasis on the divine origin of the process. Instead, one can make an empirical explanation of the emergence of events, and use empirical sources to justify the search for certain elements in their makeup. Theological appeals are not required for an adequate historical explanation of this type. On the other hand, the transactional model does provide ways to analyze the relationships between events that do not arbitrarily polarize one's understanding. It is not only easier but more fruitful to assume that the relationships result from one event's response to another event's conditions, than to assume a one-way influence.

The next part of this chapter will attempt to describe the nature of the transaction through which antecedents are assimilated into the initial phase of the emerging event. The description will show in more detail why indeterminism, novelty, and error are essential to the historical process, and why positivist and genetic approaches to historical explanation are so often in conflict about it.

Aspects of the antecedent world are not assimilated into a new event in their concrete actuality. Rather, they are perceived as images of the environment having symbolic reference to the actual world from which they emerge. For example, the event known as "Catholic Emancipation" does not actually appear in the parliamentary debates over the Reform Bill of 1832. Instead, it is referred to in symbolic ways that use language, action, thought, and objects.

Perception through symbolic means is the primary mode of understanding the past, especially in human history. And, consistent with the general argument of this book, we must assume that the symbolic means used in accounts of the past (narratives) are in some way analogous to the symbolic means used by events themselves to account for their past. The problem is to describe symbolism as a function of understanding and of assimilation.

Classical philosophy is not much help in this regard because its theory of perception was limited to consideration of sense impressions received from the external environment. Also the nature of time was assumed to be a succession of discontinuous moments; the assimilation of the past by the present was inconceivable. Our understanding of historical change and causality, therefore, was held to be the product of mental operations using data from sense impressions in a derivative fashion.

Both Hume and Kant, in their different ways, argued that people perceive momentary states of the external environment directly, and then construct the notion of a causal relationship between one state and another. This argument was in accord with a common-sense impression that people see the immediate environment distinctly but have only vague impressions of its relation to past and future. The classical notion of perception, and its corollary notion of time, have been carried foward in positivist models of explanation, which seek to derive a logic of causation from the evidence of empirical investigation.[6]

In Chapter 4, I showed that the classical notion of perception did not extend to lower organisms or inanimate objects, that other side of the mind-matter duality. But in modern science, perception has returned in a broader conception to become the cornerstone of research and theory. In the modern context, perception means the reception of, and response to, signals from the environment. It can encompass the reaction of stone to changes in temperature and the excitement of memory cells by electrochemical changes in the human brain at a level of consciousness.[7] The process is interactive or transactional,[8] as Bertrand Russell argued a long time ago:

> Philosophy has taken over from the Greeks a conception of passive con-
> templation, and has supposed that knowledge is obtained by means of
> contemplation. Marx maintains that we are always active, even when we
> come nearest to pure "sensation": we are never merely apprehending our
> environment, but always at the same time altering it. . . . In place of
> knowing an object in the sense of passively receiving an impression of it,
> we can only know it in the sense of being able to act upon it successfully.[9]

Whitehead refined Russell's argument by pointing out that humans perceive the world from a definite perspective (our bodies) and with some awareness of the functioning of the sense organs: we see with our eyes and hear with our ears.[10] But far below the level of consciousness, one finds material things that interact with the environment in nonpassive ways. Atoms react to each other according to electrical charges that scientists have systematically charted. Cells typically assimilate foreign substances in a highly selective fashion at particular locations in their walls. The environment may be full of stubborn fact, as Whitehead is fond of saying, but we are also part of that environment. The relation between a percipient and its world, therefore, is transactional, having both subjective and objective features.

The transactional nature of perception has its corollary in the modern conception of time as defined durationally by events in the process of their interaction, past with present. Each event creates continuity by its perception and assimilation of impressions from its antecedents. This sense of continuity, of the conformity of the present to past conditions, is the meaning of causality.

In his discussion of causality, Whitehead reversed the arguments of classical philosophy. He maintained that, far from being a derivative construct produced by mental operations, the sense of causality was the most primitive mode of perception, enjoyed by every kind of object and organism regardless of its level of consciousness. The causal efficacy of the world impinges on each entity, enjoining it to conform to the brute reality of external conditions. Lacking consciousness, most entities respond directly to these conditions, without the mediation of symbolic elements:

> A flower turns to the light with much greater certainty than does a human being, and a stone conforms to the conditions set by its external environment with much greater certainty than does a flower. A dog anticipates the conformation of the immediate future to his present activity with the same certainty as a human being. When it comes to calculations and remote inferences, the dog fails. But the dog never acts as though the immediate future were irrelevant to the present.[11]

Perception in the mode of causal efficacy is vague, and the feelings associated with it are indeterminate regarding definite objects in space and time. It represents a subjective relation to the world. By contrast, the world objectified through our sense impressions of the immediate present is clearly delineated from our perspective. What is missing in the immediate present is that sense of temporal interaction, of causality, that gives the world its significance.[12]

Were the two modes of perception to remain separate, we would be faced with the choice of recognizing clearly how the world is arranged now without being able to understand its meaning, or of feeling the import of the world's movement without understanding its arrangement. There are times, of course, when people experience one or the other of these situations. A historian coming across a new document, for instance, may identify clearly what it says but wonder what context of thought or action might make it significant. And most people have experienced the feeling of impending developments in the environment without being able to discern the location or boundaries of the developing phenomena. Children have this experience much of the time: studies of their perceptual activity show that the sense of oneself as distinct from the surrounding world, and the arrangement of sense data into meaningful patterns, are relatively late developments in evolution and in human life. A child is immersed in an ocean of causal impulses, primitive and vague. The world happens *to* him. Only later does he develop a perspective on the immediate present as an ordered environment.[13]

In the higher organisms, and hence in human history, the two modes of perception are linked together by a function that Whitehead called "symbolic reference." Typically, elements derived from the sense data of the immediate present serve as symbols of the real world of causal efficacy. The elements have a correspondence of their own to recognized objects located in space and time, but they also refer symbolically to the dimly perceived conformity of the present to past conditions, and to the inclusion of past elements in present events.[14] I greet my child in recognition of her presence, but her image symbolizes for me a whole train of occasions in our relationship assimilated from the past and anticipated for the future. The recognition is of objective form; the assimilation is subjective feeling. Thus in the mixed mode of symbolic reference, which Whitehead says characterizes almost all perception among humans, form and feeling are brought together. It is in this synthetic guise that aspects of the past become elements in the emergence of new events.

The importance of symbolic reference is this: while perception of causal efficacy is direct and errorless, and perception of the immediate present can be put to the test of simple correspondence, the synthesis of form and feeling is open to novelty and error.[15] The words, actions, and objects we associate with the dynamics of the actual world are notoriously flexible and creative. Freud and Jung have provided thousands of dramatic examples, and the relation of symbolic form to subjective feeling is the basic problem in modern communications theory. I can say "There goes a bad black cat" in a dozen different ways; and my audience, depending on its cultural background, may respond with fright, laughter, derision, or curiosity.

Criticism in the arts is focused on the adequacy of the symbolic reference in particular works. The critic asks whether all the elements of the painting or piece of music work together to give a satisfactory and invigorating reference to our subjective feelings. Do some elements seem out of place, inhibiting the function of the whole? This critical approach is also appropriate for literature, including historical narratives. One wants to know, in judging a narrative, whether the language, its terms and stylistic arrangement, adequately connect the empirical data with feelings associated with the historical experience.

Which brings us back to the problem of historical explanation. The positivist approach centers on the abstraction of symbolic elements perceived in the mode of presentational immediacy: clearly defined words that can be systematically manipulated to produce correspondences with elements in other events. The aim is to discover correspondences that have a lawlike regularity. The drawback to the positivist approach, as I have shown earlier, is that symbols divorced from the subjective experience of emergence reflected in narrative lose their historical significance. They are like pristine flags representing nonexistent nations.

The advocates of the genetic approach to explanation believe that narrative accounts, with their subjective contextual dynamics, are so direct in their reference to the actual past that they require no other mode of perception to justify them. However, it is obvious that narrative does make a symbolic connection between the arrangement of words and sentences and the feelings evoked regarding the past which those words and sentences describe. As an analogue to the emergence of historical events, the narrative develops its own temporal pattern. But that pattern is a synthesis of feeling and form, and it is therefore amenable to the same kind of critique used for other types of literature.

Let me illustrate this point with another incident from the Reform Bill proceedings. The duke of Wellington stood before Parliament in the first week of November, 1830, having previously consulted with many important people, and having endured the jeers and advice of the street crowds. His sense organs were generating all sorts of last-minute impulses, and his body continued its mindless internal conversation. Wellington responded to all of these forms and feelings, raising certain forms to a position of significance and clarifying certain feelings by their origin, scope, or intensity. Articulating those elements that had reached consciousness, he spoke: "The system of representation possesses the full and entire confidence of the country."[16]

Obviously, Wellington's objective view of the situation presented from his immediate environment was influenced by, and symbolized, his subjective feelings about the causal significance of antecedent events. And, as his colleagues immediately told him, the connection he made was disastrously different from that made by most other Englishmen. The lesson of his misjudgment is that the opportunities for creative novelty provided by symbolic reference are also opportunities for error.

A deductive hypothesis abstracted from this incident would lose altogether the irony and pathos of Wellington's action. A strictly narrative account, on the other hand, might make inappropriate references between its empirical sources and the feelings it engendered. Only a narrative subject to the type of analysis I have proposed can fulfill the goal of an intelligible reconstruction of historical experience.

In this chapter I have tried to describe how emerging events assimilate aspects of their antecedent worlds. The assimilation process is a perceptual transaction in which the settled data of the past are objectified for the new event. The forms and feelings associated with these data are synthesized through symbolic reference into the constituent elements of the new event. There are valid empirical reasons, associated with modern concepts of time and perception, why assimilation should occur, and why certain aspects of the past should emerge as nuclear elements in the initial phase of a new event. In describing assimilation, I have pointed to the dangers of emphasizing one or the other modes of perception involved and have returned to the idea that reciprocity between analysis and narrative must be the hallmark of mature historical inquiry.

Assimilation is only the first phase in the emergence of historical events. The elements synthesized through symbolic reference are more closely tied to their past than to each other. Their relationships have still to be sorted out before the event becomes decisively what it is.

8. Symbolic Transformation

If you can look into the seeds of time,
And say which grain will grow and which will not,
Speak then to me....
Shakespeare, *Macbeth*, act 1, scene 3

In previous chapters it was argued that historical events are best thought of as patterns of development, having some temporal duration, rather than as mere points having simple location on a spatio-temporal grid. When analyzing the relationship between an event and its antecedents, one has to spatialize the event's form somewhat, so that it appears to be an object with a hierarchical structure. This type of analysis, which is useful for clarifying the terms of explanation and for identifying broadly regular relationships, is always done with the caveat that events are essentially temporal processes. They appear objectified only in the past, and the very act of perceiving them in the past is itself a temporal process. In Chapter 7 it was shown that in human history the perceptual process has a mixed character: antecedent events are assimilated as elements for a new composition in two ways, which might be termed "causal" and "conceptual," and which have symbolic reference to one another.

The term "symbolic" means that there is no direct, physical reference between the conceptual elements of the event, which are derived from the immediate environment, and the causal elements derived from the past. The reference has to be created anew in each event. There are, of course, strong impulses toward continuity in the world, so that much of the potential for creative novelty is overwhelmed by patterns of reference inherited from the past. But in the events historians are used to dealing with, there is a considerable element of novelty. The relation of causal to conceptual elements may change quickly and dramatically as historical characters work out new ways to respond to the conditions they perceive.

When novelty enters the process at any level of abstraction, it is necessary for the whole pattern of elements to be adjusted, and a new synoptic resolution achieved, in order for the organism or event to assume its objective identity in the external world. A rather crude illustration of this point is the introduction of barbed wire onto the field of battle in World War I. The wire was not accommodated as something "different" in an essentially unchanged style of attack and defense. Its introduction required a complex adjustment of people, guns, and tactics in order for any kind of "attack" or "defense" to occur. In fact, the principle that novelty requires readjustment in the whole system is a commonplace warning to students of history who focus too sharply on a single cause for complex events.

The implication of symbolic reference, then, is that events in human history require something more than mere conditioning from the past. They require a phase of adjustment, during which the symbolic elements derived from the external past are integrated into a new pattern. This phase may be relatively trivial (the case of sparrows entering the Crystal Palace in 1851, endangering the hats of visiting ladies and gentlemen) or it may be relatively important (the spread of the Black Death).

Because the elements of an event are transformed from their initial appearance as raw data into complex parts of an overall pattern, this phase of emergence is termed "symbolic transformation." I make no apology for using what looks like jargon at this point. The process itself is too complex to be identified with a simple term. In any case, the words chosen will be readily understood by those acquainted with creative processes in the arts, in language, and in mathematics. And they describe accurately enough what happens when a historian sets out to explain why a certain set of circumstances issued in an event that betrayed the obvious promise of its past.

Symbolic transformations occur for aesthetic, rather than for mechanical or strictly logical, reasons. Just as there is no formula for working out beforehand the impact of the opening notes in Beethoven's Fifth Symphony, or for capturing the appeal of Monet's garden pond and bridge, so there is no logic that will account for the contrasts and combinations of elements in the emergence of a historical event. Historical narrative reflects the problem rather nicely, for what makes it frustrating to analyze is its peculiar mix of formal chronology and nonsequential, aesthetic relationships. In narrative, events often occur in defiance of the calendar so that their special importance can be emphasized. Aspects that appear trivial at one time are given center stage at another. There is a clear and typical example in Palmer and Colton's assessment of German unification:

> The consolidation of Germany transformed the face of Europe. It reversed the dictum not only of the Peace of Vienna but even of the Peace of Westphalia. The German Empire, no sooner born, was the strongest state on the continent of Europe. Rapidly industrialized after 1870, it became more potent still. Bismarck, by consummate astuteness, by exploiting the opportunities offered by a Europe in flux, and with no more fighting than that involved in a few weeks in three short wars, had brought about what European statesmen of many nationalities had long said should at all costs be prevented.[1]

Most historians are so used to this style of exposition that they don't notice its chronological transpositions. But critics are aware of them. One reason for criticism is that, in modern technological societies, there is a tendency for the mechanical aspects of timekeeping to overshadow the more aesthetic experience of historical change, so that the latter, embodied in narrative, appears devoid of explanatory value. Another reason is that the power of narrative to evoke reconstructions of past experience is increasingly denigrated in favor of quantification and logical analysis. This is unfortunate, because the human value of studying the past lies in extending one's personal experience and, through a lengthened perspective, enriching it by reflection. The dissection of past events in the name of an anachronistic science has only revealed the irrelevance of data when divorced from their particular contexts. Thus, while the study of historical causes and effects has all but disappeared from American schools during the last twenty years, historical fiction in the form of the "dramatic documentary" or "nonfiction novel" has become the leading vehicle for historical understanding. To give just the most obvious example, Alex Haley's *Roots,* both in book form and on television, stirred an incredible social and personal reassessment of slavery in America in ways that quantified analyses of the antebellum South never approached. It is too soon to tell if the new mode of history will prevail. Perhaps the traditional forms of the discipline are still needed. But the changes are a warning to historians who would turn their backs on the aesthetic sense that informs their humanistic heritage.

This is not a call for all historians to turn into writers of popular fiction. It is simply that the techniques of enhancing the dramatic impact of narrative, and of thus evoking a desirable kind of historical understanding, are not the exclusive province of fiction. As demonstrated in Chapter 1, they can be used responsibly by historians who understand the principles of composition shared by most of the creative arts. And they must be considered if one wants to explain how a definite actual event can emerge from the array of conditions in its antecedent world.

In this chapter I intend to outline a set of concepts that describe the internal, temporal development of a historical event and, by analogy, the development of a historical narrative. The concepts are drawn from the realm of literary criticism, which has a tradition of analyzing temporal patterns. Historical writing is, after all, literature; and I have tried to show that the literary style used by modern historians expresses their understanding of past events better than any theory adapted from outmoded conceptions of "science." To talk about that understanding, to compare and criticize historical accounts, we need terms that science has not yet formulated.

This chapter is not intended as an excursion into minor concerns that lie outside the theoretical framework of the book. It is instead central to the whole enterprise. It brings theory and craft together by showing that the process of emergence, common to all events, can be described critically and systematically for the purpose of studying history and writing narrative accounts of the past. The particular descriptive terms borrowed from fiction and other arts may appear awkward and, at times incompatible. They are of course open to refinement. But they are not to be dismissed as irrelevant to the central purpose of historians.

The literary term for a process of development is "composition." I will first discuss some general features of composition in events, and then move to a closer study of compositional forms in narrative.

The elements of composition for a historical event are those relationships in its past perceived in the mode of symbolic reference, and focused on one or another "nucleus." As I pointed out previously, these elements are linked to each other in fragments that include several levels of abstraction. The fragments are of more or less complexity and intensity. Just as the novelist might begin with an idea of a change of character, or a line of dialogue, so the historical event begins with an assembly of episodic fragments. Catherine of Aragon proves barren of legitimate sons; Henry VIII's appeal to Rome for an annulment is rejected; his conscience is awakened regarding marriage to his dead brother's widow, in conjunction with the conquest of Rome by his imperial rival. Wolsey's ambitions rise; Thomas Cromwell advances his career—and a hundred other fragments emerge in this early phase of the English Reformation. Each fragment—a blend of feeling, fact, valuation, and potential—expresses a proposition, a statement of one possible configuration of elements for the final resolution of the creative process for that event.[2] A proposition may be identical to one illustrated in the antecedent world. But it is equally likely to be a novel configuration, giving each element a different relative significance than it had in the past. For example, the proposition "unification of Germany" is quite evident in the period 1862–71 in European events. It is also evident in events prior to this duration. For some elements (individuals, groups, institutions) present in 1862, the proposition "unification of Germany" meant virtually the same thing it had meant previously. But to Bismarck and a few others, the proposition meant something quite different. The contrast between the propositions was a major feature of events in the period 1862–71.

It is evident that propositions are not mere collections of data, mere arrangements of fact. Each is a complex judgment regarding the causal influence of its antecedents. Each illustrates a form (the pattern of significance attributed to the past) and a feeling (the tension involved in holding the elements together in a complex unity). In symbolic transformation, the forms and feelings of an event's propositions are combined, adjusted, and integrated into ever more complex compositions. Each element in a proposition is transformed from its initial state into a constituent of a larger whole. The process continues until a synoptic judgment is reached, accounting for every item in the universe perceived by that event from its perspective.[3]

Some writers will recognize in this outline a description of their own approach to the composition of historical narratives. Especially in diplomatic history, one tends to set out the plans and perspectives of each of the countries involved, and then tell the story of their interaction leading up to some climax. The compositional outline is not just historical, however; it applies equally to events in the biological and artistic worlds. In fact one of the nicest illustrations of symbolic transformation is provided by the critic Lucy Lippard, describing the work of contemporary artist James Rosenquist:

> Most of his paintings go through myriad transformations, sometimes as many as five major changes a day.... He begins by making scribbled "ideagrams," pastel or pencil drawings with color and conception notes, and apparently non-objective oil-on-paper studies. Color areas stand for the images, which, when chosen from magazines, newspapers, or other commercial sources, are stapled onto a piece of paper, in approximately their final shape or order. But between these work sheets and the finished product, the scale and color of everything may be completely revised. Change of scale gives the artist complete flexibility and provokes new ideas even after the original decisions have been made. In the work sheet a man's trouser leg and a candy bar may be about the same size, while on the final canvas one is ten times larger than the other.[4]

It is often said that creative processes cannot be analyzed into any particular sequence, because each artist or writer proceeds in his or her own way, the idiosyncracies usually overshadowing any method suggested by critics. Certainly the excerpt above shows why mechanical or logical explanations do not do justice to aesthetic development. However, at the same time the excerpt indicates some features that may help historians explain the internal structuring of events and their narrative analogues. Put simply, symbolic transformation deals with contrasts between propositions; it proceeds generally from the realization of the most abstract contrasts to the most particular; and it expresses a temporal pattern or form that is amenable to classification. Each feature deserves further comment.

A contrast between two propositions is made possible by the juxtaposition of similar and different elements. If the propositions had absolutely nothing in common, there would be no ground of reference by which to relate them. Yet they must be different in some respect. Contrast does not mean simple opposition or contradition: red and green are contrasting colors, just as William IV and Victoria had contrasting personalities. In fact, elements in total contradition to each other could not coexist in the same event. If an event includes Napoleon, then it cannot also include the absence of Napoleon. But "unification of Germany" as Bismarck intended it, may be contrasted with "unification" related to some other focus, such as Vienna.

The advantages of the term "contrast" over "cause and effect" may be obvious. Explaining how one event may become a constituent of another requires an emphasis upon relatedness rather than autonomy. Put red and green next to each other, and each becomes more intense. It is more accurate (and easier) to say that the contrast between them enhances the intensity of each, than to say that green enhances red, and red enhances green. Similarly, it is more accurate to say that the significance of Bismarck's unification of Germany was intensified by contrast with its past and potential alternatives, than to say that one or another alternative caused it to be significant. The term "contrast," then, which avoids the spurious question of causation, is useful for describing the internal development of an event.

The task for the historian is to identify the salient contrasts in the emerging structure of an event, and to describe the transformations through which they are gradually integrated. One may begin by identifying pairs of significant elements, one from each proposition, but the analysis will quickly proceed to more complex combinations. For instance, in the Reform Bill action one might sort out contrasts among Tories and Whigs, Whigs and Radicals, gentry and urban magnates, workingmen and aristocrats, fiscal conservatives and progressives, the House of Lords and the House of Commons, Lord John Russell and Lord Brougham, and so on. But soon it becomes necessary to deal with the complex contrasts between gentry, urban magnates, rural laborers, and industrial workingmen; between moderate Tories, ultra-Tories, and reform Whigs; and among the issues of French revolution, abolition of slavery, fiscal reform, and rotten boroughs. In historical accounts, as in fiction, these contrasts are often illustrated through episodes involving their nuclear elements. Lord Grey, representing the moderate Whigs, tones down an amendment by Lord John Russell, of the more adamant reformers, but argues its merits against Wellington, of the conservatives. Alternately, a single individual may be split up into his or her various relationships to other elements (that is, the several sides of his or her character), and then these may be contrasted to illustrate the complex personality of the individual. This is a standard fictional technique that historical novelists have used for a long time. In *The French Lieutenant's Woman,* for instance, John Fowles surrounds his subject, a nineteenth-century gentleman of leisure, with people reflecting the various paths and beliefs open to the gentleman at that time. One woman stands for respectability, another for adventure. Each character, from his or her singular perspective, offers a judgment on the entire cast.[5]

History writers are well aware of the difficulty in this approach. After a certain group of elements has been sorted out, and their relationships within a configuration described, one has to depend upon the reader to hold everything together as the story progresses. The careful distinctions are lost when the proposition is necessarily indicated by a more general, shorthand label in subsequent episodes. And using even an important element, such as Francis Place, to represent a whole perspective, such as Benthamite Radicalism, one grievously neglects all the other aspects of the man and the movement that ought to be kept in mind.

Historians may alleviate this difficulty, however, by pointing out what types of contrasts are being integrated, so that even if readers lose sight of the particular subjects involved, they can still appreciate the aesthetic transformations. This is akin to a fiction writer exposing, in the story, the principles of his composition. It gives the game away—which is awkward in fiction, but quite helpful in history writing.

The types of contrast have different labels depending on the artistic field, medium, and artist or critic involved. It seems natural for historians to look to literary criticism for their terminology; there is certainly a valuable group of long-established works in this field.[6] However, the adoption of a whole array of overly refined terms at this point would be premature. Historians need to get used to the major types of contrast, and to find out through experience how they operate in explanatory narratives, before borrowing from other disciplines. At first, one wants some general terms that help bridge the gap between analytical and genetic modes of explanation.

One category of contrasts involves a distinction between elements that are larger, more important, more comprehensive, or more intensely involved and elements that are less so. Also there may be elements of roughly the same significance. No scheme of analysis could account for all gradations of relative scale, but one can usefully begin with a simple division into contrasts of relative parity and of relative disparity.

In addition to the above, one needs terms to distinguish between elements that support each other and elements that undermine each other's importance or influence. For example, the proclamation of the German Empire resolved some of the conflicts inherent in the Franco-Prussian War, but the tensions between Germany and France over Alsace-Lorraine, and the conflict between constitutional and imperial forces in Germany, remained active. The new empire gained some support from the way it came about, but its resolution of past conflicts was weakened by that same character. Very generally, then, there are discordant, concordant, and neutral contrasts. (The category of neutrality is added for convenience to include elements whose relationship is either obscure or of low intensity.)

These contrasts appear at all levels of abstraction in the developing hierarchy of any given event. Analysis proceeds by identification of the salient types of contrast in each phase of transformation, up to and including the final synoptic judgment. Such analysis is bound to be somewhat subjective, for the terms "parity" and "disparity," "concordant" and "discordant" represent ends of two continua rather than discrete categories. In the following examples, every contrast is assumed to be identified with the phrase "relatively speaking" attached to it.

A short digression is necessary here. The terms "positive" and "negative" might be substituted for "concordant" and "discordant," except that Whitehead used the term "negative" to identify perceptions, by the emerging event, of antecedents that contradicted some element in its constitution.

Such perceptions are felt subjectively but not assimilated as objective elements. So they are accounted for in a "negative" sense. For instance, the U.S. presidential election of 1932 includes the presence of Franklin D. Roosevelt as an objective element. It does not include the absence of FDR; but that proposition is a real possibility in the antecedent world and must be accounted for by any event emerging from it. Thus the inclusion of FDR's presence as a positive element implies also the negative perception of his absence.

Strictly speaking, then, all the elements of an event are felt positively, being in accord with its final complex judgment about their roles in its constitution. The Axis powers may hate to lose, but their feelings are concordant with the Allied victory. The two elements enhance each other's meaning.

The term "discord" is therefore a departure from the Whiteheadian scheme, expressing a historian's feeling that in many events there are elements that detract from the final synthesis, leaving the exact disposition of their relationship to other elements undecided, and the prevailing tensions unresolved. This is true, of course, of other compositions in the arts: the judgment about quality in music or painting is based on the appearance of discordant fragments, whose form and feeling seem out of keeping with the primary thrust of the work. The fact of discord in actual events explains why historical narratives often appear less satisfying than their fictional counterparts—why they have a problem with "loose ends." Historians do not have license to arrange all the elements just as they would like them. The way to cope with this problem is to make it explicit and to account for it in a constructive way, by showing its implications for the future. For example, the Frankfort Assembly of 1848 failed to find a way to resolve nationalist ambitions with liberal-constitutional ideals, and the revolutionary movement stumbled. This event ends in ambiguity and discord. One can make it intelligible only by showing what that ambiguity and discord meant for subsequent events, as they incorporated aspects of the Assembly of 1848 into their own constitutions.

The identification of discordant contrasts has two heuristic functions in history. One is a critical function in which one points out the strengths and weaknesses of given narratives, both as analogues to the events they describe and as evocations of experience in the minds of readers. Failure to deal reasonably with discord is a drawback, and that knowledge should help historians write better narratives. Similarly, early attempts at temporal analysis by historians may uncover a lot of elements considered discordant because the analytical perspective is still naive. But attempts to account for so much discord will lead to more elegant explanations.

Contrasts of concordant parity occur between two or more configurations whose primary elements have about the same size and intensity, and whose function in the overall composition of the event is mutually supportive. Examples in the arts are the *duetto da camara* which evolved into the show-stopping love duets of nineteenth-century opera; similar duets in modern dance and ballet; *Romeo and Juliet;* and the groups of disciples in Leonard's *Last Supper.* In historical events, concordant parity between primary elements at the higher levels of abstraction is infrequent, though interesting. One might include the balance between religious and political elements in the Lutheran revolt, between political and military in the unification of Germany, between cultural, economic, and technological in the Luddite attacks on early English industry. Though such elements are not always in harmony, the tensions between them tend to enhance the significance of each.

It is more common, however, to find concordant parity between elements subordinate to some primary focus, as in a war where economic, political, and technological patterns become temporarily less significant than military ones, though of equal importance among themselves. As one proceeds down the hierarchy through institutions, groups, and individuals, the instances of concordant parity normally increase, simply because there are more instances to account for. Thus in the Reform Bill legislation of 1830–32, the House of Lords and monarchy are often mutually augmentative; the political unions and the Reform Whigs work in tandem; Brougham and Russell and Palmerston enhance each others' roles. And though their general configurations seem so far apart, even the ultra-Tories and the Radicals, in their common fear of Wellington's power, achieve a sporadic concordance. In this sense, concordant parity does not necessarily mean cooperation or expressed support, only a relationship in the overall composition of the event characterized by reciprocal intensification.

Contrasts of discordant parity, especially in the higher echelons of elements, are found typically in signficant events which lack the decisive resolution of the Reform Bill. For instance, the discords between technology, culture, and politics which pervade accounts of the industrial revolution (and lately the works of C. P. Snow and Lewis Mumford) are seldom resolved in any actual event. Walter Ullmann has chronicled a similar tension between religion and politics during the European Middle Ages.[7] On a smaller scale one finds discordant parity between liberalism and nationalism during the German revolutions of 1848, particularly in the deliberations of the Frankfort Assembly; between Gladstone and Disraeli in the middle of Victoria's reign; and between workingmen and urban magnates in many of the cities (other than Birmingham) during the Reform Bill agitation of 1830–32.

The identification of discordant parities at any level of abstraction should warn the historian that the final pattern of relationships in the event will not yield a "satisfaction" of all conflicts, and that these discords are the most likely nuclei for future creative process. However, discord in the early

phases of integration may be resolved later on, with a corresponding enhancement of intensity for the elements involved. An example illustrating
both possibilities was the question of the creation of new peers to carry the
Reform Bill in the House of Lords after the Whig government was defeated
there in October 1831. Asa Briggs relates that Grey was wretchedly un-
happy about the consequences of creating peers on a large scale even if the
king was willing to go through with it.[8] At issue were two principles: that
king-in-parliament must ultimately be responsive to the changing legitimate interests of the kingdom, and that no one part of government, least of
all the one with a popular constituency, must force its demands upon the
others, especially on a controversial issue. The Commons, and Lord Grey,
were caught between their fears of democracy and of autocracy. While Grey
characterized the creation of peers as "a measure of extreme violence" and "a
certain evil, dangerous as a precedent," he had to admit that if the bill were
defeated in the Lords, he and all his ministers would be "utterly and entirely
ruined in character," and the country might well rise in open rebellion.

In January 1832 Grey obtained a vague promise from William IV to create
the required peers if the need for them became "certain." But he resisted the
pressure of his more liberal colleagues to go ahead at the time, and must
have been relieved when the Lords passed the second reading of the bill on
April 13 by a slim majority. During this phase of the internal development
of the event, it was not clear whether the discordant parity would turn to
some degree of subordination of one principle to another, nor was it clear
which principle would emerge as the more significant.

On May 7 the government was defeated in committee. Grey demanded
the creation of peers, but William, who was reported to have listened to his
queen's blandishments, refused. The government had no choice but to re-
sign. At this stage it appeared that relative parity had disappeared and that
Grey's ministry would no longer be able to resolve the discordant contrast.
For several days, Briggs reports, there was a grave political and constitutional
deadlock. Elements such as the political unions, Francis Place, Wellington
and Peel, and the concepts of "a run on the bank" and "armed insurrection"
suddenly emerged into prominence in place of Grey. The configurations
brought into focus by these elements represent potential alternative solu-
tions to the discord existing between the two political principles. They are a
reminder that the internal constitution of an event is no mere procession
from initial causes to final effect. At any stage, its symbolic elements may be
transformed in their relationships of scale and intensity, while remaining
consistent with the conditions of the antecedent world.

By early May it was evident that Grey's cabinet and its bill were the only
alternative to widespread rebellion. But when the king's secretary relayed to
Grey the vital note granting permission to create the necessary peers, he also
advised the Tory opposition in the House of Lords that no creation would

be necessary if they absented themselves from the legislative process.[9] Thus, although the principle of ultimate responsiveness to the kingdom emerged as the primary focus of this event (at its level of abstraction), the discordant contrast was never fully resolved, and the degree of subordination of the aristocratic and monarchic principles illustrated by the House of Lords and the king was not certain. As a result, the contrast was heightened, and the discordant issue became a focus with high potentiality for inclusion in subsequent events. One may put the matter another way, by saying that the tension between the actual resolution of the conflict in this event, and the potential alternative patterns of resolution, remained very high. In some events, the primacy of one configuration is so great as to reduce alternatives to impotence. But in occasions characterized by discordant parity at the higher levels, such an outcome seems almost impossible.

The importance of such contrasts is of course relative to the level of abstraction from which analysis proceeds. In an event such as the unification of Germany a quarrel between two provincial magistrates may pass unnoticed. If one is using their lives as foci, however, the situation becomes discordant indeed. For this reason, it is the duty of historians to remind themselves and their readers of the level of abstraction on which they are discussing their subject, so that the judgments as to types and significance of contrasts may be kept in reasonable perspective. It is not wrong to depict a moral crisis in the life of a public figure in terms of discordant principles of high abstraction, but it is unreasonable to proceed from that conceptual level to a discussion of institutional crises as though the relative proportions of scale and intensity remain constant.

Yet, there are instances of symbolic transformation in which elements at one level appear commensurate with those at another. The most common example is the relation between a group or institution and its leader. The National Political Union, based in London but with connections to Birmingham and other activist centers around England, was certainly important in the passage of the Reform Bill of 1832. But its chief strategist, Francis Place, was equally influential, not only in organizing the group but in representing its demands to parliamentary leaders. His actions and those of the union were mutually reinforcing; the contrast between them approaches concordant parity. On the side of discord, one could cite the struggle between Bismarck and the German Diet over the constitutionality of German unification. In a historical narrative, such elements are legitimately set against each other as foci of equal weight.

It is well to remember that any attempt to define contrasts between isolated pairs of elements is doomed to failure. The configurations brought into focus by those elements are what really matter; these are the propositions that must be welded into a single definite statement about the past. Thus, instead of dealing with Place and his union as separate entities, the historical writer needs to place one configuration of relationships among Place, the union, and its principles, over against another consisting of Grey, the reform Whigs, and their ideals. Admittedly this is a more complicated business than describing interactions between isolated elements (which tend to become "causes" and "effects"), but it can be done without undue interruption of narrative continuity. As I suggested in Chapter 1, the dynamics of narrative produce such complex configurations in the reader's mind as he follows the sequence of events. What the historian needs to do is to identify the relevant configurations explicitly, as benchmarks for the rationalization of the "following" process.

The difficulty of sorting out relative degrees of abstraction in the later phases of the Reform Bill event, so as to present coherent configurations of elements for comparison, is that the discordant parity between constitutional principles remained unresolved almost to the last. In less controversial events the primary contrasts at this fifth level are integrated fairly early, and the relative weight of institutional forces established soon after, so that the disposition of groups and individuals in the emerging pattern is worked out within a relatively narrow framework of possibilities. For example, the issue of Catholic Emancipation was for many people a matter of strong feelings and grave consequences. Yet almost everyone except the king saw the bill as inevitable from the time that Daniel O'Connell announced his candidacy for an Irish seat in the House of Commons. George IV tried to dig in at the institutional level by recalling his father's conscientious defense of the Church of England. But as everyone knew that George IV had no conscience to speak of, the appeal was ignored. Wellington bullied the king into submission, and all that remained was the determination of contrasts between the various groups and individuals with respect to the conceptual and institutional fact of Catholic Emancipation.[10]

The passage of emancipation is a type of event in which the propositions offered for symbolic transformation are so close.together at the higher levels of abstraction that the contrasts between them are relatively weak. The degree of organization required for a final decision is correspondingly less, and the internal constitution of the event, displayed synoptically in its formal hierarchy, will be simpler. This assessment is in keeping with the notion of a continuum of organic complexity as the foundation of a unity of science, developed in Chapter 4.

However, it is axiomatic in process explanations that no part of the constitution of an event may be dismissed from consideration prior to the resolution of the whole. The meaning of an event is not expressed solely by its major contrasts, any more than a symphony can be reduced to its main theme, or a novel to its basic plot. The historian must find a place in his analytical scheme, and in his narrative, for all those elements and propositions that appear in subordinate relation to the primary foci, providing those subtle gradations of value and intensity that make the event decisively what it is. Such contrasts may be concordant or discordant. They may emerge from the interaction of propositions in the initial phases of the event, or they may appear as novel elements in later, more complex arrangements.

Contrasts of relative concordant disparity show how the pattern of relationships focused on one element is reflected and augmented by that of a less significant one. In painting or sculpture, dance or music, this is often achieved by the repetition and variation of a motif in various parts of the composition. In literature, the effect is gained through subplots, minor episodes, and secondary characters, which clarify and strengthen the main ideas. Such contrasts appear at all levels of abstraction in a historical event, and express how the elements at each level are graded in relevance within a given configuration. As the configurations are gradually integrated, the degrees of subordination may shift considerably. The earlier alternatives are not eliminated from the temporal constitution of the event but remain as overtones of value for the one pattern realized in its final decision.

The interplay of the principles of disenfranchisement and enfranchisement in the Reform Bill proceedings may illustrate this idea. The first version of the bill was introduced with a strong emphasis on getting rid of the rotten boroughs, those comprising dying or long-dead villages, stone walls, or plowed fields. The enfranchisement of the urban-industrial areas to the north appeared as a subordinate program, for it was paired with a reduction in the total number of seats in Commons. The contrast was not discordant, because each principle enhanced the others. However, in May 1831 an old conservative, General Gascoyne, carried an amendment retaining the previous number of seats, intending thus to weaken the thrust of disenfranchisement. The pattern of subordination proposed by the government was therefore challenged by a different one.

The subsequent transformations are instructive. Grey and his colleagues resigned at once, mounted a campaign for "the whole bill," and won passage, with the principle of reduction, in the new Parliament. But after the Lords threw the bill out (with yet another outburst of public violence, and another election), the government decided to compromise. The third version of the bill, introduced in December 1831, modified the earlier clauses on disenfranchisement, while reinstating Gascoyne's principle retaining the number of seats in Commons. Thus the pressure to guarantee new seats to the industrial constituencies overcame hostility to the rotten boroughs, so that the initial disparate contrast between them was subtly reversed. Yet in the final hierarchy, which the actual event presents for incorporation in subsequent processes, the earlier, alternative patterns of relationship are displayed as real possibilities, adding significance to the one determinate pattern. Their efficacy as historical agents does not disappear, as students of later British reform bills can testify.

Each level of abstraction in a proposition achieves some gradation of relevance among its elements. There is a gradation among the pure concepts guiding the initial process of assimilation, and there are gradations among fields, principles, institutions, groups, and individuals. For example, in the Zollverein created by Friedrich List in 1834, which bound many of the states of Germany into a customs union, the economic field served as a primary focus, while the political, the military, the technological, and the socio-cultural were ranged in descending degrees of concordant subordination. During the Reform Bill agitation in England, the institution of Parliament was enhanced by contrasts with the Birmingham and London political unions, which were less significant in the general scheme of relationships. Blucher's army arrived in the nick of time in a concordant, disparate contrast with Wellington's troops at Waterloo. And so on, down to the level of individuals. In a narrative, the historian may just point out the more important of these contrasts, allowing each to suggest the tone of its relevant configuration. In an analytical study, however, the whole complex of interwoven contrasts is to be made explicit.

It is common in narrative accounts to mention concordant elements: one brings up the "primary causes" and then the "secondary" ones. Major conflicts are also commonly described, though not in the context of temporal development proposed here. But narrative writers often overlook the relatively minor discords, which detract from the resolution of the whole, cast doubt on its judgment and its perspective on the past, and remain as potential seeds of change for future creative process. These are the contrasts of discordant disparity. For example, the general support of the working classes for the Reform Bill of 1832 gains in significance when placed against their bitterly disappointed aspirations for voting rights and their increased awareness of class discrimination. The experience of the Anglican bishops, die-hard opponents of reform, also ran counter to the process of resolution. Their contrariness was not in itself discordant, for its presence is perfectly consistent with the triumph of reform; but the obscurity of their position, and the fact that in the end they were absent rather than present from the legislative process, makes their role discordant. It muddles instead of clarifies the final form of the event.

Discordant contrasts represent mistakes in the process of symbolic transformation. Some of these may be only apparent, as I suggested previously, and with a more sophisticated view of the situation they cease to be disparaged. The others need to be recognized for what they are: signs that historical events, like artists, rarely achieve perfection. When they do, the result is a kind of immortality, a durability of judgment through myriads of subsequent events. The Athenian temples, with their beautiful proportions, remain aesthetic standards even today, while the death of Socrates, a historical event reported to us from the same context as the temples, remains consistently satisfying. It is perhaps for this reason that historical episodes are most often remembered as they appear in literary rather than analytical works. The former aim at concordant integration of all elements, while the latter display discord more openly.

Having named the types of contrast expressed in the continuum of parity-disparity in relation to that of concord-discord, I now aim to show how the interplay between them develops. The relevant descriptions of creative process in the arts and in inventive thinking imply that the temporal pattern of transformation is usually scrambled. Since integration is the rule, what happens in a later stage to some major element may require a wholesale readjustment of minor contrasts previously considered "settled." Every historian who has constructed a narrative knows the frustration of this task. Two-thirds of the way through a passage of inspired description, one realizes that this new insight invalidates the arguments of two whole chapters, and that an agony of revision is the price one pays for creativity.

On the other hand, even from this experience we can see that the more particular and complex elements are not finally settled as to their role in the overall composition until those on higher levels of abstraction have been arranged. The particulars cannot be pinned down until the generalizations which they illustrate are fully defined. In historical events, this means a progressive judgment regarding the contrasts between propositions focused at the level of fields, then principles, institutions, groups, and individuals, ending with the most complex decision as to the actual event.

The gradations of relevance among pure potentials, guiding the emergence of a given event, are determined in its initial phase. This decision puts a limitation on the creative process from the perspective of that event. But it also expresses the range of potentiality available to elements at lower levels of abstraction. In effect, the pure potentials establish what is *not* going to happen in this event, from its particular perspective, and then give the creative process free rein with what is left.

In each phase of symbolic transformation, there is a decision about the contrast between the several field elements, a decision that influences the development of contrasts between conceptual, institutional, group, and individual elements pertaining to the contrasted fields. The individual contrasts are worked out last, and the integrated actual event is drawn from their level. In some events it appears that an institution or concept is the final aspect to be settled, as in the Reform Bill proceedings when the legislation emerged swiftly from the king's concession on creation of peers. But in actuality, the feeling of the participating groups and individuals could not be determined prior to a decision about the relative weight of the principles they espoused. Their role in any particular configuration prior to the final phase may be quite definite. But the status of that configuration is indeterminate.

This notion of progression from higher to lower levels of abstraction is consistent with the patterns of change discerned by Crane Brinton in political revolutions and by Thomas Kuhn in scientific ones.[11] Conflicts build up in groups from disagreement between individuals (and in individuals from discords in their experience of actual events); then between groups within institutions, between institutional expressions of the relevant principles, and so on. This pattern may be displayed synoptically in the antecedent world, as discussed in Chapter 6. The emergence of a novel event from that world follows a reverse pattern. Thus, prior to the Russian Revolution there was buildup of tensions among particular events, individual behavior, groups, and institutions, which came to involve the principles of political, economic, religious, and social organization. There followed a disruption of the prevailing matrix of perceptual fields, and an attack on the fundamental order of pure potentials delimiting the potential range of resolution, for example, the ideals of autocracy and orthodoxy held by the ruling authorities. The "revolution" involved a creative response to these conditions. But the form of that response, from the perspective of the actual event and its individual or group elements, was not fully resolved until novel relationships were established at the higher levels of ideals, fields, complex concepts, and institutions, in that order.

Similarly, in scientific revolutions it is the increasingly discordant contrasts between individual experimental results and predictions that lead to conflict between groups, challenges to institutional imperatives, the questioning of intermediate hypotheses, the breakdown in definitions of the "field" or discipline in relation to other fields, and the subsequent rejection of the laws of order governing the whole paradigm. The feelings engendered at each stage of disintegration are strikingly similar to those displayed during political revolutions. And the emergence of a new paradigm follows the same pattern in reverse, from the discovery of new laws to the particular experimental results which illustrate their heuristic validity.

"Revolution" is a relative term, indicating a type of change significantly more intense, by reason of its compressed duration and the involvement of more abstract elements, than "evolution." What is perceived as revolutionary on one level, therefore, may be viewed as evolutionary on a higher level. Thus the "Glorious Revolution" of 1688 in England, in which a corrupt but legitimate ruler was displaced by an invader representing a different constellation of interests, may be viewed as a less drastic change when placed in the context of constitutional development during the whole seventeenth century.

Reference to revolution indicates again that there is a continuum of events based on the relative complexity and degree of innovation involved in their temporal organization. For events at the level of inanimate material and primitive life, the stability of relationships on the higher levels of abstraction (those expressing principles of order more than organic function) predominates. Change is therefore minimal and overwhelmingly incremental.

Similarly, there are many historical events having such continuity from their antecedents as to make the term "change" almost inappropriate. This fact suggests the possibility of classifying historical events according to the levels of abstraction significantly involved in their emergence. For example, the Reform Bill passage was a "conceptual" event, because change occurred at all levels up to and including the conceptual, while change at the field level, and the level of pure potential, was insignificant. And there will be "institutional" events, "individual" events, and so on. Narrative historians usually work with some such classification, describing the general conditions prevailing in a given era and ranging the various events under them as illustrations of the scope of change made possible within the general configuration. The critical evaluation of such narrative explanations presupposes an explicit analysis of their implied classificatory schemes, in comparison with those of other accounts.

Granted, the identification of contrasts and the analysis of their transformations are matters of judgment for historians. Consideration of relative stability or change at the several levels of abstraction is also open to dispute. No one familiar with the discipline can expect such an analytical scheme to bring about a new era of reconciliation and peace. One can expect, however, a gradual narrowing of gaps between alternative interpretations, a movement from uncertainty toward certainty, as historians refine their critiques within a common framework. This expectation (or blind hope) is all that the proud designation of "science" comes to: a disciplined approach to inquiry. It is prevalent also in such "subjective" fields as literature, where criticism is directed toward the delineation of categories of meaning shared by most informed members of the field.

Recent work in literary criticism, in fact, suggests a way to diminish controversies that may arise from analyses of temporal organization in historical events. The whole sequence of transformation, from the initial phase of assimilation and symbolic reference, to the final resolution of contrasts, may be thought of as a story-line or a plot. And what the critics have done with the concept of a plot is very instructive.

In a well-known essay, R. S. Crane discarded the notion that plot referred simply to the sequence of action, the bare chronology of events, in a story. Rather, he argued,

> the plot of any novel or drama is the particular temporal synthesis effected by the writer of the elements of action, character, and thought that constitute the matter of his invention.[12]

The difference between these two notions of plot may be illustrated by considering any event, say the confrontation between Henry II and Thomas Becket. The more primitive notion may be expressed as a chronicle: Henry appoints Becket as chancellor and archbishop, quarrels with him over jurisdiction, and evinces a desire to be rid of him. Becket is murdered, and Henry does penance for his death. Such a story-line only prompts more questions: What were Henry and Becket like as people? Why did Henry do penance? What did he expect from Becket in his new offices? And so on. Answering these questions involves action, character, and thought in a developing synthesis.

According to Crane, in any plot one of these elements will predominate. That element will be the subject of change, and the other two elements will react to it and not primarily to each other. Thus there are plots of character, plots of action, and plots of thought. (By "thought," Crane appears to mean an awareness of circumstance and implication, past and future.) Beyond these basic forms, however, one must consider the power of the whole pattern to evoke analogous experiences in the reader, to affect his feelings and opinions. We are concerned not only with what happens, but also with how it is expressed. The primary focus, then, is on the composition as a whole; analysis of its symbolic elements is secondary.

Crane's critique of plot can be adapted for historical narratives, and even for historical events, if we make the necessary transition from a "person-centered" type of literature to an "event-centered" type. Thus, the characters in an event are, for analytical purposes, its propositions or potential configurations. These are the entities which undergo adventures of change with respect to a given set of conditions. "Character" expresses the content of the proposition, its various elements and their complex pattern of relationships. In a plot of character, this pattern undergoes qualitative change in response to its adventures with other propositions (action), and to the emerging implications of its perspective on the past and anticipation of the future (thought).

In fiction and drama, characters represent configurations of elements also. In *The Great Gatsby,* for instance, Tom Buchanan is described in terms of his group memberships ("the most powerful end in Princeton football history") and his institutional affiliations (his "contacts" expose Gatsby's secrets); and he expresses a few blunt principles borrowed from Lothrop Stoddard and the eugenicists. His "field" is primarily physical, and his ideals (which he is too dense to articulate) are those of East Egg. Thus "Tom Buchanan" identifies a proposition, a configuration of elements focused at the individual level of abstraction.

In historical narrative, propositions are also used as characters. Unfortunately, historians are less likely than fiction writers to study and delineate the links between a primary element and the rest of its proposition. This is especially important because, unlike most fiction writers, historians use institutions, groups, principles, and even fields as protagonists in their accounts. One can't assume that an individual stands for a set of historical elements in the same way that he might stand for a set of fictional elements.

In Chapter 1, I quoted a passage from Halphen's account of Charlemagne that showed both the use of abstract elements as characters and the problems of doing so. Halphen personalized his account by attributing human qualities to groups, institutions, and ideas, as in the following:

> in the course of the events which had unfolded in Italy since the intervention of Charlemagne in the affairs of the Lombards, the West had, around him and through him, come to be conscious of its unity as opposed to the "Roman Empire" which, following its eight-century-old career in the Eastern Mediterranean, continued to embody the tradition of ancient Rome.[13]

In this passage, Halphen sketched two propositions in a contrast of discordant parity. One is made up of Charlemagne, Lombards, "the West," Italy, and "unity." The other includes "Roman Empire," Eastern Mediterranean, "tradition," and Rome. These propositions, although focused at the institutional level, are treated as individual characters with consciousness and careers. There may be ways to avoid such personalization, but it is not a particularly acute difficulty. What matters more is the accurate characterization of the primary elements ("the West" and "the Roman Empire") as symbols of their relevant propositions. One needs to know, more exactly than Halphen has explained, what pattern of relationships is represented by "the West" and "the Roman Empire," so that each time they or one of their associated elements is mentioned, the pattern emerges clearly in our minds. In Halphen's case the propositions are traceable through most of his account; in the work of lesser historians, it is difficult even to identify the primary elements.

There is a tendency among historical writers toward spurious variation of terms of reference, that is, the use of an individual or group label to signify an institution or concept, and vice-versa. "Moscow" or "Washington" is used instead of "Chairman Khrushchev" or "the president and secretary of state." "Ghandi" walks to the sea to make salt in defiance of British rule, instead of the thousands who formed his group. This type of variation, a standard technique in almost all forms of literature, is not prohibited to historians. But it needs to be done deliberately, with the aim of rendering the full scope and exact meaning of the whole proposition involved. Otherwise the narrative will lack intelligibility.

Treating the potential configurations of an event as characters in its plot is therefore a matter of borrowing a very useful approach from literary criticism. The idea of action is also easy to transfer. The action of a plot consists of the adventures of its characters. In a historical event, this means the transformations of propositions as they are brought into contrast with each other. We can describe changes from parity to disparity, from concord to discord, from significance to insignificance, and back again. Action means, then, the process of internal organization of any event. R. S. Crane speaks of this process in terms of cause and effect, because he is viewing the plot as a sequence of events. Considered as one complex event, however, the plot does not involve causality; its action is aesthetic.

It used to be thought that plot meant action and nothing else. When children read Dickens's *A Tale of Two Cities* in school, for example, they dutifully outlined the "plot" as a sequence of incidents, and then went on to discuss the characters and the ideas contained in the novel. This attitude is also found in critiques of historical narrative, with the result that most narratives turn out to be linear sequences of action, or are treated as such. They wind up little more than adventure stories, and lack explanatory value. Crane's reformulation of the concept of plot should make historians and their critics aware of the shallowness of the earlier approach. The action in historical accounts must be intimately associated with their characters and thought, and any critique must begin with such association as an assumption.

The element of thought in a plot may be harder to transfer to history from fiction, especially for those who try to keep consciousness and human thought out of the definition of historical events. But in fictional or dramatic plots, thought is something different from mere mental activity. For R. S. Crane, it means an awareness, either by characters or author, of the implication of some configuration of change as a potential judgment of the past, and as an anticipation of the future. This awareness may rise to the level of clear consciousness, or remain relatively intuitive or instinctive. It may grow gradually or arrive with a shock.

Whitehead termed the element of thought in an event its "perspective." The emergence of perspective is guided by the "subjective aim," the organizing principle first established by a matrix of pure potentials and then articulated during the phases of symbolic transformation. The subjective aim of an event is a vortex of valuation, through which propositions are related to the antecedent world which they judge and to the future which they anticipate. In a fictional story, a character may realize what a fool he's been, and resolve to act differently in future situations. That is a change of perspective, of thought. Similarly, the coronation of Charlemagne involved changes in the way certain propositions (focused on Charlemagne, on the papacy, and on the Byzantine court) perceived the past, and organized themselves for subsequent interaction. These changes may be described in terms of institutions or concepts, not just human consciousness. The awareness of circumstances manifested in an institution such as the papal curia shows up in its relations with other elements in an event. If it develops contrasts of extreme disparity or discord, there is reason to believe that its perspective on the past and future is naive or perverse.

Crane's concept of plot seems to be a useful way to approach the temporal composition of historical events and of their narrative analogues. It provides both a sense of the whole pattern (which is the best starting point for intelligent criticism) and a means of distinguishing the constituent changes of character, perspective, and circumstance. By delineating the plot of a historical event, we establish a common referent for critical analysis of contrasts, and thus reduce the range and intensity of arguments that are admittedly bound to occur.

The general division of plot forms into action, thought, and character does not exhaust the critical framework developed for literature. Norman Friedman, in a later essay based upon Crane's ideas, described some fourteen plot forms, distinguished by the direction or type of change involved.[14] Friedman's analysis is actually a summary of critical concepts that have been in use for a long time, and because they have proven their heuristic value in dealing with human experience (fictional or not), their adaptation for historiographical purposes seems quite justified. In the following outline, I have paraphrased Friedman's definitions of some forms, and substituted actual historical events for his fictional illustrations. Some may argue that this or that example belongs in a different category than the one I have assigned it to; I claim no final authority in such matters. An analytical scheme is only worthwhile if the disagreements it provokes can be clarified by reasonable application of its principles. It is the muddy conflicts one has to avoid.

The forms of the plot, adapted from Friedman, are as follows.

Plots of Fortune

In this category, change of circumstance overwhelms any modification of character and perspective. The latter two elements undergo relatively little development, being dependent on fate or destiny.

1. *The Action Plot.* This is the most primitive and most common plot in pulp literature. John Masefield satirized it in a story entitled *ODTAA,* an acronym for "One Damn Thing after Another." Usually it involves the solution of a puzzle or the winning of a contest. Benvenuto Cellini's *Autobiography* falls occasionally into this form. Accounts of Viking invasions, the battles of the Thirty Years' War, and the development of industrial technology also tend toward simple action sequences. The action plot represents the ideal of nineteenth-century positivist historians, who wanted to strip narrative of all interpretation. The form can be entertaining for awhile, but it is almost devoid of explanatory value.

2. *The Pathetic Plot.* A sympathetic protagonist, somewhat deficient in character, suffers misfortune through no particular fault of his own. Accounts of the coming of the Civil War in the U.S. are often cast in this form, as are the later years of Napoleon III and Harold Godwinson (ca. 1066), and the narratives of some utopian communities whose good intentions failed to

overcome circumstances. Liberal renditions of the "moderate" stage of revolutions tend toward the pathetic form. The moderates are viewed as victims of their own ideals of liberty and tolerance, which are turned against them by unscrupulous radicals. Recent assessments of George III have moved in a similar direction, but here the character is sympathetic because of his sincerity rather than his ideological correctness. Revisionist accounts of the "winning of the West" have stressed the pathetic plight of the Indians.

3. *The Tragic Plot.* A sympathetic protagonist with strength of will and sophistication (and corresponding moral responsibility) suffers misfortune through an error of judgment and realizes it too late. Unlike the pathetic plot, where the main character never understands what went wrong, the tragic hero or heroine must face the knowledge of his mistake. And his tragedy is not due to a change of character but rather to a change of circumstance which exposes him to error. Oedipus, Hamlet, and Antigone are three dramatic examples. The confrontation of Henry II and Thomas Becket has been cast in the same form, as have the stories of Maximilian and Carlota in Mexico, Neville Chamberlain in the 1930s, and Mary Tudor. The form is rare because it demands nobility of spirit, misfortune, and self-realization together. In earlier discussions of events, I have suggested a kind of tragedy that occurs every time a particular event makes its final synoptic judgment. There is the realization of character and value, but there is also the realization of loss in terms of what might have been. Because human beings have historical consciousness, this aura of tragedy is present in most recorded human events, and the historian who wishes to emphasize the contrast between potentiality and actuality can construct a tragic plot for any of them.

4. *The Punitive Plot.* Here an arrogant, knowledgeable character who is a satanic hero-villain suffers well-deserved misfortune. Shakespeare's drama *Richard III* is a good example. James I and Bolingbroke are often caught in punitive plots, as is Italy under Mussolini and Spain from the perspective of the Netherlands. Few concepts or principles fit in this category, although Russian "autocracy" from about 1815 to 1914 is sometimes portrayed as an evil thing that gets is comeuppance.

5. *The Sentimental Plot.* As the label suggests, this form involves a sympathetic character who suffers awhile and then arrives at a happy ending through a change of fortune. The thought or perspective of such a character does not really change; in fact, it may be vindicated. The sentimental plot is the all-time favorite for popular romance. Some of the recent accounts of the princess Elizabeth (I), which have her narrowly escaping exile or death at the hands of her various rivals to the English throne, fall into this category. The Dreyfus affair is often handled in the same way. But both the punitive and the sentimental plots have become unfashionable in academic history since their abuse at the hands of Whig historians and chauvinistic

textbook writers. The whole business of bad kings and good kings and the ultimate triumph of parliamentary rule or Manifest Destiny or whatever, had its heyday in the nineteenth century. It is still current in some accounts of reform movements, such as the abolition of the British slave trade.

The difference between the action plot and the sentimental plot is that the former puts the hero in a jam, but one does not feel pity for him, because one knows that he is going to turn the tables on his opponents in the end. In the latter, suffering evokes sympathy because it seems to be undeserved and unprovoked. The sentimental plot may be valid for historical events, if the historian takes care to make explicit the ground of his emotional involvement. For example, he can explain that the subject of his study is an event through which some institution, now generally admired, was first established; and he can admit that admiration as the ground of his critical approach. Nothing has bedeviled academia more than the equation of scientific objectivity with denial of emotional feeling. Freud saw what would happen: every feeling repressed becomes projected into the surrounding world, making inanimate objects into potent symbols and infusing so-called objectivity with a profound emotional tension. In identifying the sentimental plot we at least avoid such duplicity.

6. *The Admiration Plot.* Here the protagonist not only survives misfortune but outperforms expectations when circumstances permit. The saga of Winston Churchill and England in the Battle of Britain is wrapped up in this form, as is the story of England and the Spanish Armada. One's admiration is excited not because the protagonist gets a happy ending (as in the sentimental plot) or renounces a temporary weakness (as in the testing plot—see below) but because one did not really see his or her strength of character before. The administration of Harry Truman has been worked into this form also. It is not used much for the War of 1812, the Compromise of 1877, or other events characterized by discordant elements.

Plots of Character

In these plots, the character of a proposition undergoes a transformation, either in response to or in spite of changes of circumstance and perspective. The character plots involve the crucial element of choice, accompanied by action, which is less apparent in plots of thought. In the description of historical events, one can portray a proposition as experiencing a change of values in its internal relationships, so that its contrasts with other propositions, and its perspective on the past and future, are subsequently altered. This amounts to a change of character.

1. *The Maturation Plot.* Here a sympathetic character corrects misconceptions and weaknesses to achieve nobility through adverse circumstances. The happy ending is not just circumstantial but results from the

decision to change character. This form is very popular among serious novelists. It differs from the education plot (see below) in that a change of perception is accompanied by a decision to follow some other course of action.

In old high-school histories, the replacement of the Articles of Confederation by the U.S. Constitution was presented as an example of maturation. Accounts of the emergence of Parliament in the seventeenth century sometimes follow this form, as do biographies of William Wilberforce, the evangelical reformer. Frantz Fanon's *The Wretched of the Earth*[15] outlines a general maturing plot for colonial independence movements: the insurgents first learn to talk about their own culture instead of "home"; then get rid of their attachment to colonial forms of behavior and thought; and finally achieve a new cultural identity based on indigenous values. Using Fanon's outline, one could discover a maturing plot in the independence movements of India, Algeria, China, and many other former colonies.

2. *The Reform Plot.* An unlikeable protagonist is forced to give up his mask of nobility, as in a punitive plot, but is then redeemed by confession and reforms his behavior. Friedman's fictional example was *The Scarlet Letter*. DeGaulle's reform of French colonial policy after Algeria and Vietnam follows such a pattern, as does Emperor Hirohito's denial of his own divinity at the end of World War II. The abolition of the slave trade appears as a reform plot in accounts by British historians, although the fact that by 1807 England was the only country still transporting slaves from Africa lessens the impact of her change in character. The life of St. Paul is built on a reform plot.

3. *The Testing Plot.* In this form, a strong, sympathetic character wavers under the temptation of illicit gain and then chooses noble misfortune. Many martyrs fit this pattern: Thomas More, Bishop Cranmer under Mary Tudor, and, in this century, Martin Luther King, Jr. One can also see it in Elizabeth I's sorrowful renunciation of her love for Prince John of Austria in the interest of her kingdom. Perhaps Belgium's resistance to the German advance in World War II follows the form, though one would have to evidence a period of hesitation on the part of her leaders. Wellington, in the final stages of the Reform Bill agitation, tried to scuttle the Whigs by forming a cabinet that would put through a more conservative measure; but, seeing it was hopeless, he advised the king to recall Lord Grey, and prepared himself to accept the outcome. Propositions focused at higher levels of abstraction are difficult to imagine in a testing plot. But there are events in which a principle or an ideal is compromised during some phase of transformation, only to emerge strengthened in the final judgment. The enmity between Communists and Nationalists in China, which was temporarily suppressed during the common war against the Japanese, is a possible example.

4. The Degeneration Plot. Here a character who is initially strong and admirable suffers misfortune, gives up his goals, his strength, and his nobility, and becomes resigned or contemptible. More than just a disillusionment, this pattern goes on to encompass a change of character and thought. Benedict Arnold may be a candidate, though only from a certain perspective; in some accounts, the later career of Lloyd George is plotted as degeneration. Henry VIII is often cast in accounts with this form, as is the French Republic from 1934 to 1944. The House of Lords seemed to be working toward degeneration during most of the nineteenth century, just as many church hierarchies succumbed to secular pressures during the twentieth. Perhaps the career of Boniface VIII, which led to the Great Schism, should be understood in this form as well.

Plots of Thought or Perspective

In these plots, a dramatic change of feeling or judgment regarding the significance of the external situation takes place. The change usually implies both a new perspective on the past and new anticipation of the future. It does not necessarily lead to a change of character or to a change of circumstance. Instead, the true character of a person, or the truth about the past, is gradually or suddenly revealed.

Plots of perspective seem to work better at the higher levels of abstraction. The focus is on the maturation or degradation of some complex principle or perceptual field or ideal, and the feeling of faith, belief, or loyalty attached to them.

1. The Education Plot. A change of perspective for the better in conceptions, beliefs, attitudes: a stronger awareness of reality, or a more noble aim. This is similar to the plot of maturation but does not emphasize the change in character and behavior. The protagonist may move from a set of wrong ideas to a right set, or from naiveté toward relative sophistication. *Candide* is one example, though a bit jaundiced. The American experience of Watergate and its related scandals may one day be told as an education plot, a "coming of age" story. Such was the perspective of the positivists of the nineteenth century, and of idealists in almost any age, such as Hegel or Whitehead. In their accounts, the past is portrayed as a period of wrongheadedness or innocence, gradually progressing toward the enlightenment of the present. Werner Ohnsorge, in the work on Charlemagne discussed in Chapter 1, argued that the coronation and its associated problems opened the Frank's eyes to the wider reality of the Mediterranean world and led to a more sophisticated conception of the Empire as a Frankish-Christian power.

There is also the charming story of the Synod of Whitby in 663, when the flight of a sparrow through the great hall of the synod, as though in brief passage through life, led the assembly to join the Roman church instead of the Celtic. In a more realistic vein, one could mention the struggle of Charles Booth, Victorian businessman, who married into the liberal "cousinhood" of Trevelyans, Darwins, Macauleys, and other intellectuals. Booth was so challenged by his wife's circle that he suffered a nervous breakdown. After his recovery, he founded the science of social statistics, compiling the first great study of the London poor.

2. *The Revelation Plot.* When the change of perspective is dramatic and sudden, and the protagonist discovers his self-deception or the deception of others just before making a vital decision, we have a plot of revelation. The result is usually a feeling of relief. The transition from Neville Chamberlain to Winston Churchill prior to England's entry into the Second World War is often narrated with an emphasis on the failure of appeasement and the last-minute appreciation of Hitler's real intentions. In fiction, the revelation plot commonly concerns a prisoner, initially deceived as to his situation, who figures out where he actually is before he yields the information that would harm his side. The youth and reign of Queen Elizabeth I are replete with incidents of this kind. And there was a dramatic case of revelation in 1788, when George III went temporarily insane (displaying symptoms that are now viewed as evidence of a hereditary disease) and the government almost collapsed under the vicious infighting of politicians ranged for and against the regency of the Prince of Wales. Fortunately—or not—George recovered before he could be disqualified from the throne. Beyond these few examples, the revelation plot may have limited applicability to historical events. It is not likely that the internal constitution of an actual event would display a significant proposition persisting in an inappropriate set of contrasts through most of its phases of transformation, only to change dramatically in the final phase of judgment. That would amount to a revolution in the subjective aim of that event.

3. *The Affective Plot.* In this form, a character changes his feeling toward another character as a result of seeing him in a different and truer light. The result is pleasant and hopeful, or unpleasant and sad. This form seems more useful than the revelation plot, because it applies directly to the various changes of contrast displayed in symbolic transformation. Two propositions in apparent discord during the initial phases of an event may be reconciled later on, because of a shift of emphasis in one or the other, or because of their mutual involvement with a third. Or they can move from harmony to discord. For example, prior to the end of the Civil War the Southern slaves and their Northern liberators had a number of, shall we say, naive ideas about one another. During Reconstruction they saw each other in a new light, and changed their feelings. Similarly, the working classes in England saw the political-industrial system of the 1830s in a new light and developed new feelings as a result of their disappointments in the passage of

the Reform Bill. During that same time, on the individual level, the duke of Wellington approached Mrs. Fitzherbert on the delicate matter of a pension from the estate of the late George IV, whose mistress she was assumed to have been. Mrs. Fitzherbert, pilloried in the press for many years, showed Wellington the marriage certificate which, as a loyal but humiliated woman, she had never made public after George abandoned her for a Protestant princess. Wellington's feelings toward her were indeed changed.

4. *The Disillusionment Plot.* In this plot a sympathetic character gradually loses his or her initial faith, hope, or ideals in a trial or loss. He or she may die of a broken heart (as they used to say) but his or her character doesn't change, and the circumstances become almost irrelevant. *The Great Gatsby* is one fictional example. Woodrow Wilson at and after Versailles, and Warren Harding in his last months, are nonfiction counterparts. The experience of the younger generation in World War I is often narrated in this form. There is a kind of disillusionment also in some education plots, but in those the lost ideal is replaced by another, presumably more realistic one. In the true plot of disillusionment, the loss is complete, and despair takes the place of restored confidence. Both patterns, however, begin with a proposition that is out of touch with the actual past and relevant future, as perceived by the majority of other propositions. Were history causally determined, disillusionment would be impossible, because the creation of alternate propositions, and their perception via faith or hope or fear, would be precluded. In fact, the whole idea of a plot would be utter nonsense, not just in historical writing but in fiction as well.

The fourteen plot forms outlined above provide an initial perspective on the emergence of historical events. As I argued before, appreciation of the whole pattern must precede analysis of its elements, when the creative process is being dealt with. The various types of contrasts and phases of transformation illustrated during the emergence of an event cannot be assessed intelligibly until one has some idea of the overall subjective aim that guides them. As Friedman argues, "if we would examine the pertinence and efficacy of the parts and devices of a given plot, we must begin with a hypothesis as to *what* those things are relevant *to* and effective *for*."[16]

It may be said that I have borrowed another set of pigeonholes for the irrelevant game of classification that substitutes for "solid" empirical research and writing. On the contrary, I have sought only to reduce, through reasonable criticism, the irrelevance of most "empirical" work now done in the name of history. The scheme of plot forms adapted from Friedman is a heuristic device to force careful study and reflection on the temporal forms of events, which no other method seems to do.

There are some problems in using the scheme as it has been presented here. First, the examples given for each of the three categories of plot may be inappropriate, requiring amendment to be useful as illustrations. Such examples are as subject to reassessment as the experimental results and other data to which scientific concepts are applied in physics and chemistry. That is, after all, what a conceptual framework is for.

Second, the examples have not been extended into the realm of published narratives. There is not enough space in this book to even begin such a task, although it is a legitimate one and greatly needs doing. The writing of better historical accounts must be preceded by criticism of those already accepted as adequate, so that historians will know what to preserve as well as what to change. My own brief excursions into this area indicate that, from a literary standpoint, many historical narratives are a strange mixture of insight and awkwardness. But at least when analyzed via a framework of concepts based on creative process, they look far more intelligible than they do in a deductive-law system.

The plot forms outlined above are not answers to the question, "What happened?" They are simply guides to further inquiry. Also, they are not strictly objective labels, for they refer to complex combinations of form and feeling that give events their intensity in the historical process. This fact revives the question of interpretation encountered in Chapter 2: the historian has to distinguish between his own feeling about the event he explains and *its* feeling about itself and its constituent elements. One may find Mary Tudor tragic, because she had to live with the realization that her cherished hopes were misdirected and that she had failed in so many ways. But Mary's contemporaries, especially her victims, might have cast her as villainess in a plot of punishment or disillusionment. Again, this is not necessarily a weakness in the analytical scheme. To recognize that there are differences of feeling, and to have the means of identifying them, is a step forward in historical understanding.

There is another kind of trap in the scheme to which historians, as intellectuals, are susceptible. This is the use of one plot form to interpret all the others, bringing all events under a single umbrella. This tendency, also found in the analysis of Freudian symbols and Jungian archetypes,[17] is like the old Mesopotamian practice of having the conqueror's gods eat up or destroy the gods of the conquered cities and tribes. In other words, if one wants to outdo other historians, one can show that one's favorite plot form is fundamental to all the rest. Thus the testing plot can be seen as the controlling form, the tragic being a tangential example of a failed test, the sentimental merely reducing the phase where the hero "wavers" in his determination, and the education and maturation plots providing a series of tests wherein the protagonist's sense of reality is gradually strengthened. And so on. It is possible to bring all the plots under the rule of any one of them, because in any complex event they are all usually involved in some way. They are complementary forms of creative process. For example, in the 1066 conquest of England, Harold Godwinson plays out a tragic or pathetic role, having to realize the consequences of his errors of judgment in the midst of very difficult circumstances. Fortune seemed to play against him. At the same time, William of Normandy seems the hero of a basic action plot, which might be changed to a sentimental or admiration plot if one were on William's side.

The point is that since the elements and propositions and contrasts of an event are supposed to fit together into a more or less coherent pattern, the plot forms that express how that pattern emerged will necessarily fit together as well. and there will be as many plots as there are propositions undergoing transformation. So one's choice of plot form for a given event depends on what proposition one selects as the protagonist, or agent of most significant change, in the story. And it is certainly possible to choose one that fits an existing mold.

One way to guard against this trap is to look at the event as a whole rather than as an assembly of parts, and as a complex expression of value rather than as an object. In this way one can grasp the aesthetic significance of the various subplots and decide which is the primary plot form for the whole event. The procedure is similar to the search for elegance in scientific explanations: one wants to find the single form that sheds the most light on all the others. There will be a certain logic to this approach as well, but the relationship between logical and aesthetic patterns in emergence is too complicated to deal with here.

There are some plot forms more appropriate to the lower levels of abstraction, and some to the higher. Also, some may turn out to be more generally useful than others. These distinctions will emerge in the course of the historian's experience with the framework and should not be attempted prematurely. What is offered in this book is a guide for exploration and cooperation, not a set of absolute rules. The present framework, however, does give historians a systematic array of categories with which to classify and compare the temporal structures of events, the need for which was suggested by my discussion of scientific research in Chapter 4. The fourteen plot forms together with the seven levels of abstraction provide a taxonomy of ninety-eight categories of development, to which any event or narrative account could be assigned. A taxonomy is an indispensible reference for critical inquiry in any discipline. It allows researchers and their critics to sort out similarities and differences among various accounts of a given subject, and to maintain consistency of terms when discussing problems of explanation. In history, it would permit historians to key their individual narrative accounts more explicitly to a general scheme of investigation, and it would give philosophers a more comprehensive view of the historical enterprise.

If the taxonomy of historical events seems too elaborate, one only need compare it with others. The periodic chart of the atoms lists from 92 to 104 elements (depending on the inclusion of the ephemeral trans-uranium elements) and, like the taxonomy presented here, can predict and accommodate new discoveries. And the taxonomy developed for modern biology has labels to distinguish among 250,000 species of spiders alone. Next to these systems of classification, without which scientific progress would be chaotic, the one offered for history is undeniably modest.

The investigation of contrasts and propositions, phases and levels of transformation, simple and complex plot forms, is to be primarily based upon, and applied to, the critical evaluation of narrative explanations in history. It does offer the possibility of analyzing relatively invariant or normative relationships at the levels of abstractions presupposed by deductive-law models of explanation, but this aspect of inquiry is only a prerequisite to the other. The final purpose is not predictability, but appreciation of creative process as a response to the indeterminate conditions of the historical world. It is a recognition of the need to cope with tragedy— the realization of what is, in contrast to what might have been—and an appeal to hope, through the creative resolution of potential discord and disintegration. The analytical purpose is not thwarted; it is even advanced. But it is subordinated to the more comprehensive, humanistic function of historical explanation.

9. Metamorphosis

The relationships among actual occasions are as unfathomable in their variety of type as are those among eternal objects in the realm of abstraction. But there are fundamental types of each relationship, in terms of which the whole complex variety can find its description.

Alfred North Whitehead, *Science in the Modern World*

In previous chapters, the analytical scheme has been focused upon the relationship between a historical event and its antecedents. This relationship is genetic: the conditions of the past are inherited by some newly emerging event, which transforms them into elements of a definite pattern. The process of transformation is completed by the final phase of synoptic judgment, which establishes that event as a determinate matter of fact. In this guise, the event passes on to subsequent durations, to be included in the emerging constitutions of still other events.

Now it is necessary to explain what "passing on" means, and what aspects of events are inherited by subsequent occasions. Briefly, the argument is that events undergo a kind of metamorphosis. Their symbolic form and significance change as they are assimilated by events in future durations, even though their objective identity remains actual fact. They are perceived differently by different events.

It will not be possible to predict exactly how a particular event will undergo metamorphosis, or exactly in what manner it will appear in subsequent events. But the dynamics of the process, and the several types of metamorphosis, can be indicated, so that historical explanations become more systematic and adequate. For instance, one can indicate how the concepts of "period" and "trend" fit into the general critique of events and their narrative analogues. Also, it will be seen that any event undergoing metamorphosis becomes an antecedent to some other event; the future orientation of this chapter complements the backward-looking discussion of Chapters 6 and 7.

Whenever one looks at a historical event, one finds traces of past events in its constitution. Most of these, or the most obvious, stem from the conditions of the antecedent world, that is, from the state of affairs immediately preceding the event in question. But there are also traces of events from the

more distant past. Their appearance may be quite vivid, or it may be diffused and subtle. At one time they emerged as actual fact; now they are
undergoing further adventures, as perceived by their successors. An aspect
of the Catholic Emancipation movement in England illustrates the possible
adventures nicely. George IV, faced with widespread pressure to sign the
Emancipation Bill in 1829, pleaded that he must honor his father's conscientious objection to such a measure (on the grounds that the king was head of
the Church of England and Defender of the Faith). There was a fourfold
historical irony in this plea. In the first place, everyone agreed that the
conscience of George IV was negligible in comparison with his father's. The
son's life was one long example of dissipation. Second, George IV had had a
secret liaison with a Roman Catholic woman for over thirty years, although
he had abandoned her to marry a Protestant princess to ensure his succession
to the throne. Third, the "church" and the "faith" of which he was so
solicitous had undergone many changes of form and meaning since the titles
were invented. Henry VIII's church was not that of his son, nor of his two
daughters. Charles I interpreted the church one way, James II another.
George I was a Lutheran. In fact only George III, of all the rulers, seems to
have been a sincere advocate of the Church of England as he found it upon
his accession. The fourth and final irony of the case was that the title
"Defender of the Faith" had been bestowed upon Henry VIII by the pope, in
honor of Henry's erudite and vigorous defense of the Roman doctrine
against the Lutheran heresy, prior to 1529.

The past lives in the present, then, in a variety of ways. But it obviously
does not live on in its original guise of actual events; only symbolic elements
are assimilated and transformed by events as they perceive them. Yet it has
been traditional, in the historical sciences, to conceive of events as unchanging objects, or unchanging objective data. There is a Battle of Waterloo that remains essentially fixed for all time, with its definite causal
significance becoming the same for all subsequent events. If the Battle of
Waterloo is discovered as a factor in some future event, it is still considered
the same object, though changed in status. Alternately, one can trace its
effect upon the next event in a series, showing how the conditions laid
down initially carry through the whole set. The assumption is made that the
historical event fully determines the ways in which it influences the future.
To have a different influence than that inferred from its initial form, it
would have had to be a different event.

In the approach I have outlined, the adventures of events are more complex. The synoptic judgment that completes the internal development of an
event presents the world with three related decisions: a definite form and
structure; a complex feeling pervading the form; and a hierarchy of contrasting elements, representing potential propositions not realized in this
event but aesthetically and logically related to it. Each decision is final with

regard to its own antecedent world, and conditional with regard to its relevant future. It is "given" in the sense that its synoptic pattern cannot be altered and must be accounted for by future events. But it is "open" to interpretation from the perspective of any future percipient. Its form and feeling, assimilated in the mixed mode of symbolic reference, become compositional elements whose meaning will be finally determined by *that* percipient for itself. Thus, in contrast to the traditional view, the process approach allows an event to influence the future in many different ways, without invalidating its original character.

In traditional positivist models of explanation, it is hard to see the relation between continuity and change. There is an assumption of inertia, and the world is expected to continue on its determined course unless moved by some agent of change. But where the change comes from is a mystery. Obviously, it could not come from the antecedent world, for that was determined by *its* antecedents. Sometimes the mystery is avoided by assuming that the causal influence of the past is different for each subsequent event, because of the change of location. But this opens the door to perceptual relativity, which undermines the whole principle of determinism. One is left with a model that simply describes, in an abstract way, certain types of regularities. It is often very useful to do this. But one does not thereby explain anything.

In the approach presented here there are three features of events that, together, show how continuity and change are interrelated. First, the assumption is borrowed from physics that causal influence is impossible between contemporary events. The decision made by any event about its past, therefore, is made in relative ignorance of the decisions being made elsewhere in the same duration. Since each decision involves some degree of novelty, however small, the result is a variety of events that all share the same general past but make different judgments about that past. And the whole variety is presented to the future for its consideration. Thus there is ample reason for novelty and change in the historical process. In fact, this feature of the process, taken alone, would leave one wondering how continuity arises.

But individual events are not wholly divorced from the activity of their contemporaries. There is an indirect perception of the immediate environment, derived from the past, which has been discussed in Chapter 7 in connection with "symbolic reference." And there is a similar anticipation of the future environment inferred from the conditions of the antecedent world. Without the possibility of anticipation (as has been argued from the beginning of this book), history would simply not be intelligible. For example, the overthrow of Richard III by Henry VII in 1485 involves a good deal of change. But it only makes sense if the major conditions of the antecedent world could be expected to obtain for its contemporary duration and for its relevant future. England, it is assumed, will have the same general type of government, the same general population and geography, the same general interests to consider.

Thus the ignorance of other events in the same duration, which produces a measure of uncertainty and change, is offset by the continuity of history presupposed by every event in its perception of the past. Also, in its final synoptic judgment, every event conditions the future to adjust to its own expectations. Subsequent events do not often ignore such presuppositions and conditions, for they provide the measure of continuity that every system needs for its existence.

The third aspect of events that relates continuity to change is the presence of unrealized potential in their temporal constitution. Propositions that are not fully realized in the final form of an event are nevertheless thrown into relief and are available, indirectly, for incorporation in subsequent events. For example, the principle of universal suffrage was not embodied in the final version of the Reform Bill of 1832, although it was a subordinate element in some phases of transformation. But in subsequent events whose major focus was the English working class, the principle of universal suffrage became a significant element, relating to a variety of individuals, groups, and institutions.

Though unrealized propositions may influence the future, they are not an arbitrary or random set of alternatives to be used by any subsequent event. As outlined in Chapter 5, they are logically and aesthetically linked to the one pattern realized in a particular event. However dramatic their contrast to that pattern, they must be consistent with its antecedent world. They therefore offer limited alternatives for future development. At higher levels of abstraction especially, the number of elements that might instigate radical change, consistent with past conditions, is relatively small.

In a process approach to historical explanation, then, change is a function of continuity. Both stem from the creative, temporal nature of historical events. On the one hand, the past is filled with momentum and inertia; on the other hand, the past is incomplete and indeterminate regarding the future.

The final judgment of an event may be compared to the ending of a novel or drama. In pulp fiction, the ending tends to settle a small number of tensions without suggesting any new reflections on the past or additional visions of the future. The hero wins, or solves the problem, and will live happily ever after. Sometimes the hero explains the situation, showing the reader some minor detail that gave the clue to the whole, and sometimes the hero is apparently done in at the last moment, so that one has to buy the next book in the series to find out whether he lived. But all such stories leave the reader free from significant reflection, just as a deductive proof of inevitability does.

In serious fiction and drama, on the other hand, the resolution of the major conflicts of the plot provokes renewed reflection on previous phases of development, because what is finally realized is a selection and synthesis of the available propositions, and not always the most obvious ones at that. The resolution also, for the same reason, suggests a number of possible future developments, in which subordinate contrasts and unrealized elements of this ending might undergo further adventures. Plots of tragedy, maturity, education, and affection especially leave the reader at a new beginning.

When a historian follows some event through its adventures in later durations, he is not dealing with a fixed object fitted out with detachable, changeable properties. Rather, he is dealing with a complex of form and feeling that remains decisively what it became in its own time. However, the significance of this form and feeling in the constitution of some future event is not given. One has to wait and see what will happen. The historian who can convey the contrast between decisiveness regarding the past and openness regarding the future has a far better sense of historical explanation than one who merely shows that the past was "inevitable."

Examples of the subsequent adventures of events abound in accounts of the past. The Peace of Vienna, 1815, was consciously referred to over and over in the century following its settlement. Its provisions served sometimes as discordant elements, sometimes as concordant. They formed the background of political discussion in the Frankfort Assembly of 1848, the same year that Metternich, guardian of the peace in its more repressive aspects, was hounded out of Vienna. The provisions were negated by Bismarck's diplomacy and ripped apart by World War I. Yet, half a century after that war, the diplomatic strategy behind the Peace of Vienna was revived by an American statesman for use in the modern world of superpowers.[1]

Another example: in 1966 I was reconstructing the efforts of the West India Committee, a commercial representative for West Indian interests in London, to prevent the abolition of the British slave trade in the late eighteenth century. Everyone knows that there were such efforts, and that it took the abolitionists a long time to overcome them. Yet, one day officers of the Committee (which is still in existence) approached me to ask that the committee not be credited with any help in the research and that if possible the research not be published at all. The reason? In 1966 there were several nonwhite governments in the former British West India colonies, whose relations with the Committee were already strained. Revival of the subject of slavery at this time was, in the words of the Committee's director, "political dynamite."

There are more complex instances: the revival of aspects of the Roman Empire in the time of Charlemagne and then of Napoleon in the West or, later, by Moscow in the East; the inspiration of the American Revolution for Europe, Latin America, and Vietnam; the influence of classical architecture upon later schools of design. In 1919, the German National Assembly met at Weimar because, according to Koppel Pinson, the heritage of Prussian hegemony symbolized by Berlin was distasteful to the delegates; Frankfort, the home of the ill-fated National Assembly of 1848, was out of the question; and Weimar was the home of Goethe and Schiller, symbols of classical humanism. The final condition, that Weimar offered military security from the proletarian rioting in Berlin, is perhaps more precise but less significant. There were other cities with security forces, but none with the appropriate historical associations of Weimar.[2]

These examples indicate that the adventures of an event in the subsequent world take place symbolically and not literally. The actual event perishes; its form and feeling, woven together by symbolic reference, live on to condition the emergence of other events. It is easy and tempting to intellectualize such symbols, emphasizing their conceptual form and ignoring their emotional qualities. In this way, events become ideas, and history becomes the manifestation of ideals and principles amid the flux of corrupting material embodiments. Such was the interpretation of Hegel, of the Whig historians, and of modern idealists.

Now it is true that every event involves the articulation of some matrix of potentiality. Such a matrix, however, expresses more potential than can be articulated in that particular event. This discrepancy is clearest when one compares the highest and lowest levels of abstraction—in other words, when one compares the ideal with the individual behavior. But it also exists in less dramatic forms throughout the hierarchy of any event. What is decided at one level represents a choice among the alternatives permitted by the next highest level. For instance, the potential for parliamentary reform was not exhausted by passage of the Reform Bill of 1832. The contrast between what actually happened, and what might have happened or could happen, is a measure of the significance of that event. Thus, it is not ideas that drive history forward, nor is it customary behavior from which ideas arise, but rather the contrast between actuality and potentiality.

To summarize the argument thus far: an event in its final phase of synoptic judgment establishes concrete conditions to which subsequent events must conform. It thus becomes an objective datum in the world beyond itself. At the same time, the event in its symbolic form expresses a contrast or a pattern of contrasts between its own concrete actuality and relevant forms of potentiality. This aspect of events also passes on into subsequent occasions. Thus, the "fact" established by any event as a condition for the future presupposes the possibility of a wider application of the principles that inform it. There is therefore a continuity in history arising from the concrete conditions passed on from past to future, and from the logical and aesthetic relevance among actual and potential elements in any event. And there is change in history due to the inherent contrast between what happens and what could happen, together with the forms of novelty introduced during the emergent phases of other, contemporary events. Continuity and change do not stem from different roots; they are reciprocal functions of the genetic character of historical events. The metamorphosis of an event expresses the changes undergone in the process of its assimilation and transformation in subsequent durations. The symbolic form is interpreted anew, in relation to other elements, but always in conformity to the conditions established by its temporal constitution.

The coronation of Charlemagne illustrates this duality clearly. The objective conditions from which it emerged could not be changed by any of its participants. There had been a Roman Empire, whose ruler became semidivine within the context of a Christian community. The Empire had been divided for administrative purposes, and the Western portion had lost its cohesiveness under pressure from barbarian incursions. The Franks had conquered most of the West and, having converted to Christianity, entered into close relations with the papacy at Rome. Meanwhile, the Eastern portion of the Empire had continued the old traditions.

In A.D. 800 there were three major nuclei for assimilating these conditions into the constitution of a new event. Each nucleus was fairly accurate in its perception of the objective situation. The differences between them related to the ways they perceived the symbolic significance of past events. For Charlemagne and the Franks, the contrast between the traditional authority of the Roman church under the old emperors, and the growing isolation and weakness of the pope in the more recent Empire, bespoke a need for resolute action on their part. For the pope, the important contrast was between the relative disunity of the Church and the potential for a united Christian empire, spiritually governed from Rome, that could be discerned in the records of the past. And for the Byzantine court, what mattered was the retention or reestablishment of the Roman Christian imperium which, even during the centuries of turmoil in the West, remained a potential configuration infused with great energy.

Each of these viewpoints represents a contrast between what actually happened, what might have happened, and what could happen. The coronation of Charlemagne was consistent with the objective content of all three propositions; but the symbolic content, which had undergone metamorphosis through countless intermediate events, emerged as an array of highly charged contrasts. One cannot say that the idea of imperial or Christian Rome was the "driving force" behind this event, any more than were the objective conditions of disunity, competition, and decay. The contrast between them is what counts.

Thus far, metamorphosis has been described in the simple case of one event appearing as an element in the constitution of another. But the example of Charlemagne's coronation indicates a more complex arrangement, in which one past event is perceived from many later perspectives, becoming transformed in many different ways. For instance, the balance of authority between pope and emperor, a feature of many occasions prior to the eighth century, was assimilated as an element in the coronation of Charlemagne. But in the tentative proposition for that event focused on the Frankish king, the balance of authority was perceived one way. In the proposition focused on the pope it meant something else. And in the "Byzantine" proposition(s) it had still other meanings. Moreover, the coronation was not the only event at that time to incorporate the historical balance between pope and emperor as a symbolic element. There must have been dozens of other events perceiving the same data from their own perspectives. As each perception is transformed into a proposition, and then realized in the final form of some actual occasion, the original contrast between papal and imperial authority must undergo kaleidoscopic elaboration. Any subsequent event will, therefore, assimilate that contrast in a great variety of forms and will have to recombine those forms to establish its own particular feeling for its meaning.

In Chapter 6, it was explained that events do not assimilate data from the distant past except through the mediation of their antecedents. From the perspective of an emerging event, the occasions in its antecedent world are roughly contemporary with each other: they belong to the same temporal duration. But from the antecedents' own perspectives, they are not exactly contemporary. They enter into one another's constitutions by the usual processes, because some of them are in the "past" of others. For example, the passage of Catholic Emancipation, and the death of the duke of York, lie in the antecedent world of the Reform Bill. But the duke's death is also antecedent to Catholic Emancipation, which in turn took place before the revolutionary disturbances in France. In the analysis of an antecedent world presented in Chapter 6, these events were construed to have contemporary durations. But even then it was remarked that, in actuality, their temporal relationship was polychronic. Thus, some of them will contain perceptions of the others, perceptions that will be offered for assimilation by the Reform Bill event. The latter will thus receive direct impressions from each of its antecedents, plus indirect impressions of some of them, through others. The final result is that an event such as the Reform Bill passage must, in order to understand and evaluate its past, integrate a multitude of impressions, each one giving one aspect of the antecedent world. Antecedents do not enter into new events as simple objects; the more distant the antecedent, the more complex its assimilation will be.

An analogy with organic systems is again appropriate. Sense perceptions traveling through the human neurological network do not describe a straight path between origin and receptor—nor is the impression unified all through the process. Instead, there are a number of feedback loops, enhancers and inhibitors, that together build up a complex field of neurological impressions. By the time the "datum" reaches its goal, it has already become enmeshed in a dynamic pattern of communication, which is rightly described as a "field" rather than as a sequence. Whitehead himself used the network-path of sense impressions to illustrate the creative process in actual events.[3] He thus tried to unite the principles of physiology, epistemology, and metaphysics. Subsequent research in all these fields has tended to confirm the validity of his approach.

The analysis of complex patterns of development is required for both the symbolic transformation of elements in the internal constitution of an event and the metamorphosis of that event in the subsequent external world. In this chapter, only the latter pattern is considered.

The ramification, or "branching out," of a particular event via its inclusion in various later ones may be illustrated by accounts of the coming of World War I. Bismarck's style of diplomacy in the unification of Germany established concrete conditions for subsequent events, and these conditions were interpreted differently by statesmen in the various capitals of Europe. In that situation, the responses of each nation followed a path of development that intersected the paths of other nations, building up contrasts of increasing intensity, complexity, and discord that exploded in 1914.

Another example of metamorphosis that culminated in 1914 was the British guarantee of Belgian neutrality. Proclaimed in 1831 after the Belgians revolted from Holland, and confirmed in 1839, Belgian neutrality was a continuation of policy long followed by the British (and incorporated into the Vienna settlement of 1815) of keeping that vital military and commercial area out of the hands of any one continental power, especially France.[4] In itself, the guarantee was a reintegration of various aspects of past incidents as perceived by the several European powers.

Belgian neutrality played a part in British and German opposition to a proposed Belgian-French tariff union during the 1850s.[5] But it gained more significance as an element in the decision of Kaiser Wilhelm and his generals to invade France through Belgian territory, following their revision of the Schlieffen plan that had earlier incorporated the idea. It was an element in France's decision to concentrate its army near Lorraine, leaving the Belgian frontier relatively open, and in Britain's delayed decision to declare war on Germany. Each percipient assimilated the Treaty of Neutrality from the past in a different way, and each made a judgment about the others' perceptions. There may have been no error in their perception of the concrete conditions established in 1839, but their judgment about the symbolic contrast between actuality and potentiality, derived from those conditions, was open to error.

The Germans seriously underestimated the determination of the British to defend Belgium, just as the French overestimated the alacrity with which Britain would act. If one asks what the status of the guarantee of Belgian neutrality was in the period immediately antecedent to 1914, one won't get a simple answer. It is as if the guarantee had become a set of colored fragments at the end of a kaleidoscope: when the instrument was turned, they formed countless patterns of contrasting value, all different, but all consistent with the original data.

Full analysis of metamorphic development thus involves the linear changes undergone by an event, as it is incorporated into a series of later events. And it involves the diffusion of its symbolic potential through the network of events in a sequence of durations. Obviously, analytical comprehension must give way to some kind of selection, and there are three ways to do this. First, the historian can simply follow the metamorphosis through the length and breadth of its adventures until its appearance as an element in other events can no longer be ascertained. This is the most general type of analysis, answering the question, "What influence did this event have in its relevant future?" The historian may conduct such an analysis to determine the definition and significant elements of an event prior to its retrodictive explanation, as suggested in Chapter 5.

Second, the metamorphosis may be analyzed from the perspective of the antecedent world of a given future event. The question then is, "What is the status of the formative event in this antecedent world?" One wants to know the array of conditions, stemming from the formative event, that will be available for assimilation by the new events emerging from this antecedent world. This type of analysis may skip over intermediate durations in order to describe the variety of forms appearing in the later one. For example, most historians would not bother to describe what happened to the Treaty of Belgian Neutrality in every year between 1839 and 1914; such descriptions are not necessary for an adequate explanation of the treaty's multiple appearances in the pre-1914 duration.

The third method of selection is that some aspect of an event—its primary configuration, a primary contrast, or its plot form—may be considered as it appears in a sequence of select future occasions. This is the analysis of a trend. A trend is an abstraction from the whole metamorphic pattern; the historian abstracts in order to explain the increasing intensity of a particular contrast or proposition. As the intensity becomes greater, the ability of the proposition or contrast to serve as a creative nucleus for new events broadens, and its significance in relation to other elements increases. The twentieth-century trend toward automobiles in place of mass transit in America illustrates all of the above features.

Now, these same aspects of events may be considered as they are diffused through a particular duration, without the temporal dimension stressed in the previous approaches. Usually the duration is longer than that of an "antecedent world," because the perspective from which it is defined is broader. This results in the analysis of a period. Most historical narratives swing back and forth between trend and period approaches, suggesting (but not fulfilling) a more comprehensive analytical scheme. It should be the task of historical analysis to elucidate such schemes and to either justify or amend their application to narrative accounts. The full metamorphic analysis of an event is admittedly a formidable challenge. On the one hand it is an extension of the analysis of a single event, and on the other it is an extension of the analysis of an antecedent world. Thus it requires a thoroughness and a talent for painstaking clarification that reasonable historians may not care to claim. Yet it is a necessary prerequisite to the reestablishment of narrative as a valid form of historical explanation.

Fortunately, the analytical scheme presented here is based upon the incredible body of research already published by historians. There are innumerable studies of trends and periods, and descriptions of "the state of Europe" or "the economic situation" in specific durations. The development of an analytical scheme begins with the organization and critical appraisal of these efforts, not with a whole new edifice of raw information. The compatibility of the scheme with previous approaches, and the meaning of some of its concepts, may be illustrated by some other examples of trends and periods.

A trend is a temporal pattern of appearance, in a sequence of events, of a selected proposition, contrast, or plot form. The subject undergoes change during its transition from one event to the next and is reconstituted in new patterns of relationship from one duration to another. Usually a trend refers to an increase in comprehensiveness and intensity, but it could also describe a decrease in both features or a reciprocal change. Also, it is common to contrast an increase in one subject with a decrease in another: automobiles displace horses, decreasing productivity is associated with increasing inflation.

A trend may also refer to the adventures of a single type of element at any level of abstraction. For example, Bolingbroke's attitude toward Spain during the 1620s changed from intense affinity to equally intense dislike. Or one can trace the sequence of changes in the attitudes of W. E. Gladstone, whose maiden speech in 1833 was a passionate defense of Caribbean slave owners, but who ended his career as a reformer too progressive for many of his Liberal allies. These are trends concerning elements at the individual level, although they might be studied at the level of complex concepts as well.

Trends concerning groups have been widely studied, both in history and in other social sciences. The social and political evolution of the Mormons, the Bolsheviks, and the early Christians are familiar examples. At the institutional level, numerous examples follow a common pattern of change from ideals of external service toward policies of self-service and consolidation. But one might also describe the development of committee organization in Parliament during the early seventeenth century, or the army reforms in many countries during the nineteenth century, as a sequence of related changes concerning institutional elements.

The adventures of ideas have already been discussed with reference to idealist historians. Above that level, there are perceptual fields that undergo alternations, not only internally (as with physics under Newton and Einstein) but in relation to other fields as well (such as the growing prominence of economics during the last two centuries). The important thing to remember when studying such trends is that the primary element is not the only part of a proposition undergoing change. Proper analysis of the trend requires some attention to the other levels of abstraction as well.

The historian may also pick out a contrast, or type of contrast, to follow its adventures in a sequence of events. The rivalry between Gladstone and Disraeli during the reign of Victoria is a favorite subject. It could be analyzed in terms of particular contrasts between the two, as in their manner of addressing the queen or in their attitudes toward poverty. Another illustration is the contrast between church and state in medieval Europe, or the relative status and role of each sex during any century. When the historian studies a trend involving contrasts like these, he is not so interested in the whole pattern of elements on all levels of abstraction in a single proposition, as he is in the changing relation between two or three elements at the same level of abstraction, belonging to separate propositions. One can compare the two approaches by looking at the unification of Italy in the nineteenth century.[6] There was a primary proposition focused on the Kingdom of Piedmont-Sardinia, which came to include Count Camillo di Cavour as its chief minister. Early in the century this kingdom became the object of dreams for a united Italy. Its soldiers fought against the Austrians in 1848 and again in 1859 and 1866. It tended to espouse principles of constitutional liberalism and was economically and technologically progressive in relation to the other Italian states. One can follow the adventures of this set of elements from its inception as a vague "proposition" in the post-Napoleonic era, through the frustrations of 1848 and 1859, to its final realization in the Kingdom of Italy proclaimed in 1861 and completed in 1870. By following this one configuration, one can see how its character and status changed in different durations. It gives a consistent "point of view" and allows identification of a plot form for the extended pattern of development.

The "Piedmont and Cavour" configuration may be contrasted with another focused on Joseph Mazzini, the idealistic nationalist writer prominent earlier in the century, or with yet another focused on Giuseppe Garibaldi, the soldier-adventurer. By tracing the development of this contrast, one can get a better sense of the shifting balance of forces and of the meaning of terms such as "nation," "liberty," and "constitution" common to all three configurations. For example, Mazzini's writings stirred up a great deal of nationalist fervor, but the man himself was suspect among Italians who favored a constitutional monarchy. Mazzini's republicanism was echoed by Garibaldi, who also showed that organized military power was more effective than the pen. Finally, Cavour used "Realpolitik" to bring about a united Italian kingdom, even gaining Garibaldi's reluctant acquiescence. These are three different styles, characterizing three different propositions for the unification of Italy. The actual historical unification is explained as the interaction between them.

The point of this example is that one can isolate a single proposition, or a contrast between several propositions, to gain different kinds of information and understanding. Both kinds are legitimate abstractions from the whole web of metamorphosis. However, neither kind can stand in isolation from the other. Following a single proposition through its metamorphosis would be meaningless unless, along the way, it was brought into contrast with others. And the adventures of a particular contrast can't be adequately described without reference to the propositions involved with it. In analyzing a trend, the historian may emphasize one or the other aspect of events, but both are required for a proper explanation.

There is a third type of trend, less commonly analyzed by historians, that involves a temporal pattern or plot form common to a sequence of events. Certain episodes, such as the French Revolution of 1789–92, the Crusades, the conversions of St. Paul and St. Augustine, or Napoleon's retreat from Russia in 1812 have plot forms that seem to remain as paradigms for future generations, showing what that kind of event looks like. Consequently, subsequent events illustrating similar elements, contrasts, or propositions are likely to be perceived as repetitions of the same pattern or plot. Moreover, the percipients expect the pattern to repeat itself, and they tend to direct their behavior accordingly. The original event thus assumes archetypal proportions and generates a self-fulfilling prophecy. One has only to look at remarks made by participants and observers in the French revolutions of 1830, 1848, and 1870 to realize how much they depended upon the revolution of 1789 for their understanding of what happened in their own time.

The archetypal function of certain events depends upon the historical consciousness of humans. Other organisms apparently do not experience events this way. Though they may respond to stimuli in predictable ways, they are not conscious of previous events, or they respond to them as symbols of potentially recurrent patterns.[7] Human awareness of history accounts for the fact that the archetype, like an ideal form with pure potentiality, is not repeated exactly in any subsequent occasion. Perceiving the archetypal character of an emerging event means integrating the perceived archetype with a new and different set of propositions. The result is a type of metamorphosis which, given enough instances, one can analyze as a trend.

It was shown in Chapter 8 how plot forms enter into the construction and analysis of historical narratives. If these forms reach archetypal proportions, the narrative account may do so too. The question then is, has the writer of the narrative constructed a valid analogue to the event being explained? Is there empirical evidence that the participants in that event were conscious of some historical archetype, or have the proportions of the plot been exaggerated by later developments?

That such questions are important was demonstrated by Donald R. Kelley in his discussion of the massacre of St. Bartholomew's Day.[8] The French Protestants who were killed during the autumn of 1572 were, according to Kelley, conscious of the emerging pattern of events as a repetition of previous incidents, stylized as "massacre," in which the proper Protestant role was that of "martyr." Their preparation for and willingness to play that role helped bring about the very drama they expected, and the survivors' perception of what happened was immediately cast in the preconceived mold of "massacre," which colored many subsequent historical accounts. The problem of explaining this situation was vividly described by Kelley in his opening paragraph:

> How, from a distance of four hundred years, can we obtain a clear view of the Massacre of St. Bartholomew? The refractory powers of time always present difficulties, but in this case our vision is further distorted by a screen of false and conflicting evidence and by an endless stream of partisan debate. Perhaps the answer is that we should discard altogether the idea of describing some objective set of circumstances independent of ideological presuppositions and the passions aroused in witnesses and interpreters. Perhaps we should try rather to restore the event to its various contexts, conceptual as well as historical, and from a point of view that accommodates political and religious consciousness as well as social reality, that recognizes the mythical as well as the historical dimension. For it is upon some such symbolic level that the historical significance of events is to be found.[9]

Kelley's argument that separate points of view might be more enlightening than the traditional omniscience of the historian is similar to the argument, in Chapter 5, that a story told from the perspective of a particular participant might reveal more about the event than a general overview. And Kelley seems to be pointing toward a type of account in which contrasts between complex propositions provide the main focus of study. Each witness and context he mentioned signified a proposition, that is, a judgment about the form and significance of the past, energized by an anticipation of the future. Because the propositions were so discordant, subsequent interpretations of the event were bound to vary widely. Kelley sums it up as an archetypal occurrence that transcended its historical context—transcended it not only in the direction of the future (by endless debates over premeditation, guilt, and consequences) but also in the direction of the past (by seeming to symbolize, summarize, and confirm long-standing fears and anticipations and indeed to repeat earlier misfortunes on a grander scale). It was, in other words, an almost generic human experience that came as no surprise in the event, that followed a familiar pattern in its course, and that would be relived in various ways afterwards.[10]

The metamorphosis of plot forms has been discussed in some detail because the two other types of trends are more familiar to historians. All three types can be applied to advantage in explanatory narratives and in critical analyses, if care is taken to inform the readers of their proper function within a deliberate pattern of historical inquiry. The same general rule holds for the analysis of periods, which require a different kind of abstraction from the metamorphic pattern.

In historical narrative, the temporal flow of events has to be interrupted from time to time by consideration of related elements in a particular duration. For instance, the development of nationalist sentiment among German revolutionaires in 1848 is often accompanied by descriptions of contemporary matters in France and in the Hapsburg lands. To keep the story line from disintegrating, a historian often incorporates such related elements into a general description of the period out of which, or within which, the trend emerged. A period may be defined as a duration in which a given element, contrast, or proposition assumes a primary role, becoming the focus of a significant number of actual events. Its analysis requires a different approach than that used for trends: instead of isolating a sequence in which a stated element is illustrated, one must describe a set of roughly contemporary events in which the element appears.

The period is not a static concept, however. Within its duration, some events are bound to be antecedents of others, and there will be some temporal change no matter how abstract the level of inquiry. This fact is illustrated in historical accounts by strands of narrative woven into the more spatialized description of a period. For instance, a historian might describe the eighteenth-century Enlightenment by condensing its many developments into categories such as "belief in natural law" or "admiration for the noble savage." Within this scheme, however, the historian would insert short narrative accounts showing how each category emerged—that is, how it reached the scope and intensity it needed to become a significant element in the stated duration, or a significant focus for subsequent events.

A period is not, therefore, just a cross section of history devoid of temporal dimensions. Like an "antecedent world," it is a quantum of temporal activity with a given duration. Unlike antecedent worlds, however, periods are not usually formed from the perspective of any particular event. Instead, their internal relationships are treated as expressions of some intrinsic principle of order.

The concept of "period," with its genetic undertones, may be one of the few concepts historians can claim as their own. According to Trygve Tholfsen, other disciplines describe trends, states of the world, and orderly patterns of data, but none combines the spatial and temporal qualities of the historical period.[11] The closest relative of the concept of "period" might be the concept of "culture" developed by anthropologists. Each element in a culture (like elements in a period) is functional in terms of the whole complex, even though it may contrast with other elements in a variety of ways. Some anthropologists assume that cultures tend toward harmonious equilibrium of their several functions, while others assume a constant tendency toward disequilibrium. The argument between the two groups is like the argument between genetic and analytic critics of historical explanation: it is an endless argument because it begins with an arbitrary dissociation of first principles, a false dichotomy. If one assumed that each of the functional elements of a culture aimed at a general equilibrium, but inevitably from its own singular perspective, then frequent disequilibrium would be the natural outcome to expect. This becomes clear when one turns from short-term examinations of particular tribes and villages to long-term studies of historical periods. There, one can see both the harmonious relationships among a great many elements at different levels of abstraction, and also the metamorphic change in those relationships over the duration of the period. Depending upon the level of abstraction used for analysis, there would be periods of relative change and periods of relative equilibrium. But there are no periods exclusively one or the other. It may be, as Tholfsen says, that the period concept reflects the historization of the concept of culture,[12] but historians seem to have developed a more sophisticated (if still intuitive) view of the relationship between periods and trends, between time and space, than anthropologists have yet done. The approach to explanation outlined here should benefit both groups.

The complete analysis of a historical period requires (1) identifying its fundamental principles of order, which may be some set of pure potentials, perceptual fields, or complex principles, and (2) considering the variety of ways in which this set is articulated in the actual events of the period. Most analytical studies proceed inductively from (2) to (1), although they are written out in the reverse order. In developing his account of medieval society, for example, Marc Bloch arrived at a general definition of "feudalism" by immersing himself in the records of actual events.[13] In this way he could see when the major elements and contrasts became significant, and when they declined. He could mark the boundaries of the period, and sketch in the major trends, to form a kind of plot. Then the full meaning of feudalism, in terms of its articulation in actual events, could be understood more precisely. Bloch's narrative account of feudal society is introduced by an analytical "bracketing" of the major elements as terms in a general definition. The story of their articulation in actual events follows as illustrative material. In other narratives, of course, the bracketing may be omitted, and the reader left on his own to proceed from events to principles of order.

The elements or contrasts governing the definition of a period may themselves change over time. As I argued previously, the picture of an abstract ideal as the unchanging agent of change is a distortion of actual historical experience. By rigorous abstraction, one could delineate a small set of elements that informed all relevant events in a given period. But the explanatory value of that set is correspondingly negligible. Few historians would think themselves sufficiently enlightened if they were told that a particular pattern of behavior was, simply, "medieval" or "baroque." In most period studies, there is recognition that the general labels must be qualified as the period advances. Thus, there are studies of the "early," "middle," and "late" or "high" Renaissance; the "later" Roman Empire, the "infancy" of the Age of Steam, and so on.

One major difficulty in delimiting a period is to find the line between minor variations in its primary elements and outright anomalies. Diderot looks like a safe candidate for inclusion in the Enlightenment, but what about Maria Teresa or Rousseau? Does one include anyone or anything displaying elements of the major proposition or contrast, even though their other features be quite at odds with them? Historians overcome with admiration for their subjects have done this, of course, with predictable results.

The most common way to deal with this problem is to acknowledge at the outset that the period in question is not monolithic. It contains contrasts between its primary and subordinate elements. Such contrasts may be concordant (the notion of the "noble savage" and that of "civilized" man attaining progress through rational thought) or they may be discordant (Methodist "enthusiasm" versus "cool reason"). By using contrasts instead of isolated elements as the basis for analysis, one can avoid the tendency to stretch one label to cover everything in the period. For example, if Rousseau is too romantic for one's taste, one can use him as an illustration of the contrast between romantic and rationalist tendencies in the eighteenth-century period.

It may seem that the notion of "contrasts" has been overworked in this book. It was used in analyzing the internal constitution of an event and in explaining how one event becomes a symbolic element for others. There have been examples of contrasts obtaining at all levels of abstraction. And there is good reason for such emphasis. Previous theories of explanation have tried to objectify events, and to reduce the relationships between them to a matter of causal regularity, logically abstracted from the actual flux of interaction experienced historically. It was the aim of Whitehead's metaphysical work to correct this distortion, on the basis of new discoveries in science which overturned Newtonian views. By adopting the subjectivist bias of modern science and philosophy, Whitehead made it possible to investigate the noncausal relationships that characterize actual events. He grouped relationships into a general category of contrasts, because in that way he could talk about events without getting trapped in the old cause-effect approach. This work has highlighted contrasts for the same reason. The Newtonian attitude toward explanation so pervades the ordinary language of historians that only a frontal assault can begin to change it. An acute awareness of noncausal contrasts among historical events is the primary prerequisite for bringing historical theory into line with scientific theory and making it consistent with the dynamics of narrative explanation.

The concept of metamorphosis, and the guides to its analysis presented in this chapter, complete the basic approach to historical explanation derived from Whitehead's work and related research in the arts and sciences. This approach is based on the compatibility, even the mutual necessity, of analytic and genetic (narrative) modes of explanation. Because it is evident that the traditional approaches cannot bring about this integrative goal, a great many changes have been suggested, based on a fundamental shift in the perception of reality. Also, the examples of past events and published accounts used to illustrate parts of the theory have suggested the need for critical reappraisals of much previous work. Obviously, I cannot ask acceptance of the explanatory scheme without showing more concretely what needs to be done, and what can be done, as a consequence of that acceptance.

10. Analytical and
Narrative Explanation

It is quite possible . . . for fundamental conceptual revolutions in historical thought to occur without being preceded or accompanied by fundamental changes in the modes of historiographical production.

Haskell Fain, *Between Philosophy and History*

In various sections of this book I have alluded to the dissension and disarray characterizing the present state of historical studies. Historians, mindful of neopositivist criticism, have been using the vocabulary of cause-effect determinism as though they were generating lawlike hypotheses from the data presented in raw narrative. Analytical critics rightly chide historians for the logical frailty of these attempts. Meanwhile, advocates of the genetic approach rightly deplore the loss of coherence in narrative accounts that results from the interjection of logical analysis.

The main theme of this book is that both sets of critics have overlooked the dual nature of historical events and historical understanding that is reflected in narrative. The "self-explanatory" character of narrative lies in its ability to evoke imaginative reconstructions of past experience. This evocation has as its purposes the enrichment of the present, through integration with forms of experience based on other conditions and assumptions than one's own; the corollary critique of present-mindedness based on an increased sense of perspective; and the enhancement of one's appreciation for imperfect 'achievement, that is, the contrast between actual and potential that inspires feelings of hope and remorse and thus increases one's ability to cope with the inevitable indeterminateness of the historical world. These purposes have informed historical writing at least since Herodotus's day. The modern reformers of history have lost a lot of credibility by ignoring them.

I have also argued that the effectiveness of the narrative form lies in its ability to evoke in the reader's mind a cumulative sequence of configurations and contrasts representing potential patterns of development. These configurations and contrasts, while looking forward to realization, also serve as tentative reflections upon the past. The plot of a narrative is the complete sequence of configurational changes, through which the initial elements bequeathed by the antecedent world are brought into a single determinate pattern. I indicated earlier that these aspects of narrative were not merely subjective, "literary" notions. Compositional elements, the propositions of which they are members, and contrasts between propositions are all amenable to logical analysis and clarification. Their internal relationships may be clarified in terms of levels of abstraction and types of transformation, inferred from what actually happened. Their external relationships to elements and contrasts of the antecedent and subsequent environments (and indirectly their relationships with their contemporaries) may also be analyzed, in terms of regularity or probability.

The dual nature of explanatory narrative invites reciprocity between analytical and narrative historians. If history is to become a mature discipline, analysis must proceed with the aim of elucidating and refining the problems of explanatory narrative, while narrative must be based on the considered judgments of critical analysis. Without a model that provides terms for analyzing the temporal dynamics of narrative, reciprocity is all but impossible.

Thomas Kuhn points out in *The Structure of Scientific Revolutions* (1970) that disciplines with long-established, coherent bodies of theory rarely discuss theoretical problems in published reports. Publication of research usually takes the form of articles rather than books, or more recently of "notices" and "letters" more than articles. In many social sciences, on the other hand, there are more books, and they more often begin with a discussion of relevant theory and methodology. This, says Kuhn, is due to the relative immaturity of the latter disciplines. In history, of course, very few books and articles include sections on theory or methodology, but this is because of the discipline's backwardness, not its maturity. The theoretical issues are left to historiographical manuals and to philosophers.

I hope that, if the approach to explanation outlined in this book is found useful, more and more historians will preface their narrative accounts with explanations of their theoretical and methodological presuppositions. Also, philosophers of history will relate their analytical arguments more directly to actual examples of historical writing. In this way, communication can increase within a framework that grows gradually more intelligible to both sides.

Two types of historical criticism have been drawn from the model of events. One type is the logical analysis of abstract elements and their patterned relationships. The other is the criticism of narrative "literary" devices: plot, point of view, and types of dynamic contrasts. Probably the latter type should be undertaken before the former. That is, it is necessary to draw from the vast body of established historical writing a systematic survey of the plot forms, symbolic contrasts, and other devices commonly employed by historians. These, then, would provide material for logical analysis.

The proposed approach may be illustrated in two ways, using a concrete historical event as an example. First, the plot forms of the event can be identified by comparing different accounts of it. This composition is done first because it provides a great deal of other material for later reference. Second, the internal and external relationships of the event can be outlined, beginning with the question of its proper time-limits or duration. As mentioned before, such an outline will of necessity include some narrative, in order to show the scope and intensity of the elements in the relationship.

The event selected for illustration here is the abolition of the slave trade, by act of Parliament, in England in 1807. This event is useful because it has been extensively researched, because there are different accounts of its emergence, and because I am familiar with it. As with other examples in this book, no attempt is made to break new research ground to to provide a new interpretation of the facts. Space does not permit a full-blown illustration of the explanatory method, so what follows is admittedly sketchy and tentative.

In accounts of the abolition of the British slave trade there are three general plot forms. One is a sympathetic plot: the abolitionists are described as a hardy band of enlightened enthusiasts whose moral superiority gradually wins out over an array of reactionary, parochial interests. Combined with this are two subplots: a punitive plot concerning the West Indian planter aristocracy and an education plot concerning the gradual enlightenment of the English people and their representatives in Parliament.[1]

A second form, favored by Marxist-oriented historians, is a rather cynical action plot, supported by the story of degeneration among the planters of the West Indies. In these accounts, the growth of British industry makes slavery obsolete, and abolition is merely an expression of bourgeois self-righteousness in the face of economic necessity.[2]

The third plot form, which might be labelled the pathetic, sees abolition as the outcome of circumstances that broke the defenses of the West Indians and brought them little by little toward surrender. In this plot, filled with irony, the accommodation or compromise that might have secured abolition much earlier than it actually occurred is finally achieved by seasoned politicians skillfully maneuvering legislation through Parliament during a brief period of helpful circumstances, while abolitionists and slave-owners both take back seats.[3] Unlike the sympathetic or punitive plots, the pathetic does not consider the winners to be better than the losers: the focus is at the institutional level, where moral questions give way to functional ones.

Each of the plot forms emphasizes different contrasts between the primary elements of the event. To adherents of the sympathetic plot, the abolitionist proposition shows moral feelings, intensity, articulation, and anticipation of future developments far superior to those of the West Indian proposition. The contrast develops from discordant disparity in favor of the latter proposition, to an equally discordant disparity in favor of the former one.

The Marxist action plot concerns a more complex contrast between a developing capitalist-imperialist proposition on the one hand, the aristocratic proposition represented by the agricultural West Indians and their leisure-class abolitionist opponents on the other. Neither of the contenders realized the true nature and strength of the economic forces in their time. One might point to the antiabolitionist propagandists who criticized William Wilberforce for crying over Africans while neglecting the wretched factory workers in his own constituency, or to the belated and generally futile attempts to mechanize the production of sugar in the West Indies. But these are mere fragments of the larger movement from land-based to machine-based social patterns.

The pathetic plot emphasizes the discordant contrast between the planters and abolitionists but assigns no inherent moral superiority to the latter. Their discord is itself contrasted with the view of many politicians who, taking a more comprehensive look at Britain's economic, political, and military situation, tried throughout the campaign to arrange a compromise measure for gradual abolition. It was the change of circumstances accompanying war after 1800 that, in this view, enabled the politicians to overcome the discord that had frustrated their efforts for so long. On another level, the pathetic plot emphasizes the group and institutional contrasts of the event: the conflict between West Indian interests and those of the Empire as a whole; the difference between legal relations in England and legal relations between planters and slaves in the Caribbean; and the growing dissension between West Indian planters and the English merchants who financed them and brought them slaves.

Each of the plot forms with its relevant patterns of contrasts is drawn from a different point of view and emphasizes a different level of abstraction. The sympathetic plot focuses on individuals and their relevant groups: Wilberforce and his Clapham sect, the West Indians in Parliament, William Pitt the Younger, Charles James Fox. It thus reflects the point of view of the abolitionists themselves, who were motivated by personal evangelical feelings to redress the wrongs done to other individuals. The action plot focuses more on the shift of perceptual fields and the set of pure potentials governing historical epochs. The "mode of production" approach may appear materialist in theory, but in practice it uses terms of high abstraction to describe the forces of change. In the action plot, institutions, groups, and individuals are merely symbols of the more general transition to a new order. Finally, the pathetic plot tends to look at relations among institutions and large groups, with individuals illustrating their special features and complex principles influencing their behavior. Abolition then appears as the result of a fortuitous combination of interests among Parliament, monarchy, navy, industry, and the slave-based West Indian system itself. Neither the highly abstract perceptual fields and pure potentials, nor the more particular individual elements, can be used to explain a basically institutional transformation.

Analyzed in terms of its plot forms, the abolition of the slave trade ceases to be a subject for argument between irreconcilable schools of thought. Each of the three plots may be criticized at its appropriate level of abstraction without detriment to the others. And all three may be woven into the framework of a more comprehensive account, based on a full critical model of the event. Such a model would show the place of each plot in the scheme of explanation, assess its contribution to the intelligibility of the whole, and suggest a more coherent and comprehensive structure for narrative explanation. The model would then be ready for analytical refinement and for comparison with models of other events.

Constructing a critical model means setting out systematically all the elements, and their relationships, at every level of abstraction. The duration of the event must be defined in terms of the level of abstraction used for explanation. The major elements, propositions, and contrasts must be identified, and the phases of their transformation accounted for. The relation of the event to its antecedent and subsequent worlds also has to be outlined.

At the start, one has to decide on the duration of the event, and the elements to be included within it. The abolition of the British slave trade presents an intriguing problem of definition in this respect. The abolition campaign lasted roughly from 1784 to 1807, but the dates are deceptive. Although Parliament did not debate abolition until 1788, there was a pamphlet war about it from 1784 on, and that year also saw a wholesale review of imperial commerce policies as a result of the end of the American war. So the beginning of the duration seems clear enough. At the other end, however, there were four measures that together prohibited the slave trade. In August 1805 Pitt's cabinet issued an Order-in-Council preventing further trade to colonies captured from France and her allies since 1801. A bill extending this order to cover all non-British colonies passed Parliament in 1806, under the leadership of Charles James Fox. Fox then introduced a resolution calling for effective restriction of the remaining trade. This resolution passed both Houses in June 1806, due in large part to parliamentary tactics used by Fox and Grenville. The final bill for abolition was passed March 25, 1807, after an election in which Grenville pulled out all the stops in influencing voters.

Should this campaign be treated as one complex event with a twenty-three-year duration? Or should the historian isolate the passage of the four abolition measures in the period 1805–7 as one event, and discuss the previous developments as aspects of the antecedent world? The second approach might be more immediately intelligible, because it sets up an antecedent duration of (roughly) 1802–4 that includes most of the political, economic, and military changes that made abolition probable in the short run. But the first approach has the advantage, from a narrative point of view, of showing the intensity and significance of the event as it emerged over years of frustrating argument and effort. Moreover, it is more likely than the second approach to reveal long-term changes at the levels of complex concepts, fields, and pure potentials, though it will give correspondingly less attention to small groups and individuals.

Both approaches can explain why that event happened just the way it did at that time. The shorter duration accounts for the passage of specific legislation in 1805–7 in terms of the institutions, groups, and individuals through which the legislation was realized, and links it to the conditions of the antecedent world of 1802–4 on similar levels of abstraction. The longer duration concerns the whole campaign for abolition along with contrasting developments in imperial economic and political patterns. By reference to an antecedent period extending from 1756 to 1783, it explains why that campaign should have emerged with its peculiar character during the last decade of the eighteenth century.

Strictly speaking, since the two durations are different, they refer to two different events. But of course it is possible to include the shorter duration within the longer in a more complex account in a systematic way. The two events are mutually significant. They also have an equivalent richness of meaning. One cannot say that the explanation of the longer campaign is less valuable or less "meaty" because it tends to be more abstract than the other. Ernest Nagel has countered such a notion with his formulation of the principle of the inverse variation of the extension and intension of terms. This means, the wider the scope of the term, the less intensive its content.[4] An explanation for an event with extended duration will contain just as many items as for a shorter duration. Its overall density or richness will be the same, although the terms of explanation will be wider in scope. For the same reason, the short-term explanation will use terms with narrow scope, without loss of validity. Its comparative wealth of detail will offset its lack of temporal comprehensiveness. The two explanations, then, could have roughly the same complexity, the same "size" in historical accounts, and the same number of data, though the data will be on differing levels of abstraction. Further, as argued above, one can make the terms of the shorter duration compatible with the terms of the longer by respecting their different levels of abstraction.

For these reasons the "short" explanation of abolition, defined as the passage of legislation in 1805–7, has no inherent advantage over the "long" explanation of the whole abolition campaign from 1784 to 1807. But they have different antecedents and futures. If the duration is the "long" one, the terms of explanation must be general enough to show connections with an antecedent world of roughly the same length, say from 1756 to 1783; and also with a future world of events from 1807 to about 1833, the date of the end of slavery in the West Indies. One may use details of individual and group activities to illustrate the long-range developments, but these details do not explain why the abolition campaign should have emerged over a period of twenty-five years the way it did. Thus, the emphasis in this duration will be on elements at the levels of complex concepts, fields, and pure potentials, all of which have longer periods of articulation.

The abolition campaign, defined in this way, displays three primary propositions: the "abolitionist," the "mercantilist," and the "West Indian." The first is focused on the principles of liberty for slaves, righteousness for Englishmen, and public campaigns for reform. In the campaign's relevant future, abolition will appear as a significant symbol of evangelical reform to many people. It will also seem to be a triumph for Enlightenment principles of natural rights and human liberty. Finally, the individuals and groups who organized the abolition campaign will carry with them into subsequent occasions the conviction that moral crusades are effective instruments of public change. This conviction will become a common feature of later reform movements. Each of these elements in the "abolitionist" proposition has its referents in the antecedent world, the period from 1756 to 1783. The religious impulse can be traced to Methodist and Anglican evangelical movements arising in that era, and the Enlightenment idea of natural rights has a similar background in the philosophical writings of the time. The campaign tactics themselves show a novel element, derived from the antecedent world to be sure, but quite unlike anything that had gone before.

The second major proposition in the abolition struggle was a "mercantilist" one. Most members of the House of Commons, most peers, and most cabinet ministers believed in the right of Parliament to protect imperial commerce from foreign competition and to arrange its regulations for the economic welfare of Great Britain. The American revolt had not really dimmed this belief: in 1783 the king issued an Order-in-Council denying all British colonial trade to the new United States. War with France and her allies during the period 1793–1807 also strengthened British determination to keep her colonial trade intact. This included both the slave trade and the shipments of cane sugar from the West Indies that paid for slaves and other plantation necessities. Besides the general belief in mercantilism, many institutions, groups, and individuals were financially interested in the British Caribbean. And on a more abstract level, the perceptual field of economics was undergoing a slow transformation from the agrarian-aristocratic orientation long dominant in Europe toward a bourgeois-industrial one that would perceive the colonies as markets for goods rather than as suppliers of sugar.[5] Thus the proposition labelled "mercantilist" during the period 1784–1807 was not static. If one follows its adventures after 1807, one can see the relaxation of mercantilist views in relation to the United States during the Napoleonic war, with a corresponding movement toward free trade in many articles. Also there was a long effort by the British navy, then in control of the Atlantic, to enforce the provisions of the abolition measures. Between the navy and her industrial growth, England became an imperial power of the first rank. However, the strict protection of colonial trade that characterized the period 1784–1807 began to disintegrate. Knowing this, the historian can better gauge the significance of the mercantilist elements during the campaign for abolition.

Antecedently, in the period 1756–83 Britain fought two great wars to gain and protect her empire. The first war, against France, ended with a new era of prominence for the British West Indies, now augmented with French territory. The second war wrecked a valuable section of the colonial trade pattern by separating the West Indies from their primary source of supplies and transport in America. But taking this duration as a whole, it is easy to account for the intensity of interest in the slave trade as a cornerstone of West Indian (and therefore imperial) prosperity after 1783. One can also discern the growth of the British navy as an instrument of imperial expansion—an element noted in abolition's future, and one that became crucial to the monopoly of the West Indian market in the period 1805–7.

The third proposition of importance to abolition is focused on the West Indies themselves. It includes the West Indian planters, their creditor-merchants in England, and a large number of people who made livings of one sort or another from ownership of interests in the plantation economy. It includes the slave trade as an institution, tied in with sugar production and with the commercial network between plantation and merchant. The principle of imperial protection is emphasized over that of imperial welfare: the West Indians wanted all the benefits but none of the handicaps of the mercantilist system. The perceptual field is predominantly economic. Though religion and politics are subordinate, they are also quite different in tone than similar fields in the other two propositions. In fact, the general outlook of the resident planters was so different from that of abolitionists in England that effective communication between the two groups was often impossible.

Perhaps the most important element in the "West Indian" proposition was indebtedness. From 1784 to 1807 (and beyond) the decline of West Indian economic power was steady and steep. In the post-1807 world, the trend continued for at least half a century. The outlook of the resident planters did not change prior to abolition, but the conditions of trade turned against them, and when slavery was abolished in 1833 Parliament prevented their utter ruin with £20 million in compensation.

The planter's debt was already increasing prior to 1756, but the future

seemed secure in that antecedent period. What developed was a pattern of
financing the West Indian and African trades that involved many of the
major institutions of England, which gradually took control away from the
plantation owners. As one result, the owners came into conflict with government during the two periods of war, when West Indian demands that the
navigation laws be relaxed to permit the purchase of supplies from non-
British sources were viewed at home as attempts to evade repayment of
debts. This growing discord between the West Indian proposition and the
mercantilist proposition is a primary contrast in the emergence of abolition.

The phases of transformation can be described briefly. In 1784 the
abolitionist proposition was fragmentary and weak, while the mercantilist
and West Indian ones were not only strong but mutually concordant.
Therefore, for many years abolition made little headway in Parliament.
However, the idea was received positively by some mercantilists who
thought the slave trade could be gradually reduced by economic incentives
and colonial reforms. The mercantilist proposition thus became the crucial
focus for resolution of the conflict.

By reviewing relevant events in the antecedent world, one might form a
prediction that if there were another war, in which the West Indians sought
to break the navigation laws, foreign merchants took away British colonial
trade, so that the West Indian debt repayments were imperiled, then the
West Indian proposition would find itself in subordinate, discordant contrast to the mercantilist one. And that is what happened. Following the
resumption of war in 1803, the British navy swept all other nations (except
the United States) from the Atlantic and captured all the sugar colonies
formerly owned by France and Holland. The West Indians clamored to
reopen trade with the United States, and did so without waiting for official
approval. At the same time, the planters asked that the newly captured
colonies be prevented from competing with them—by the simple expedient
of prohibiting their access to slaves.[6]

For a brief phase in 1805 all three propositions reached a concordant
contrast: all three groups agreed that prohibiting the slave trade to foreign
and captured colonies would be a good thing. Because this prohibition
wiped out three-fourths of the entire African trade, there were few defenders left to prevent abolition of the rest of it the following year.[7] The
final phase of this event thus exhibits a general pattern dominated by mercantilist ideas, institutions, groups, and individuals, with abolition in concordant subordination on all levels except the conceptual, and the West
Indian elements in discordant subordination.

This analysis, of course, is open to dispute. Others may decide that the
abolitionist proposition is the primary one. If so, the plot form of the event
will change, and there can be informed discussion of the heuristic benefits of
the new approach. But no matter what choice the historian makes, his

analysis of the event, with the duration defined above, will deal with propositions focused at the more abstract levels, because only these elements can account for the emergence of an event with such a long duration.

An account of abolition covering the period 1784–1807, with commensurate antecedent and subsequent durations, need not exclude details about individual and small-group activities. If one claims that the mercantilist proposition is the most dynamic of the three, one has to give some empirical evidence in support. That will often appear, as admitted previously, in the form of narrative episodes. Similarly, in showing how the three propositions interact, one would have to narrate incidents in which they formed significant contrasts. The amount of information supplied this way depends on whether one is demonstrating the importance of mercantilism as a proposition in the critical model of the event, or simply illustrating a statement, relative to mercantilism, that has its warrant in some other study. But in either case, the information about groups and individuals does not explain how the mercantilist proposition emerged; it simply indicates aspects of it at some stage. So the rule remains: the terms of explanation must be on the same level of generalization as the terms of definition. If one defines abolition as "a movement to change the terms of British colonial and African trade via parliamentary legislation, 1784–1807," one has already determined that the explanation will be focused on elements at the higher levels of abstraction: larger groups, institutions, concepts, and perceptual fields. This does not mean that small groups and individuals play no part, but that no group or individual serves as the focus for transformation in all phases of the event.

By comparison, defining the event as "the passage of legislation, in the period 1805–7, prohibiting involvement in the slave trade by British subjects and territories" focuses attention on the functions of groups and individuals within the institution of Parliament, which is itself contrasted with the institutions of the slave trade and West Indian plantation economy. The same three propositions are evident in the final phase of this event as are evident in the final phase of the longer one, but in the shorter period the conceptual or field elements of the propositions are not emphasized so much as the people that got the measures through Parliament. The principles of abolition, of mercantilism, and of West Indian protection are less important because, in this short period, they undergo little change. Value-relationships among the perceptual fields remain relatively stable also; in Marxian-based accounts, the abolition of the slave trade is often just lumped together with the abolition of slavery in 1833, to show the slow change of economic priorities.

To trace the adventures of the various propositions and contrasts in the subsequent world, in order to assess their general significance, one will need to look at a comparably short duration, say from 1807 to about 1810.

Beyond that, the metamorphosis of elements at the individual and group levels becomes too complex for clear analysis. For example, the fact that William Wilberforce was still alive to celebrate the abolition of slavery in 1833 has symbolic importance when one considers the abolition campaign in the extended duration of 1784–1807. But so far as the maneuvering for legislation in 1805–7 goes, his longevity is irrelevant.

I should note here that the short-term focus on groups and individuals often reveals changes and gaps that are not evident at longer range. For instance, the abolitionist cause in the period 1805–7 is represented more vividly by Lord Grenville than by Wilberforce. It was Grenville who guided the final bill for abolition through the Lords in January 1807, and it was his political influence and talent that packed the new Commons with a majority of "friends," who passed the abolition measure by an overwhelming vote in March. This in itself should make the historian curious about changes in the antecedent world. But one also notes that Grenville, Grey, and the abolitionists went out of power on the day that the bill passed (March 25, 1807) and that Grenville was never again associated with the reformers in the same way. One has to guess that there were some extraordinary transformations in the period 1805–7, or that the antecedent world of 1802–4 contained unusually unstable configurations. Both guesses, in fact, seem to be correct. During the antecedent period, William Pitt's role as a focus for abolition efforts declined along with his general political power. Grenville, Pitt's former ally, made common cause with Charles James Fox and the Whigs, while Wilberforce decided that Pitt was no longer serious about abolition. These developments conditioned (but did not determine) what happened in 1805–7. Wilberforce, by threatening to join the opposition, forced Pitt to issue the Order-in-Council prohibiting the slave trade to captured colonies. And when Pitt died in January 1806, Wilberforce threw his support to the new Fox-Grenville coalition. Thus, the significant changes between the antecedent world and the emerging new event have to do with groups and individuals within an institutional setting. There were no striking changes in institutional or conceptual relationships. But a new proposition did emerge from the older ones, and the relative intensity of its elements was altered. Before, it was Pitt and Wilberforce at the center of abolition; now it was Fox and Grenville who deliberately kept Wilberforce in the background to avoid antagonizing the opposition.

As mentioned above, elements in the world antecedent to 1805–7change in similar ways: the individual aspects are less constant than the institutional or conceptual. But in describing antecedents, one must remember to include telescoped images of developments reaching into the more distant past. These narrative sketches of metamorphosis indicate the scope and intensity of certain significant elements as they were presented for assimilation by the new event in 1805. For example, the style of public crusade invented by the abolitionists, and used for twenty years previous to 1802, appears in muted form after that date. The big campaigns of the 1790s had done their work. People were tired of hearing about the Cause, but the feelings engendered by atrocity stories and sermons on natural religion and humanity turn up in a variety of incidents. This may explain why Wilberforce could say, about this time, that a new generation had grown up ignorant of the arguments for abolition—and yet discover, in 1807, dozens of young M.P.'s jumping up to speak with the old abolitionist phrases spilling from their lips.[8]

This example shows why it is important for the historian, when identifying aspects in the antecedent world from the extensive past, to indicate the variety of elements in which each aspect is manifested. There may be no single element that presents the aspects in a forceful, complete way (e.g., the pro-abolition feelings of the younger generation); and yet it is possible for the emerging event to bring all of these minor manifestations together in a new way that does stand out. Without carefully distinguishing the manner of their appearance in the antecedent world, the historian would be unable to explain how such aspects gain importance in the new event.

Other metamorphoses relevant to abolition that might be telescoped into elements of its antecedent period of 1802–4 are the growing indebtedness of the planters, the gradual domination of the Atlantic by the British navy, and the many attempts by mercantilist politicians to force a compromise bill for gradual abolition. Each of these aspects can be described with an appropriate narrative account leading up to the antecedent duration and showing the scope and intensity of the pattern at that time.

Telescoping long-term developments into short-term antecedents for the period 1805–7 helps avoid the fallacy of explaining such a concisely defined event by using grossly over-generalized terms of reference. Although field, conceptual, and institutional elements may be included in the explanation, the main focus will be upon groups and individuals. Thus the principle of British imperialism is significant in relation to a person such as Lord Hawkesbury, an old opponent of abolition who nevertheless began to see how dangerous the slave trade was as a stimulus to foreign colonies. And abolition as an ideal enters the event in relation to the brief reign of Charles James Fox as leader of the Whigs in 1806. Only by tying abstract elements to their more concrete allies can one explain clearly what their role actually was.

In reputable histories of England one can find assertions to the effect that "the Parliamentary abolition passed by Fox represented the triumph of moral persuasion over economic interest." What is the meaning of such a statement? It asserts that a contrast that developed over a twenty-five-year period (the triumph of morality over interest) was directly responsible for an individual's legislative achievement in a particular three-month period. One has to ask, why then? Why not some other time, in some other form, by some other person, through some other institution? The scope of potentiality represented by the stated contrast could account for a great many alternatives to what actually happened. One has to explain how that potential was articulated through more complex, more precise levels of elements, down to the level of the actual event. Then the questions can be answered.

It has been the aim of this book to alleviate problems, such as the above, that are due to confusion about levels of abstraction and patterns of temporal development, by providing a systematic approach to the critical analysis and composition of explanatory narratives. A primary task in this approach is the construction of critical models of carefully defined historical events. The critical model for abolition, for instance, would include a macroscopic study of the duration 1784–1807 and its relevant future and antecedent periods, together with microscopic studies of the important transformations within it. Because the internal process of transformation is analogous to the external process of metamorphosis, it is possible to analyze short-term episodes separately, and then to integrate the findings into a long-term framework. The metamorphic changes of short episodes will translate into transformational changes in the long ones. For example, one can analyze Bismarck's handling of the Schleswig-Holstein affair, 1864–66, as one complete event. This approach will emphasize details at the lower levels of abstraction but suggest lines of inquiry at all levels. Then, one can move to an analysis of Bismarck's role in the unification of Germany, which spans a longer period. The elements of the Schleswig-Holstein affair now involve one phase of transformation in the more extensive patterns of German unification. The relevant propositions and contrasts are already known and the lower levels of elements already accounted for. There is a solid base for inquiry at the higher levels, using terms of broader scope.

The analytical framework through which historians may arrive at useful critical models of events can be applied rather piecemeal to separate research questions without loss of coherence, if care is taken to adopt consistent terms of reference, levels of abstraction, and procedures. More importantly, one needs to pay attention to the structure and compositional dynamics of previous related studies when planning a new one. It is not enough to cite other works in a footnote, as if only the authority for raw data or isolated arguments matters. Each reference should be considered in comparison to the common analytical framework, so that further research makes a critical difference to our understanding of the past. If the comparison is not made explicit, then "contributions to knowledge" remain useless additions, like hulks of old automobiles piled one on top of another in a salvage yard.

Narrative explanations, it was argued, cannot deal with all levels of abstraction at once, even if based upon critical models of events. But as the narrative unfolds, the transitions from one level to another, or from micro- to macro-explanations, can be made intelligible by having the writer identify and make explicit the process of "following" expected from the reader.

The narrator should first decide on the main plot form and subplots that make up the temporal constitution of the event. Then the major propositions and contrasts can be identified. These become the bases for selecting and arranging the data into meaningful episodes, for deciding when to use details about individuals or groups, and when to remind the reader of more abstract elements in the emerging pattern. Such decisions help avoid superfluous detail in accounts of broad scope, and avoid superfluous concern with general concepts in narrower accounts. The explicit inclusion of these compositional principles and decisions within the body of the narrative separates it from the "story" level of fiction and raises it to the level of explanatory narrative.

Throughout this book, I have sought to unify theory and practice. The principles of narrative composition described in the previous paragraph are consistent with the principles of the analytical framework described in previous chapters. They are also consistent with the pattern of emergence displayed by actual historical events and with the pattern of perception by which people understand events as they unfold. Thus the process approach to historical explanation unifies the discipline, grounds it securely upon our direct experience of reality, and demonstrates its harmonious connnections with other areas of intellectual inquiry.

Notes

Chapter 1

1. For an elegant summary of the relation between perception in physics and in psychology, see David Bohm, *The Special Theory of Relativity* (New York: W. A. Benjamin, 1965), chap. 6.

2. Carl L. Becker, "What Are Historical Facts?" *Western Political Quarterly* 8, no. 3 (September 1955):329.

3. Werner Ohnsorge, "The Coronation and Byzantium," in Richard E. Sullivan, ed., *The Coronation of Charlemagne: What Did It Signify?* (Boston: D. C. Heath, 1959), p. 80.

4. J. H. Hexter and Hayden White are two notable exceptions.

5. Louis Halphen, "The Coronation as the Expression of the Ideals of the Frankish Court," in Sullivan, *Charlemagne*.

6. Ibid., pp. 28–29.

7. Ibid., p. 34.

8. Edward Hallett Carr, *What Is History?* (New York: Vintage Books, 1967), p. 167.

9. Marc Bloch, *The Historian's Craft* (New York: Vintage Books, 1953), p. 143.

10. Ohnsorge, "Coronation."

11. Isaiah Berlin, "The Concept of Scientific History," *History and Theory* 1, no. 1 (1961). See also Berlin's *Historical Inevitability* (London: Oxford University Press, 1955), in which he terms the application of scientific models to history "one of the greatest and most destructive fallacies of the last hundred years."

12. Ohnsorge, "Coronation," pp. 87–88.

13. Carl C. Hempel, quoted in J. H. Hexter, *The History Primer* (New York: Basic Books, 1971), p. 31.

14. Hexter, *History Primer*, p. 8. Elsewhere (p. 253), Hexter mounts an extended and forceful critique of philosophers of science who "reduce discussion of history to discussion of causal explanation in history, because it is at this point, they think, that the structure of history most nearly converges on that of the natural sciences. Having singled out this casual structural similarity, they imply or even state that whatever else historians do is not relevant for whatever truth value history may have. Therefore, by assuming that it has none, they absolve themselves from even asking what truth value a large part of the activity of historians has."

15. G. R. Elton, *The Practice of History* (New York: Crowell, 1967), p. v.

16. Ibid., p. 84.

17. Ibid., p. 85.

18. Ibid., pp. 11, 27 ff.

19. Louis Gottschalk, *Understanding History, A Primer of Historical Method* (New York: Knopf, 1950). Gottschalk has one of the better critiques of theories of causality, and makes useful distinctions regarding terms like "influence." These contributions, however, are not reflected in his discussion of style and composition.

20. Carr, *What Is History?* Carr and Elton should be read together, as they create a running battle over the functions and possibility of scientific generalization versus intuitive judgments.

21. Berlin, *Historical Inevitability*.

22. Bloch, *Historian's Craft*. Bloch accepted the "vacillating and ambiguous" language of

history "which has not derived from the rigorously organized efforts of technical experts."
23. Hexter, *History Primer*, p. 10.
24. Ibid., pp. 188.
25. Ibid., pp. 197, 205.
26. Hayden White, *Metahistory: The Historical Imagination in Nineteenth-Century Europe* (Baltimore: The Johns Hopkins University Press, 1973).
27. Sullivan, *Charlemagne*, 3.
28. Hexter, *History Primer*, 266.

Chapter 2
1. Thomas S. Kuhn, *The Structure of Scientific Revolutions*, 2d ed. (Chicago: The University of Chicago Press, 1970), esp. chap. 7, "Crisis and the Emergence of Scientific Theories."
2. Arthur C. Danto, *Analytical Philosophy of History* (Cambridge: Cambridge University Press, 1965), p. 78.
3. Carl C. Hempel, "The Function of General Laws in History," in Patrick Gardiner, ed., *Theories of History* (Glencoe, Ill.: The Free Press, 1959), p. 344.
4. Ernest Nagel, "Some Issues in the Logic of Historical Analysis," in Gardiner, *Theories*, p. 375.
5. Hempel, "General Laws," p. 345.
6. Ibid., 346.
7. Quoted by Jacob Bronowski, *The Common Sense of Science* (Cambridge: Harvard University Press, 1953), p. 39
8. Michael J. Scriven, "Truisms as the Grounds for Historical Explanations," in Gardiner, *Theories*, p. 460.
9. Ibid., p. 450.
10. Morton White, *Foundations of Historical Knowledge* (New York: Harper and Row, 1965), p. 58.
11. See related arguments in William Dray, *Laws and Explanation in History* (New York: Harper and Row), 1957.
12. Danto, *Analytical Philosophy*, pp. 229, 237–39.
13. Alan Donagan, "Explanation in History," in Gardiner, *Theories*, p. 430; Scriven, "Truisms," p. 462; Michael Oakeshott, "Historical Continuity and Causal Analysis," in William Dray, ed., *Philosophical Analysis and History* (New York: Harper and Row, 1966), pp. 193–99.
14. Cf. Bronowski, *Common Sense*, p. 70.
15. Danto, *Analytical Philosophy*, p. 229.
16. Hempel, "General Laws," p. 345.
17. Danto, *Analytical Philosophy*, pp. 234–35. Cf. Maurice Mandelbaum, *The Anatomy of Historical Knowledge* (Baltimore: The Johns Hopkins University Press, 1977), pp. 55–59.
18. Danto, *Analytical Philosophy*, p. 226.
19. Danto, pp. 76–77.
20. Bronowski, *Common Sense*, p. 117.
21. Danto, *Analytical Philosophy*, p. 29; Scriven, "Truisms," p. 469.
22. Danto, *Analytical Philosophy*, p. 183.
23. Hexter, *History Primer*, pp. 114–15.
24. Cf. ibid., p. 199, for related arguments.
25. White, *Foundations*, p. 5.
26. Karl Popper, "Prediction and Prophecy in the Social Sciences," in Gardiner, *Theories*, pp. 279–81. Popper's emphasis.
27. Donagan, "Explanation," pp. 435, 438 n. (on G. Ryle, *The Concept of Mind* [London: Hutchinson, 1949]).
28. White, *Foundations*, p. 113.

Chapter 3

1. Louis Gottschalk, *Understanding History*, p. 10.

2. Haskell Fain, *Between Philosophy and History* (Princeton: Princeton University Press, 1970), p. 298.

3. Walter B. Gallie, "Explanations in History and the Genetic Sciences," in Gardiner, *Theories*, p. 391.

4. Morton White, "Historical Explanation," Gardiner, *Theories*, p. 357.

5. Gallie, "Explanations," pp. 392–94.

6. John Tyler Bonner, *Morphogenesis: An Essay on Development* (Princeton: Princeton University Press, 1952), pp. 9–10.

7. Fain, *Between*, p. 297.

8. Ernest Nagel, "Some Issues in the Logic of Historical Analysis," in Gardiner, *Theories*, p. 378.

9. Fain, *Between*, pp. 279–83.

10. Walter B. Gallie, *Philosophy and the Historical Understanding* (New York: Schocken Books, 1968), pp. 2–3.

11. Fain, *Between*, pp. 35, 40, 177, and passim.

12. Gallie, *Philosophy*, pp. 22–23.

13. Ibid., pp. 38, 41.

14. Ibid., pp. 72–73.

15. Fain, *Between*, p. 261.

16. Ibid., p. 262.

17. Ibid., p. 270. See also Gallie, *Philosophy*, p. 118.

18. R. G. Collingwood, "History as Re-enactment of Past Experience," in Gardiner, *Theories*, p. 252.

19. W. H. Walsh, " 'Meaning' in History," in Gardiner, *Theories*, pp. 298–99; Gallie, *Philosophy*, p. 118.

20. Michael Oakeshott, "Historical Continuity," pp. 207–8.

21. Fain, *Between*, p. 273.

22. W. H. Walsh, *Philosophy of History: An Introduction* (New York: Harper and Brothers, 1960), p. 14.

23. The relation between history as subject and history as methodology is explored vigorously in terms of the constructionist-realist argument about historical reality by P. H. Nowell-Smith and Leon J. Goldstein in *The Constitution of the Historical Past (History and Theory*, Beiheft 16, vol. 16, no. 4 [1977]). However, neither side of the argument views the past as process rather than object, so the argument seems misdirected from my point of view.

24. Gallie, *Philosophy*, pp. 63–64.

25. Danto, *Analytical Philosophy*, p. 249.

26. White, *Foundations*, p. 221.

27. Danto, *Analytical Philosophy*, p. 249.

28. Fain, *Between*, p. 211.

29. Louis Mink, "The Autonomy of Historical Understanding," in Dray, *Philosophical Analysis*, pp. 178–79.

30. Fain, *Between*, p. 249.

31. Scriven, "Truisms," p. 457.

32. Bronowski, *Common Sense*, pp. 130–31.

33. Ibid.

34. Mink, "Autonomy," pp. 186–87. See also Wilhelm Dilthey, "The Understanding of Other Persons and Their Life-Experiences," in Gardiner, *Theories*, pp. 224–25.

35. In Gardiner, *Theories*, p. 225.

36. Brewster Ghiselin, *The Creative Process* (Berkeley: The University of California Press, 1954).

37. Elton, *Practice of History*, p. 89.

38. For this chapter I have used Ghiselin, *Creative Process;* Arthur Koestler, *The Act of Creation* (New York: Macmillan, 1964); and an unpublished survey of works on creativity by Professor Albert Rabil of SUNY at Old Westbury. For the general theme, see Alfred North Whitehead, *Process and Reality,* corrected ed. (New York: The Free Press, 1978); and Susanne K. Langer, *Problems of Art* (New York: Scribner's, 1957).

39. Cf. Wolfgang Köhler, *Gestalt Psychology* (New York: Liveright, 1947).

40. R. R. Palmer and Joel Colton, *A History of the Modern World* (New York: Knopf, 1965), p. 527.

41. Dale H. Porter, *The Abolition of the Slave Trade in England, 1784–1807* (New Haven: Archon Books, 1970).

42. Hayden V. White, *Metahistory: The Historical Imagination in Nineteenth-Century Europe* (Baltimore: Johns Hopkins University Press, 1973).

Chapter 4

1. Becker, "What Are Historical Facts?" p. 328.

2. J. W. N. Watkins, "Historical Explanation in the Social Sciences," in Gardiner, *Theories of History*, p. 504.

3. Whitehead, *Process and Reality*, pp. 7–8.

4. Elton, *The Practice of History*, p. 101.

5. Ibid., p. 52

6. Carr, *What Is History?*, p. 72.

7. Ibid.

8. Marc Bloch, *Historian's Craft*, p. 72.

9. Bronowski, *Common Sense*, p. 77 and passim.

10. Specific information about time is from Gerald Whitrow, *The Nature of Time* (New York: Holt, Rinehart and Winston, 1973), but the general argument rests on research reports from current science journals and encyclopedias.

11. Cf. Whitehead, *Process and Reality*, p. 35, and his *Science in the Modern World* (New York: The Free Press, 1925), pp. 125–26 for the contrast between classical notions of the "continuity of becoming" and his own "becoming of continuity."

12. Whitehead, *Process and Reality*, p. 6.

13. Quoted in Arthur Koestler, *The Roots of Coincidence* (London: Hutchinson, 1972), p. 55.

14. Ibid., 51.

15. Bronowski, *Common Sense*, pp. 64–65.

16. Kenneth G. Denbigh, *An Inventive Universe* (New York: George Braziller, 1975), especially chap. 4, "Determinism and Emergence," and chap. 5, "Are There Any Inventive Processes?"

17. C. G. Hempel and P. Oppenheim, "Studies in the Logic of Explanation," *Philosophy of Science* 15 (1948), quoted in Bonner, *Morphogenesis*, p. 4.

18. Denbigh, *Inventive Universe*, p. 146.

19. The odds against humans are amusingly illustrated by Joan Brady's short story "A Variety of Religious Experience," *Harper's Magazine*, January 1974.

20. Carr, *What Is History?*, pp. 76–82, offers an extended argument for this position.

21. A similar argument is made on behalf of biological explanations by Michael Scriven, "Explanation and Prediction in Evolutionary Theory," *Science* 130 (1959):46–47.

22. Ernest Nagel, "Types of Causal Explanation in Science," in Daniel Lerner, ed., *Cause and Effect* (New York: The Free Press, 1965), p. 24.

23. Ernst Mayr, "Cause and Effect in Biology," in Lerner, *Cause and Effect*, pp. 42–43.

24. Arthur Koestler, *The Act of Creation* (New York: Macmillan, 1964).

25. Denbigh, *Inventive Universe*, p. 146.

26. Arthur Koester, "Order from Disorder," *Harper's Magazine*, July 1974, p. 56.

27. Quoted in John J. McDermott, "Space, Time and Touch: Philosophical Dimensions of Urban Consciousness," *Soundings* 57, no. 3 (Fall 1974):265.

28. Lewis Thomas, *The Lives of a Cell* (New York: Viking, 1974), p. 12.

29. Information on biological clocks is from Whitrow, *Nature of Time,* and Ritchie R. Ward, *The Living Clocks* (New York: Knopf, 1971).

30. Gay Gaer Luce, *Body Time: Physiological Rhythms and Social Stress* (New York: Dover, 1971).

31. Cf. references to Professor Frank Brown in Ward, *Living Clocks.*

32. Ibid., pp. 218–19, 322–34.

33. The wave-field theory and its link to creativity was discussed by R. W. Gerard, "The Biological Basis of Imagination," in Ghiselin, *The Creative Process.*

34. The definitions of time and space discussed in this chapter are consistent with the structure of events outlined in Chapter 3 with regard to creative thinking. An extension of the argument to the problem of creativity in the arts is made by Susanne K. Langer, *Problems of Art,* which may be read in parallel with this chapter.

Chapter 5

1. McDermott, "Space, Time and Touch," p. 263.

2. Georges Lefebvre, *The Coming of the French Revolution* (Princeton: Princeton University Press, 1947), p. 3.

3. William H. Maehl, Jr., ed., *The Reform Bill of 1832: Why Not Revolution?* (New York: Holt, Rinehart and Winston, 1967).

4. Whitehead, *Process and Reality,* p. 208.

5. Maehl, *Reform Bill,* p. 22.

6. Ibid., pp. 80–82.

7. Ibid., pp. 40–47.

8. Koppel S. Pinson, *Modern Germany: Its History and Civilization* (New York: Macmillan, 1954), p. 214.

9. Maehl, *Reform Bill,* pp. 94–95.

10. Ibid., p. 104.

11. This list is based on the excellent works of Carl G. Gustafson, *A Preface to History* (New York: McGraw-Hill, 1955) and *The Mansion of History* (New York: McGraw-Hill, 1976).

12. Cf. F. L. Baumer, *Religion and the Rise of Skepticism* (New York: Harcourt Brace, 1960); J. B. Bury, *The Idea of Progress: An Inquiry Into Its Origin and Growth* (New York: Dover, 1932).

Chapter 6

1. Whitehead, *Process and Reality,* p. 148.

2. See my argument in "History as Process," *History and Theory* 14, no. 3 (1975):308. Another perspective is developed in Chapter 9 of the present book.

3. Richard Aldington, *The Duke* (New York: Viking Press, 1943), p. 321; Norman Gash, "Halevy's Interpretation Disputed," in Maehl, *Reform Bill,* pp. 40–47.

4. Aldington, *Duke,* p. 321.

5. Cf. Maehl, *Reform Bill,* pp. 34–47.

6. Ibid., pp. 11–12; Aldington, *Duke,* p. 322.

7. Aldington, *Duke,* p. 299.

8. Ibid., 308–11.

9. Maehl, *Reform Bill,* pp. 40–47.

10. Aldington, *Duke,* p. 320.

11. Ibid., pp. 319–21; Maehl, *Reform Bill,* pp. 43–44.

12. Maehl, *Reform Bill,* p. 45.

13. Ibid., p. 47.

14. G. D. H. Cole, "Working-class Support Decisive," in Maehl, *Reform Bill,* p. 23.

15. Aldington, *Duke*, pp. 312, 321.

16. Ibid., p. 301.

17. Maehl, *Reform Bill*, p. 15.

18. Ibid., p. 28.

19. Edward T. Hall, *Beyond Culture* (Garden City, N. Y.: Anchor Press, 1976), pp. 14–21.

20. Danto, *Analytical Philosophy*, p. 147.

Chapter 7

1. Aldington, *Duke*, pp. 314–15.

2. Maehl, *Reform Bill*, p. 11.

3. Ibid., pp. 13, 24, 28, 30, 32.

4. Kuhn, *Scientific Revolutions*.

5. Whitehead, *Process and Reality*, pp. 342–51. The journal *Process Studies* carries many of the theological discussions relevant to Whitehead's thought.

6. A. N. Whitehead, *Symbolism: Its Meaning and Effect* (New York: Macmillan, 1927), pp. 38–40.

7. Cf. Bohm, *Relativity*, chap. 10 on "Relativity and Perception."

8. For a relevant discussion of transactionalism as a mode of explanation, see F. H. Allport, *Theories of Perception and the Concept of Structure* (New York: John Wiley, 1955), pp. 278–81.

9. Bertrand Russell in Gardiner, *Theories of History*, p. 290.

10. This and following arguments in Chapter 7 are drawn from Whitehead, *Process and Reality*, pp. 157–85, and *Symbolism*, pp. 49–57.

11. Whitehead, *Symbolism*, p. 42.

12. Ibid., pp. 42–43. Cf. related arguments regarding the perception of causality in Mandelbaum, *Historical Knowledge*.

13. Jean Piaget, *The Child's Conception of Time* (New York: Basic Books, 1969). Cf. Whitehead, *Process and Reality*, p. 177, for a related discussion of "the grades of entities."

14. Whitehead, *Symbolism*, pp. 56–57.

15. Whitehead, *Process and Reality*, pp. 168–69. Cf. Bronowski, *Common Sense*, p. 111.

16. Aldington, *Duke*, p. 322.

Chapter 8

1. Palmer and Colton, *A History of the Modern World*, p. 527.

2. Whitehead, *Process and Reality*, pp. 280–84, 391–97.

3. Ibid., p. 71.

4. Lucy R. Lippard, *Changing: Essays in Art Criticism* (New York: Dutton, 1971), p. 90.

5. John Fowles, *The French Lieutenant's Woman* (Boston: Little, Brown, 1969).

6. Especially valuable is Philip Stevick, ed., *The Theory of the Novel* (New York: The Free Press, 1967).

7. Walter Ullman, *The Growth of Papal Government in the Middle Ages: A Study in the Ideological Relation of Clerical to Lay Power* (London: Methuen, 1955).

8. Asa Briggs, "A Caution against Doctrinaire Judgments," in Maehl, *Reform Bill*, pp. 30–33.

9. Ibid., p. 33.

10. Aldington, *Duke*, pp. 312–15.

11. Crane Brinton, *The Anatomy of Revolution* (New York: W. W. Norton, 1938); Kuhn, *Scientific Revolutions*.

12. R. S. Crane, "The Concept of Plot," in Stevick, *Theory*, p. 141.

13. Halphen, "Coronation," p. 28.

14. Norman Friedmen, "Forms of the Plot," in Stevick, *Theory*, pp. 145–66.

15. Frantz Fanon, *The Wretched of the Earth* (New York: Grove Press, 1963).

16. Friedman, "Forms," p. 168.

17. As Marie-Louise von Franz points out in *An Introduction to the Interpretation of Fairy Tales* (New York: Spring Publications, 1973), pp. 9–10.

Chapter 9

1. Henry Kissinger's adherence to Metternichian principles was mentioned in newspaper and magazine accounts of his diplomacy, but it was evident earlier in his study *A World Restored: Metternich, Castlereagh, and the Problems of Peace, 1812–1822* (Boston: Houghton Mifflin, 1957).

2. Pinson, *Modern Germany*, p. 395.

3. Whitehead, *Process and Reality*, p. 226.

4. Palmer and Colton, *A History of the Modern World*, pp. 457–58.

5. Ibid., p. 506.

6. Ibid., pp. 439, 483, 513–17.

7. But recent experiments with chimpanzees and gorillas have challenged the exclusiveness of man's historical thinking. At least one primate has learned to tell lies after getting into mischief, which may be a good definition of history. Cf. *Science News* 3, no. 11 (March 12, 1977).

8. Donald R. Kelley, "Martyrs, Myths, and the Massacre: The Background of St. Bartholomew," *The American Historical Review* 77, no. 5 (December 1972):1323–42.

9. Ibid., p. 1323.

10. Ibid., pp. 1323–24.

11. Trygve Tholfsen, *Historical Thinking* (New York: Harper and Row, 1967), p. 261.

12. Ibid., p. 262.

13. Marc Bloch, *Feudal Society*, trans. L. A. Manyon (Chicago: The University of Chicago Press, 1961).

Chapter 10

1. Cf. Frank J. Klingberg, *The Anti-Slavery Movement in England* (New Haven: Yale University Press, 1926); Reginald Coupland, *The British Anti-Slavery Movement* (New York: Barnes & Noble, 1964).

2. Cf., for example, Eric Williams, *Capitalism and Slavery* (Chapel Hill: North Carolina University Press, 1944).

3. Porter, *Abolition*. The pathetic plot is also found in Lowell J. Ragatz, *The Fall of the Planter Class in the British Caribbean, 1763–1833* (New York: Century, 1928).

4. Nagel, "Historical Analysis," p. 375.

5. Porter, *Abolition*, pp. 16–32.

6. Ibid., pp. 108–24.

7. Ibid., 124–39.

8. Ibid., p. 138.

Index